GLACIER NATIONAL PARK CAMPING

BECKY LOMAX

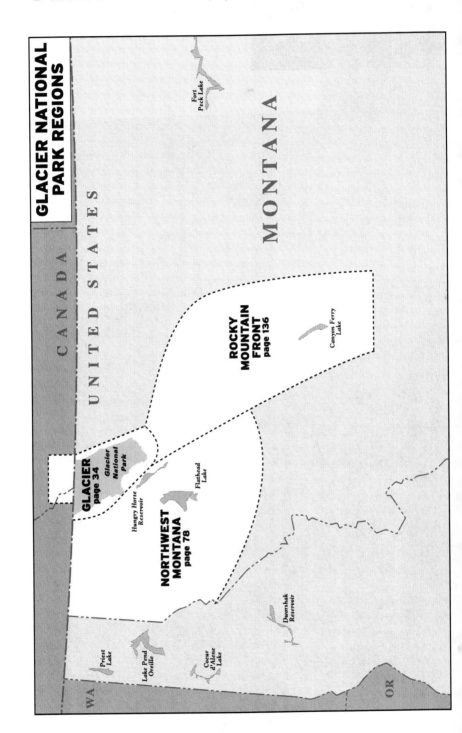

GLACIER NATIONAL PARK REGIONS

CANADA

UNITED STATES

MONTANA

Fort Peck Lake

ROCKY MOUNTAIN FRONT
page 136

Canyon Ferry Lake

GLACIER
page 34

Glacier National Park

Hungry Horse Reservoir

Flathead Lake

NORTHWEST MONTANA
page 78

Dworshak Reservoir

Priest Lake

Lake Pend Oreille

Coeur d'Alene Lake

WA

OR

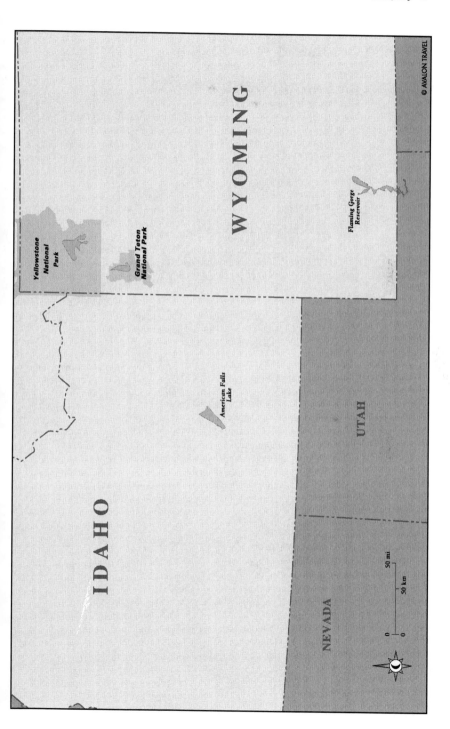

How to Use This Book

ABOUT THE CAMPGROUND PROFILES

The campgrounds are listed in a consistent, easy-to-read format to help you choose the ideal camping spot. If you already know the name of the specific campground you want to visit, or the name of the surrounding geological area or nearby feature (town, national or state park, forest, mountain, lake, river, etc.), look it up in the index and turn to the corresponding page. Here is a sample profile:

Campground name and number

Icons noting activities and facilities at or nearby the campground

General location of the campground in relation to the nearest major town or landmark

Rating of scenic beauty on a scale of 1-10 with 10 the highest rating

Symbol indicating that the campground is listed among the author's top picks

1 SOMEWHERE USA CAMPGROUND

Scenic rating: 10

south of Somewhere USA Lake

BEST (

Each campground in this book begins with a brief overview of its setting. The description typically covers ambience, information about the attractions, and activities popular at the campground.

Campsites, facilities: This section notes the number of campsites for tents and RVs and indicates whether hookups are available. Facilities such as restrooms, picnic areas, recreation areas, laundry, and dump stations will be addressed, as well as the availability of piped water, showers, playgrounds, stores, and other amenities. The campground's pet policy and wheelchair accessibility is also mentioned here.

Reservations, fees: This section notes whether reservations are accepted, and provides rates for tent sites and RV sites. If there are additional fees for parking or pets, or discounted weekly or seasonal rates, they will also be noted here.

Directions: This section provides mile-by-mile driving directions to the campground from the nearest major town or highway.

Contact: This section provides an address, phone number, and website, if available, for the campground.

ABOUT THE ICONS

The icons in this book are designed to provide at-a-glance information on activities, facilities, and services available on-site or within walking distance of each campground.

- 🥾 Hiking trails
- 🚲 Biking trails
- 🏊 Swimming
- 🎣 Fishing
- 🚤 Boating
- 🛶 Canoeing and/or kayaking

- ❄ Winter sports
- 🐾 Pets permitted
- 🎠 Playground
- ♿ Wheelchair accessible
- 🚐 RV sites
- ⛺ Tent sites

ABOUT THE SCENIC RATING

Each campground profile employs a scenic rating on a scale of 1 to 10, with 1 being the least scenic and 10 being the most scenic. A scenic rating measures only the overall beauty of the campground and environs; it does not take into account noise level, facilities, maintenance, recreation options, or campground management. The setting of a campground with a lower scenic rating may simply not be as picturesque that of as a higher rated campground, however other factors that can influence a trip, such as noise or recreation access, can still affect or enhance your camping trip. Consider both the scenic rating and the profile description before deciding which campground is perfect for you.

MAP SYMBOLS

▨▨▨▨▨	Expressway	🛡 80	Interstate Freeway	✈	Airfield
———	Primary Road	🛡 101	U.S. Highway	✈	Airport
———	Secondary Road	21	State Highway	○	City/Town
∷∷∷∷	Unpaved Road	66	County Highway	▲	Mountain
··········	Ferry	🗌	Lake	⬘	Park
—··—··—	National Border	🗌	Dry Lake	⊃⊂	Pass
———·——	State Border	🗌	Seasonal Lake	◉	State Capital

Camping Tips

TRAVELING THE NORTHERN ROCKIES
Roads and Routes

Traveling the Northern Rockies of Montana, Wyoming, and Idaho requires an understanding of roads. Interstates are few and far between. Rough, narrow, paved two-laners are common, and dirt roads are as ubiquitous as pavement.

HIGHWAYS AND INTERSTATES

Only two interstates bisect the region. I-15 runs through Montana and Idaho, connecting Calgary with Salt Lake City, and I-90 crosses Montana en route from Seattle to Chicago and Boston. State highways crisscross the region, providing the main thoroughfares. These can be two or four lanes, or they may be dirt roads. To navigate the area, use a current detailed map that shows pavement and gravel roads.

CROSSING THE CONTINENTAL DIVIDE AND HIGH PASSES

The Continental Divide skitters along the highest summits of the Rocky Mountains, making the division between water flowing to the Atlantic and water flowing to the Pacific. For campers, driving over the Continental Divide provides a challenge. In winter, some high passes are closed for several months, while others struggle with intermittent closures due to avalanches. Glacier's Going-to-the-Sun Road, the Beartooth Highway northeast of Yellowstone, and much of Yellowstone National Park closes for winter, and remote Forest Service roads convert to snowmobile routes.

But even in summer, you can encounter snow on the higher passes through the mountains from Glacier to the Tetons. Wyoming's Beartooth Pass tops out at 10,947 feet, and Togwotee Pass is 9,658 feet. Both have amassed snow in August. But perhaps the most notorious is Teton Pass on the south end of Grand Teton National Park. While it only touches 8,431 feet high, its 10 percent grade proves a grunt for RVs and those hauling camping trailers. Make a practice of downshifting into second gear for descents rather than burning your brakes.

Current pass conditions are available on each state's Department of Transportation website. Some even have webcams on the summits so you can see the weather.

DIRT ROADS

Many of the prized campgrounds in the Northern Rocky Mountains are accessed via dirt or gravel roads. The best roads—wide, graveled double-laners that may be graded regularly—hold the washboards to a minimum. Others bounce along with large washboards, rocks, eroded stream beds, and small potholes. The worst contain monstrous chuckholes that can nearly swallow small cars and grab trailer hitches. Do not bring prized paint jobs on dirt roads! Take a hint from locals, who all drive rigs with dings and window chips. Rigs with four-wheel drive are helpful to get out of rough spots, but they are not required to reach any of the campgrounds in this book. If you are concerned about your vehicle's ability to navigate a certain dirt road, call the appropriate national forest for a road update.

DISTANCES

Many campers visiting the Northern Rockies for the first time expect to whiz between Glacier and Yellowstone National Parks in a few hours. The distance between the two is the same as driving from San Francisco to Los Angeles or from Boston to Baltimore, only without an interstate most of the way. To drive between the two parks, most campers take a full day without stopping or sightseeing.

GAS

Don't wait until you're empty to look for gas. Always plan ahead for filling up, as gas stations sometimes can be 60 miles or

ENTRY FEES

While many national forests and public lands require no entry fee, national parks, national historic sites, and some special Forest Service and Bureau of Land Management sites require entry fees. Rates vary by site.

NATIONAL PARK FEES

Entry for one private vehicle to Glacier, Grand Teton, or Yellowstone National Park costs $25 for a seven-day pass. No single-day passes are sold. Those entering one of the parks on foot or by bicycle pay $12. Motorcycle entry fee to Glacier costs $12, but it's $20 for Yellowstone and Grand Teton National Parks. Passes for Yellowstone or Grand Teton National Park are good for both parks.

Yellowstone has the same fees year-round, but Glacier reduces the entry fee in winter to $15, and Grand Teton reduces it to $5. Glacier also offers free entry June 20-21, July 18-19, and August 15-16. All three parks waive entry fees on National Public Lands Day on September 26 and Veterans Day on November 11.

For those camping longer than seven days, annual passes are available, too, for each of the parks. A combined annual Yellowstone-Teton pass costs $50, and the Glacier annual pass costs $35.

INTERAGENCY PASSES

Since 2007, the America the Beautiful Interagency Pass has been available. The $80 nontransferable annual pass grants entrance to federal sites run by the National Park Service, Fish and Wildlife Service, Bureau of Land Management, Bureau of Reclamation, and the U.S. Forest Service. The pass covers all occupants in a single, noncommercial vehicle. At walk-up sites, the pass is good for the pass-holder plus three adults. Children under 16 camp for free. Passes are available at entrance stations or online (store.usgs.gov/pass).

Seniors can purchase lifetime nontransferable interagency passes for $10. The pass is available to U.S. citizens or permanent residents age 62 or over. The pass admits the pass-holder and passengers in a noncommercial vehicle at per-vehicle fee areas and the pass-holder plus three adults at per-person fee areas. Lifetime passes can only be obtained in person at park entrances. Bring proof of age (state driver's license, birth certificate, passport). The pass provides a 50 percent discount on many campgrounds in the Northern Rockies.

Access passes are available free to U.S. citizens or permanent residents with permanent disabilities. The nontransferable lifetime pass admits the pass-holder and passengers in a noncommercial vehicle at per-vehicle fee areas and pass-holder plus three adults at per-person fee areas. Passes may only be purchased in person at entrance stations with proof of medical disability or eligibility for receiving federal benefits. The Access Pass provides a 50 percent discount on many campgrounds in the Northern Rockies.

more away. Gas prices tend to be cheaper in Wyoming than in Montana or Idaho; they are also cheaper in cities compared to small rural stations.

REPAIRS

Repairs to vehicles and RVs are available. Even in the national parks or on remote national forest roads, mechanics can come take a look at your vehicle and tow it back to the shop, if necessary. In some places, mobile repair services are available. Most repair services coming to your campsite will charge by the hour for their services rather than by the mile, to account for the extra time spent traveling slow dirt roads and scenic byways.

RVs

Most RVers are well aware that different campgrounds have size restrictions based on the size of parking pads and configuration of the campground road. However, RVers will want to consider the road status in their choices of campgrounds, too. Dirt national forest roads do not usually post warnings on status. Call the local ranger station to check on road status before driving. Most paved roads, except for the Logan Pass stretch of Glacier's Going-to-the-Sun Road, are suitable for any size RV. The Logan Pass stretch is closed to vehicles over 21 feet in length, taller than 10 feet, and wider than 8 feet.

MOTORCYCLES

Montana, Wyoming, and Idaho are popular for motorcycle touring. Many bikers haul their tents and mini-trailers to camp in the national parks and ride the high scenic passes. None of the three states require helmets—except for those 17 years old and younger. Motorcyclists riding the high passes should be prepared for inclement weather and cold temperatures even in August.

Navigational Tools

MAPS

The dirt roads into many campgrounds in the Northern Rockies do not even appear on the state road maps. More detailed maps will provide you with a better view of where you are driving. Overall, U.S.G.S. seven-minute maps yield the most detail for driving forest roads, hiking, and camping; however, the dollars can rack up fast on a big trip requiring a load of maps. *National Geographic Trails Illustrated* maps (800/962-1643, www.natgeomaps.com) are available for Glacier, Grand Teton, and Yellowstone National Parks. Each national forest also sells huge maps with one-mile grids; find these at ranger stations or purchase online (www.nationalforeststore.com). Beartooth Publishing (406/585-7205 or 800/838-1058, www.beartoothpublishing.com) produces regional recreation maps for southern Montana,

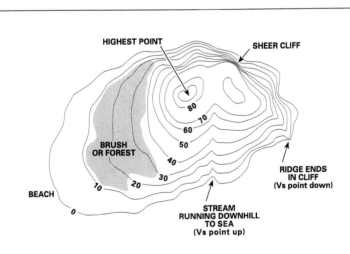

The **topographical map** is easier to read than many believe. Lines close together mean steep gradients; lines farther apart mean gentle gradients; V-shaped sets of lines pointing to higher elevations mean gulleys or stream-beds; V-shaped sets of lines pointing to lower elevations mean ridges.

northwestern Wyoming, and eastern Idaho; maps include latitude and longitude grids, trail mileages, and campgrounds.

GPS, COMPASSES, AND PERSONAL LOCATING DEVICES

GPS units and compasses are useful for navigation but require knowledge on how to use them. Learn to use them before you depart on a trip where your safety may rely on them. Large vehicle GPS units work well on most areas accessed by paved roads, but head off on remote Forest Service roads and they become useless without the detailed maps to make them functional. Both vehicle and hand-held GPS units rely on access to satellites; in many deep canyons in the Northern Rockies, you may not be able to pick up enough satellites for them to work. A compass, which always works, can provide a good backup.

While personal locating devices will transmit everywhere a GPS works, they require conscientious use. Across the West, rescue organizations are being called out for frivolous reasons or accidentally sent signals—risking the lives of the rescuers. Signals should only be transmitted in life-threatening situations. Personal locating devices should not be used as tickets to hike, climb, bike, or boat beyond one's abilities; go only those places you would visit without one and preplan self-rescue options.

Cell Phones

Visitors to the Northern Rockies expect cell phones to work everywhere as they do in virtually all populated areas. The dead zones here are vast. Even though a cell tower sits near Old Faithful in Yellowstone National Park, much of the mountainous terrain plummets into narrow canyons where signals do not reach. Don't expect to find reception deep in the forests, in canyons, or in the mountains.

One of the best inventions for emergencies, cell phones allow immediate access to help. But do not rely on a cell phone as your sole means of rescue in case of an emergency. Whether you are backpacking in a wilderness or driving 20 miles on a gravel road into a national forest, be prepared to self-rescue.

When cell phones do work in campgrounds, use of them requires etiquette. Turn off ringers because phone noise catapults hikers and campers from a natural experience back into the hubbub of modern life. If you must make a call, move away from campsites and other hikers to avoid disrupting their experience. On trails, refrain from using phones in the presence of other hikers. Be considerate of other campers and their desire to get away from it all.

CLIMATE

The Northern Rockies from Glacier to Yellowstone sit on a collision course between Arctic Continental and Pacific Maritime weather. Storms race inland from the Pacific, with accompanying moderate temperatures and precipitation. They crash into weather systems from the north that bring cold temperatures, resulting in snow in the high mountains—even in August. Yet when maritime jet streams chug north into Canada, southern heat waves creep into Montana, Idaho, and Wyoming, shooting the summer thermometer into the 90s or above.

The Northern Rockies region is a land of weather extremes. North of Helena, Montana, Rogers Pass ranks in the top 10 coldest places in the world, alongside Antarctica and Siberia. From Glacier National Park to Helena, the Rocky Mountain Front frequently makes the record books for extreme winds, cold, and heat. Loma recorded the most extreme temperature change in a 24-hour period in the United States when the January thermometer yo-yoed over 100 degrees from -54 °F to 49 °F. Lander, Wyoming, ranks in the top 10 snowiest cities in the country. Of all 50 states, Montana holds the record for the most variation in extremes—a 187-degree difference between its record high and low, and Great Falls holds the record for the most rapid temperature change recorded in the United States—47 degrees in seven minutes.

Although precipitation drops equally on both sides of the Continental Divide, wind produces more weather extremes on its east side. While winter winds often blow snow from slopes, providing forage for ungulates, they also have pushed trains off their tracks in East Glacier, Montana. Chinook winds—high warm winds with speeds reaching over 90 miles per hour—blow any time of the year, but they are most obvious in winter. Native Americans called them "snow eaters" for rapidly melting snow. In summer, high passes can rage with unpredictable winds, causing hikers to crawl on all fours across them.

Seasons

The mountains of Montana, Idaho, and Wyoming enjoy four distinct seasons, each with its own quirks. With the appropriate equipment and preparation, you can enjoy camping year-round, even in snow.

Spring

Spring first enters the lower elevations beginning in late March and April. Winter snow melts, turning miles of dirt roads into muddy tracks. While March, April, and May are appealing off-months to travel, in the Northern Rockies they are wet and cold, still clinging to winter. Weather bounces between soggy rains one day and 70-degree blue skies the next. Snow buries the high country, including scenic routes such as Going-to-the-Sun Road in Glacier National Park and the Beartooth Highway access to Yellowstone National Park, often preventing opening until after Memorial Day. May still brings tempestuous storms to the mountains, with rains and snows increasing the potential for avalanches and mudslides, but stretches of sunny days hint at summer. Spring temperatures range from the mid-50s to the mid-70s with nighttime lows from 20 to 40 degrees F.

Summer

Summer brings the most campers to the national parks and forests, but the mountainous terrain of the Northern Rockies often reels with its own weather agenda. While cool breezes are welcome on baking summer days, they can also bring snows to the mountains in August. During summer months, June habitually monsoons, but July and August usher in warmer, drier skies. Temperatures run at a pleasant 70–80 degrees with very little humidity. Most areas will see several days each summer in the 90s (locals consider anything over 90 to be sweltering), but rarely does the thermometer stretch up to triple digits. Nighttime lows dip into the 40s and 50s.

Fall

The first frosts usually descend in September. Autumn's cool nights usher in warm, bug-free days. While golds paint aspen and larch trees, temperatures bounce through extremes—from warm shorts-wearing weather during the day to below freezing at night. Plenty of 70-degree days keep summer outdoor recreation alive as schizophrenic weather jerks between rain with snow at higher elevations for a few days followed by clear, warming trends. Daytime highs vacillate between the 40s and 60s, while nighttime lows can reach the 20s.

Winter

While winter temperatures vary in elevation, most of the Northern Rockies hang in the 10–25 degree range, producing voluminous snows. While Yellowstone National Park sees about 150 inches of snowfall, Logan Pass in Glacier National Park buries under 350–650 inches of snow per year. Temperatures can spike above freezing, with its companion rain, or plummet below zero for several days with an arctic front.

Daylight and Time

Given the northern latitude and placement of Montana and Wyoming on the Mountain Time Zone's west edge, hours of daylight fluctuate wildly during the year. In June, over 16 hours of daylight floods the mountains. First light fades in around 5 A.M., and dark doesn't descend until almost 11 P.M. By late August, however, dark descends by 9 P.M. with daylight cruising on a shorter ride until December's slim 8.5 hours of daylight. Around the winter solstice, the sun rises around 8 A.M. and sets at 4:30 P.M. The Idaho Panhandle, which operates on Pacific time, sees both daylight and darkness an hour earlier.

ELEVATION

Due to the mountainous terrain, temperatures vary by elevations. Mountaintops are cooler than valley floors—up to 15 degrees cooler. Boaters may enjoy 82-degree weather camping on Montana's Flathead Lake in August, while hikers less than 60 air miles away in Glacier National Park hit trails with temperatures in the high 60s. Yellowstone National Park sits on a high-elevation plateau with most of the park above 7,500 feet, and the highest campgrounds on the Beartooth Plateau in Wyoming top out at 9,600 feet. Campgrounds in these locations are substantially cooler than those at lower elevations, such as Montana's Missouri Headwaters State Park at 4,045 feet.

Weather

Locals have a saying about the weather in the Northern Rockies: "Wait five minutes, and the weather will change." The mountain terrain lends itself to wild swings in weather. You can begin hiking in shorts but by afternoon be pulling on gloves and fleece hats as gray clouds lob sheets of sleet on slopes. Calm, glassy lakes can give way to four-foot high whitecaps as storms blow in.

LIGHTNING AND THUNDERSTORMS

Afternoon thundershowers and lightning storms are common across much of the Northern Rocky Mountains. In some locations—particularly around Yellowstone National Park and Wyoming's Beartooth Plateau—they roll in daily, almost on schedule in the late afternoon. During lightning storms, boaters should get off the water, and those enjoying beaches should move to a sheltered location. Hikers should descend from summits, ridges, and exposed slopes, and stay away from isolated trees. Some thunderstorms bring hail; other dump pelting rains.

WINDS

The Continental Divide causes high winds. With eastern air masses trying to equalize with western jet streams, the result is strong winds optimal for migrating golden eagles and wind farms. But the open, eastern slopes of the Continental Divide can pose tricky driving for large RVs, with wind gusts threatening to push them off the road. Likewise, treeless campgrounds on the prairie often bluster with winds. Montana's Rocky Mountain Front and the Absaroka Front receive the most notorious winds, on an average day blowing 7–20 mph with gusts up to 50 mph.

PRECIPITATION

While Montana, Wyoming, and Idaho are drier than the Pacific Northwest, their mountain areas receive substantial precipitation. The amount depends largely upon topography. Across the area, most snow falls November–March, but heavy snowstorms can occur as early as mid-September or as late as May—especially in the high mountains. Annual snowfall averages 300 inches in many of the mountain ranges—hence the region's numerous ski resorts. Valley floors receive about 50 inches of snowfall. Nearly half of the region's annual average precipitation falls from May through July in the form of valley rain, sleet, or snow. Heavy rains falling during the spring thaw contribute to late season avalanches and flooding.

FOREST FIRES

Like snow, wind, or rain, lightning-caused fire is a natural process. It is healthy for the ecosystem, for it removes bug infestations, reduces deadfall and nonnative plants, releases nutrients into the soil like a good fertilizer, and maintains a natural mix of vegetation. Following decades of heavy fire suppression policy, forest fuels have built up across the Northern Rocky Mountain forests to high levels, with some forests suffering under severe attack from pine beetles and blister rust—conditions that kill trees and make them ripe for fire. You can check on current forest fire locations and their status at www.inciweb.org/.

CAMPING CONCERNS

Camping Regulations and Red Tape

NATIONAL PARKS

National parks are set aside for their historical, geological, cultural, or biological significance, and geared toward public recreation. Hunting is not permitted, nor is picking wildflowers or berries for commercial use. Dogs are not allowed on trails; neither are mountain bikes. Camping is limited to designated campgrounds and generally limited to 14 days in one campsite, unless otherwise posted. Permits are needed for backcountry camping. National parks require entrance fees, and each campground requires fees.

Waterton Lakes National Park in Canada borders Glacier National Park and is used to access parts of Glacier. U.S. national park passes are not valid in Waterton. Passports are required to drive to Waterton; only U.S. and Canadian citizens with passports are permitted to travel into Glacier past Goat Haunt.

NATIONAL FORESTS

National forests are used for their resources, with timber harvesting, commercial berry picking, mushroom harvesting, mining, and recreation permitted. Hunting is permitted with licenses administered by the state. Trails permit dogs and mountain bikes as long as no special designation says otherwise. Designated campgrounds usually allow stays up to 14–16 days in the same campsite; a few high-use areas employ shorter limits. Unless otherwise designated, primitive camping is usually permitted anywhere outside of developed campgrounds. Permits are not needed for backcountry camping. National forests usually do not charge entrance fees, but some specific visitor sites do. Some developed campgrounds require fees; others are free, as is primitive camping.

Wilderness areas are administered usually by the national forest that contains the wilderness boundaries. They permit no mechanical transports, including mountain bikes. Hunting is permitted. Fido can go along on the trail, and permits are not needed for backcountry camping, which is free.

OTHER GOVERNMENT LANDS

Bureau of Land Management and Bureau of Reclamation terrain operates much like national forest land, with most developed campgrounds charging fees. Entrance fees are usually not charged; however, some sites charge day-use fees. Stays are limited to 14 days in the same spot, unless posted otherwise. Free primitive camping is permitted outside of developed campgrounds.

Montana, Wyoming, and Idaho **state parks** vary in campgrounds and amenities under the auspices of each state. State parks charge fees for day use and camping. Most campground fees include day use, too. Montana residents have free day use of Montana state parks. Wyoming residents receive discounts on day use and camping fees in Wyoming state parks. Camping is permitted in a Montana or Wyoming state park for 14 days out of a 30-day period; in Idaho, the limit is 15 days.

Camping with Children

Children learn to enjoy camping when they can participate in the activities. Have them help with camp chores—building fires, collecting garbage, and bear-proofing the camp.

Kids can earn **Junior Ranger Badges** by completing self-guided activities in Glacier, Yellowstone, and Teton National Parks. Activities, which target ages 5–12, vary by park but are an excellent way to help children learn about the park and wildlife. Junior Ranger activity books or newspapers are available at all visitors centers in the parks (free in Glacier, $3 in Yellowstone, $1 in Teton). When kids return the completed newspaper to any visitors center, they are sworn in as Junior Rangers and receive park-specific badges.

Plan ahead with kids by taking along extra clothing and shoes. If kids can get wet, they will. Replacing wet soggy clothing with warm dry gear improves their attitude and their enjoyment of camping. When hiking, even for short walks, take along water and snacks to maintain the energy level for children.

Camping with Pets

NATIONAL PARKS

Pets are allowed in national parks, but only in limited areas. Campgrounds, roadsides, and parking lots are all okay for pets. When outside a vehicle, pets must be on a six-foot or shorter leash or be caged. Pets are not permitted on national park trails, with the exception of Waterton Lakes National Park north of Glacier. Two main reasons are to protect fragile vegetation and thermal areas and to prevent conflicts with wildlife. Bears are a major argument for leaving the pooch home. Pets are also not permitted in visitors centers or at beaches. If necessary, pets can stay in your vehicle while you are viewing roadside attractions, but provide ventilation for the animal's survival.

NATIONAL FORESTS

Contrary to national parks, national forests permit pets on most trails. (Read trailhead signs carefully because some trails do not permit pets.) Keep in mind that many hikers in the Northern Rockies have heightened sensitivity to movement, due to being on alert for

In setting up camp, always be mindful of potential ecological disturbances. Pitch tents and dispose of human waste at least 200 feet from the water's edge. In grizzly bear territory, increase the distance between your tent and your cooking area, food-hang, and the water's edge threefold. In other words, if you're in grizzly country, do all your cooking 100 yards (not feet) downwind of your sleeping area. If you can establish an escape tree nearby, all the better.

bears. To prevent bear conflicts and to avoid scaring other hikers with a dog charging down the trail, keep Fido on a leash. Pets are also allowed in campgrounds, but they must be leashed, rather than running free.

In bear country, store pet food, bowls, and toys in a hard-sided vehicle or bear box when not in use. Like humans, pets should leave no traces other than footprints. Clean up and dispose of all pet feces in the garbage.

Camping Ethics

Protection of public lands and campgrounds is up to those of us who use them. Be respectful of nature and campground facilities, taking care of them as if they were your own. Follow Leave No Trace ethics when camping in developed campgrounds or the backcountry.

LEAVE NO TRACE

Visitors to the Northern Rockies need to take an active role in maintaining the environment.

Plan ahead and prepare. Plan ahead for camping with fluctuating weather in mind, and choose appropriate hiking routes for mileage and elevation gain. Carry hiking essentials.

Travel and camp on durable surfaces. In both developed and backcountry campgrounds, camp in designated sites only. Protect fragile trailside plants by staying on the trail, refusing to cut switchbacks, and walking single file on trails even in the mud. If you must walk off-trail, step on rocks, snow, or dry grasses rather than on wet soils and fragile plants.

Leave what you find. Flowers, rocks, and goat fur tufts on shrubs are protected resources in national parks. Even on other public lands, they should be left for others to enjoy. For lunch stops and camping, sit on rocks or logs where you find them rather than moving them to accommodate your camp.

Properly dispose of waste. Whatever you bring in, you must pack out or deposit in garbage receptacles. Do not burn garbage in fire pits. If toilets are not available, urinate on rocks, logs, gravel, or snow to protect

fragile soils and plants from salt-starved wildlife. Bury feces 6–8 inches deep at least 200 feet from water. Pack out used toilet paper in your trash.

Minimize campfire impacts. Make fires in designated fire pits only. Use small, wrist-size dead and down wood, not live branches. Be aware that fires or firewood collecting is not permitted in many places in national parks.

Respect wildlife. Bring along binoculars, spotting scopes, and telephoto lenses to aid in watching wildlife. Keep your distance. Do not feed any wildlife, even ground squirrels. Once fed, they become more aggressive. Maintain a distance of a football-field length from bears and wolves and 25 yards from all other wildlife.

Be considerate of other visitors. Minimize use of electronics, generators, and other noisemakers in campgrounds, and keep dogs from barking. Follow posted quiet hours, departing and arriving as silently as possible before or after hours.

RECREATION

Hiking

The Northern Rockies are crisscrossed with hiking trails—some short day-hike destinations and others stringing long miles back into remote roadless wilderness areas. While links still remain to be built, the Continental Divide Trail forms the longest trail system, running through the Wind River Range in Wyoming, Yellowstone National Park, the Bitterroot Mountains along the border of Montana and Idaho, several national forests and wilderness area, and finishing in Glacier National Park. Also, Montana's Bob Marshall Wilderness and Yellowstone National Park each contain over 1,000 miles of trails, while Glacier National Park contains over 700 miles of trails. Outfitters are available for guided hiking and backpacking in Glacier, Grand Teton, and Yellowstone National Parks.

HIKING ESSENTIALS

Hiking in the Northern Rockies of Montana, Wyoming, and Idaho demands preparedness. High elevations, unpredictable winds, fast-changing weather, and summer snowstorms can catapult a lazy day walk into a nightmare if one is not prepared. Take the following:

Extra clothing: Rain pants and jackets can double as wind protection, while gloves and a lightweight warm hat will save fingers and ears. Carry at least one extra water-wicking layer for warmth. Avoid cotton fabrics that stay soggy and fail to retain body heat.

Extra food and water: Take lunch and snacks, like compact high-energy food bars. Low-odor foods will not attract animals. Heat, wind, and elevation dehydrate hikers quickly; always carry extra water. Don't drink directly from streams or lakes due to bacteria; always filter (with a one-micron filter) or treat water sources before drinking.

Navigation: Although national park trails are well-signed, national forest and wilderness trails are not. Take a detailed topographical map of the area to best ascertain the distance traveled and location. A compass or GPS will also help, but only if you know how to use them.

Flashlight: Carry a small flashlight or headlamp with extra batteries. In an after-dark emergency, the light becomes invaluable.

First-aid kit: Two Band-Aids are not enough! Carry a fully equipped standard first-aid kit with blister remedies. Don't forget personal requirements such as bee-sting kits and allergy medications.

Sun protection: Altitude, snow, ice, and lakes all increase ultraviolet radiation. Protect yourself with 30 SPF sunscreen, sunglasses, and a sunhat or baseball cap.

Emergency bathroom supplies: To accommodate alfresco bathrooms, carry a small trowel, plastic bags, and toilet paper. Move at least 200 feet away from water sources. For urinating, aim for a durable surface, such as rocks, logs, gravel, or snow, rather than fragile plants, campsites, or trails. Bury feces 6-8 inches deep in soil. Pack the toilet paper out in a Ziploc bag.

Feminine hygiene: Carry heavy-duty Ziploc bags for packing tampons and pads out rather than burying them.

Insect repellent: Insect repellents containing 50 percent DEET work best with the mosquitoes and black flies. Purchase applications that rub or spray in a close range rather than aerosols that become airborne onto other people, plants, and animals.

Pepper spray: Use an eight-ounce can of pepper spray for charging bears, but do not bother unless you know how to use it and what influences its effectiveness. It is not to be used like bug repellent.

Cell phones: Take the cell phone along for emergencies, but don't rely on it for rescue. In much of the Northern Rockies, cell phones do not work. Plan to self-rescue. If you do carry a cell phone, turn it off to save the batteries for an emergency and to avoid offending fellow hikers who seek solitude, quiet, and the sounds of nature.

Miscellaneous: Pack along a knife, a few feet of nylon cord, and duct tape wrapped around a flashlight handle. Many hikers have repaired boots and packs with duct tape and a little ingenuity.

TRAILS AND SIGNS

Conditions on trails vary depending on the season, elevation, recent severe weather, and wildlife. In places where swinging or plank bridges are removed annually across rivers and creeks, crews re-install them in late May or early June. Steep snowfields inhibit early hiking at higher elevations until July. Avalanches and severe storms—wind microbursts, heavy snows, and torrential rains—can cause miles of downed trees across trails. Depending on the location, crews may or may not be available for immediate clearing. Some trails in Glacier, Grand Teton, and Yellowstone National Parks are closed temporarily due to increased bear activity. Yellowstone also has annual closures in feeding areas. To find out about trail conditions before hiking, stop at ranger stations and visitors centers for updates. In general, trails in the national parks are maintained in better condition than in national forests, due to funding of bigger trail crews.

National park trails tend to be well-signed with direction and mileage. Some signs, however, may be in kilometers, rather than miles. (To convert kilometers to miles, multiply the kilometers listed by 0.6.) National forests and wilderness areas tend to have both less specific signage and fewer signs. Carry a good map and a compass or GPS to navigate the maze of trails. In the Northern Rockies, some trails have names while some use numbers with names or without names. The numbers, which are assigned by the U.S. Forest Service, identify the trails on U.S.F.S. maps and many topographical maps of the region.

In the national parks, where the concentration of bears is high, you may also see **bear warning signage.** Use extreme caution and all your bear country savvy when bears frequent a trail. Obey closures: They usually mean that a bear has been aggressive or is feeding on a carcass, which it will forcefully defend.

BACKCOUNTRY CAMPING

Backcountry camping is by permit only in Glacier, Grand Teton, and Yellowstone National Parks. Backcountry campgrounds vary in size, but most separate sleeping sites from communal cooking areas. No food, garbage, toiletries, or cookware should ever be kept in the tent sites. Near the cook sites, a bear pole, bar, or box allows for safe food storage. Take along a 30-foot rope and stuff bags to hang your food in Glacier and Yellowstone; backpackers in Grand Teton are required to carry bear-resistant food containers, available for free. Many backcountry campsites do not allow fires. Carry a lightweight stove for cooking.

To plan backcountry camping trips by foot, horseback, or boat in Glacier, Grand Teton, or Yellowstone National Park, follow the directions in each park's Backcountry Trip Planner, available online (www.nps.gov/glac, www.nps.gov/grte, www.nps.gov/yell). Permits may be reserved by mail for $20–25 (a limited number of sites are assigned this way, and you still have to pay your per person fee when you pick up the actual permit), or you can pick up permits in person, no more than 24 hours in advance. Permits are not issued over the phone. Permits are free except in Glacier ($4 per person per night). Permits are not needed for backpacking in national forests or wilderness areas.

Backcountry campers in the Northern Rockies need to take a 30-foot rope for hanging food, a small screen or strainer for sifting food particles out of gray water, a water purifier, and a small trowel for human waste when a pit toilet is unavailable.

Mountaineering and Climbing

The peaks of Montana, Idaho, and Wyoming draw mountaineers for their rugged, challenging routes to the summits. The quality of the rock varies between the crumbling sedimentary shales in the north and the harder granitic rocks in the south, making the type of climbing different. Ice routes, too, are shrinking due to the rapid melting of the region's glaciers. Mountaineers shimmy routes up through most of the region's mountain ranges, but a few specific locales gain above-average reputations.

While technical rock-climbing routes are available in Glacier National Park, the bulk of the summits are reached via Class 3 or 4 scrambles. Long, loose scree fields lead to tight goat walks along cliffs. Use Gordon Edwards's *A Climber's Guide to Glacier National Park* for route descriptions. Even though more technical routes exist, all six summits over 10,000 feet can be reached via scrambles. You're on your own, though, as the park has no permitted guides for off-trail scrambles.

Teton National Park harbors the region's best rock-climbing opportunities. With over 50 major routes to the summit, the Grand Teton tops the Northern Rockies' highest elevation at 13,770 feet. For those with the expertise to climb self-guided, check out Aaron Gams's *Teton Rock Climbs* for route descriptions. Two companies in Jackson offer instruction and guided trips to Teton summits—including the Grand. Other popular rock-climbing routes string down the Wind River Mountains, particularly Cirque of the Towers in the Popo Agie Wilderness.

With the glaciers across the Northern Rockies fast melting into extinction, the routes that utilize ice are changing. However, winter ascents on skis and ice climbing are available.

Bicycling

ROAD BIKING

Road bicyclists relish the Northern Rockies for the long dramatic climbs over the Continental Divide and the miles of pedal-free descents. The **TransAmerica Trail** cuts through the region, too, as does the **Lewis & Clark Trail,** among other long-distance rides. Route descriptions and maps are available from Missoula's Adventure Cycling Association (800/721-8719, www.adventurecycling.org).

Narrow, curvy roads with no shoulders and drivers gawking at scenery instead of the road all shove the biker into a precarious position.

Wear a helmet and bright colors to ensure your safety.

Two scenic byways rank with bicyclists for both their challenge and their scenery. In Glacier National Park, the 52-mile **Going-to-the-Sun Road** requires planning. Early-season up-and-back riding is available in spring and fall while road construction has the route closed to vehicles. But due to snow at Logan Pass, riders usually cannot bike across the summit. Once the road is open (mid-June–mid-Sept.), bicycling restrictions close two narrow sections of the road on the west side 11 A.M.–4 P.M. until Labor Day. Eastbound riders must be at Logan Pass by 11 A.M. or dismount and wait.

Starting from Red Lodge, Montana, the 68-mile **Beartooth Highway** climbs a lung-busting route up to 10,947 feet to cross Beartooth Pass on a high tundra plateau. Riding westbound towards Yellowstone National Park lets you get the full wow of the snowcapped peaks of the Absaroka Range. The route, which bounces from Montana into Wyoming and back into Montana, passes scads of lakes, which produce mosquito swarms into August that plague bicyclists. Snow buries the highway much of the year, but it usually is open mid-May to mid-October.

For riders looking for flat spins instead, Idaho's 72-mile paved **Trail of the Coeur d'Alenes** runs from Mullan to Plummer, following rivers, passing wetlands brimming with wildlife, and crossing the Chacolet Bridge. Interpretive signs, picnic areas, and rest stations dot the route, which changes so little in elevation that you're never sure if you're riding uphill or down. The trail is usually snow-free April–November.

Glacier and Yellowstone National Parks maintain a handful of campsites at most of their developed campgrounds for bicyclists. The shared campsites ($5 per person) have bear boxes for storing food and room for several small tents, and the campsites are first come, first served.

MOUNTAIN BIKING

While single-track mountain bike trails are

sprouting up around the region faster than weeds, rail trail projects are converting defunct tracks into wide bike paths. Idaho's 15-mile **Route of the Hiawatha** (208/744-1301, www.ridethehiawatha.com), the region's most popular mountain bike trail, crosses seven trestles and rides through nine dark tunnels, with the longest (1.7 miles) running under the Idaho-Montana state line. The Route of the Hiawatha (open late May–early October, $9 adults, $5 kids) also offers a shuttle ($9 adults, $6 kids) for those who only want to ride downhill. Eastern Idaho's 42-mile **Railroad Right of Way Trail** also runs from Warm River to West Yellowstone.

Many national forest trails permit bicycles, except in wildernesses or areas with special designations. Mountain bikes also are not permitted on national park trails, except for special routes designated in each national park.

Fishing

The movie *A River Runs Through It* catapulted Montana's rivers into the national consciousness with dreams of clear waters and wild trout. But that's the true nature of fly-fishing in the Northern Rockies, which harbor 18 blue-ribbon trout streams populated with rainbow, brown, brook, Yellowstone cutthroat, westslope cutthroat, and bull trout—many wild-bred. Lowland lakes also fill with lake trout (mackinaw), kokanee salmon, northern pike, and bass.

NATIONAL PARK FISHING

Each of the national parks has different licensing regulations for fishing. Glacier requires no license. Yellowstone National Park requires a fishing permit for anglers 16 years and older ($15 for three days, $20 for seven days, or $35 for a season); anglers 15 and younger may fish without a permit if they are fishing under the direct supervision of an adult who has a valid park fishing permit, or they can obtain a free permit (signed by a responsible adult) to fish without direct adult supervision. Grand Teton requires a Wyoming fishing license. Waterton

Native cutthroat trout are one of the prized fish in Northern Rockies streams.

© BECKY LOMAX

Lakes National Park requires a national park fishing license (one day CDN$10 or annual CDN$35). Purchase national park fishing licenses at ranger stations and visitors centers.

Each park has slightly different fishing regulations with seasons, catch-and-release laws, closure locations, and creel limits designed to protect the resources in the area. You'll need to be able to identify species that are catch-and-release only—especially the endangered bull trout. Fishing regulations are available online and at ranger stations and visitors centers.

STATE FISHING LICENSES

Outside the national parks, state fishing licenses are required. Some states offer discounts for those who are disabled. Licenses are available online and at sporting goods stores. The one exception is on Indian reservations; each has its own tribal fishing permits and rates.

Montana fishing licenses (http://fwp.mt.gov/fishing/license/default.html) cost $13

for two days or $26 for the season for resident adults. Conservation licenses for resident seniors age 62 and older and kids ages 12–14 cost $8. Resident teens ages 15–17 pay $16 for the season. Kids 11 and under fish free. Nonresident licenses for ages 15 and older cost $25 for two days, $53.50 for 10 days, or $60 for the season. Additional permits are required for warm-water game fish, paddlefish, and bull trout.

Idaho fishing licenses (http://fishandgame. idaho.gov/fish/) for residents cost $11.50 for a single day and $5 for each consecutive day; for the season, they cost $13.75 for ages 14–17 and $25.75 for adults. Nonresident licenses cost $12.75 for one day and $6 for each consecutive day, or season licenses cost $21.75 for kids up to 17 and $98.25 for adults. Nonresidents can also purchase a three-day salmon/steelhead license for $37.50.

Wyoming fishing licenses (http://gf.state. wy.us/fish/fishing/index.asp) for residents cost $6 per day; for the season, they cost $3 for youths and $24 for adults. Nonresidents pay a daily license fee of $14 or $92 for an annual license. Nonresident youths pay $15 for an annual fee.

Boating

Small reservoirs dot the Northern Rockies, but big lakes command most of the boating interest from visitors. Montana's Flathead Lake is the largest freshwater lake west of the Mississippi. Montana, Wyoming, and Idaho each require boats to be registered. Rates vary depending on the state and the size of boat.

In **Montana,** all sailboats 12 feet long and longer and all motorized boats and personal watercraft must be registered. Nonmotorized sailboats less than 12 feet long and manually propelled boats, regardless of length, are exempt. Boats from out of state or country may be used in Montana for up to 90 consecutive days without registering with the state.

Wyoming requires all motorized boats to be registered. Motorboats that are properly registered in another state may be used on Wyoming's waters for up to 90 consecutive days without registration.

Idaho requires all boats with mechanical propulsion to be registered. Boats currently registered in another state may be used on Idaho's waterways for 60 consecutive days or less without registering with the state.

WATERSKIING

Water-skiers from warm-water areas often are shocked by their first contact with water in the Northern Rockies. It's cold. Frigid in places. The ice-fed deep lakes maintain a chill even in summer. Surface water may only heat up in August into the low 60s. Bring a wetsuit for more enjoyable waterskiing.

Rafting

The Northern Rockies spill with Class III–V white water—frothy waves with big holes. Other Class I–II rivers make for more leisurely float trips. Thirteen major rivers contain Class III and above white-water sections that you can run on your own if you have the expertise or go with local guides. In Montana, head for the Clark Fork, Middle Fork of the Flathead, Yellowstone, Gallatin, Madison, or Stillwater River for white-water thrills. Where Wyoming's Shoshone, Green, and Snake Rivers squeeze through canyons, you can bounce through rapids. In Idaho, the Lochsa, Selway, and Main Salmon provide single-day options for white water, but the Middle Fork of the Salmon requires a multi-day trip through the River of No Return Wilderness. Most of these rivers have nearby drive-to campgrounds available, and some are lined with primitive campgrounds for overnight float trips. Check on current water levels through state hydrology departments or American Whitewater (www. americanwhitewater.org).

Floating most of these rivers on an overnight trip does not require a permit. However, Idaho's Selway, Middle Fork of the Salmon, and Main Salmon Rivers do. These are acquired via an annual computerized lottery drawing. Between December 1 and January 31, you can

© BECKY LOMAX

Whitewater rafting and kayaking is available on the Middle Fork of the Flathead as well as on other rivers in the Northern Rockies.

apply for all three rivers with one application (www.fs.fed.us/r4/sc/recreation/4rivers/index.shtml); launch winners are notified in mid-February. Permits are not available by phone, except for acquiring permits from cancelled launches after the February drawing.

Outfitters guide trips on most of the Northern Rockies' major rivers and some of their tributaries. Trips include half-day, full-day, and multi-day excursions. Locate outfitters in the towns nearest the rivers. Check with state agencies to be sure they are licensed.

Canoeing and Kayaking

The Northern Rockies also harbor lakes and slow-moving rivers—gems for multi-day paddling trips. In Montana, the Missouri River through Gates of the Mountains offers paddling along the route of Lewis and Clark, plus hiking and camping. Connected lakes, such as Idaho's Priest Lake and Upper Priest Lake, include camping on islands as well as paddling the two-mile Thoroughfare to the roadless upper lake, where the Forest Service maintains four campgrounds. A paddle route

around Montana's Flathead Lake makes use of six state parks.

Canoes and kayaks are available to rent in select places, but to guarantee you have a boat, bring your own or call ahead to reserve the rental. Rentals and guided paddle trips are available in Yellowstone and Grand Teton National Parks, plus Flathead Lake.

GEAR SELECTION AND MAINTENANCE

Camping in the Northern Rocky Mountains requires planning for all types of weather and conditions. The proper equipment can make the difference between enjoying a trip when the temperatures plummet or the air drips soggy and hating the experience.

Tents

Tents come in a variety of shapes, sizes, weights, and prices—tailored to different types of camping. Any reputable outdoor store will provide comparative ratings for their tents. Due to elevation, erratic weather, and

© BECKY LOMAX

Rain flies should cover tents completely for the best protection.

the potential for snow even in August, tents for the Northern Rockies should be double walled—with a tent wall and a rain fly that covers the complete tent to the ground. Purchase a tent with sealed seams to prevent water seeping into the tent. Bug netting is also essential for the voracious mosquitoes and black flies that proliferate during June and July. While many campers go without footprints or tarps below their tents, in wet, muddy conditions or snow, ground cloths can keep the tent floor dry. They also will prolong the life of a tent. Three-season tents work the best in the Northern Rockies for camping in summer, spring, or fall—even with erratic summer snowstorms. But for winter camping, invest in a four-season tent.

After use, dry tents completely before storing to prevent mildew. They also should be stored in a dry location rather than a damp garage, attic, or crawl space. If possible, store them loose rather than folded or rolled up

tight to prevent breakdown of the fabric on the folds.

Sleeping Bags and Pads

Sleeping bags are available with synthetic or goose down insulation. Either works well in the Northern Rockies, although those with goose down need to take extra precaution to keep their bags dry because down loses its insulation value if it gets wet. Invest in a waterproof stuff sack to keep sleeping bags dry. Bags for summer camping should be rated to 20 degrees; however, if you plan on camping in spring or fall in the Northern Rockies, you'll be more prepared for the weather mood swings with a bag rated to zero. The cut of mummy bags as opposed to rectangular bags will allow your body to heat up the space faster.

A sleeping bag alone will not keep you warm without an insulating layer between the ground and your body. Sleeping pads range from a thin 0.5-inch layer of foam to large thick air mattresses that require a compressor to inflate. Assess your needs before purchasing. If backpacking, go for the lightest weight in foam or inflatable. If car camping, you can afford to pack along more weight. Self-inflating and blow-up air mattresses allow you to camp more quietly than if you must turn on an air compressor.

Both sleeping bags and pads should be stored loose to extend their life as long as possible. A tall closet works well for hanging both. Launder sleeping bags according to the manufacturer's instruction.

Day Packs

If you plan on hiking on your camping trip, bring along a day pack. While you can get away with carrying just a water bottle for a one-hour hike, you should be prepared for the weather to change abruptly on longer day hikes. Mountain weather can mutate from blue skies to rain squalls, raging winds, hail, and even snow during summer. Bring a day pack that can fit extra clothing—rain jacket and pants, warm hat, gloves, and a light

CAMPING EQUIPMENT CHECKLIST

Group Gear
- 30-foot bear pole rope
- Aluminum foil
- Camp chairs
- Camp table
- Can opener
- Coffee cone and filters
- Cooking utensils
- Cooler
- Corkscrew
- Dishwashing tubs
- Duct tape
- Eating utensils
- Firewood
- Food
- Footprint or ground tarp
- Fuel
- Garbage bags
- Hatchet
- Kindling and newspaper
- Lanterns
- Lighter and matches
- Maps, GPS, and compass
- Mugs, plates, bowls
- Parachute cord for tarps
- Pot-holder
- Pots and pans with lids
- Rain tarps
- Salt, pepper, and spices
- Soap and sponge
- Stove
- Tent with rain-fly
- Toilet paper and trowel
- Utility knife
- Water filter
- Water jugs
- Ziploc bags

Safety
- First-aid kit
- Insect repellent
- Pepper spray
- Sunscreen

Personal Gear
- Bandana
- Batteries
- Flashlight or headlamp
- Fleece top and pants
- Gloves
- Hiking boots
- Rain jacket and pants
- Sleeping bag and pad
- Sunglasses
- Sun hat or ball cap
- Swimsuit
- Toiletries
- Warm hat
- Water bottle
- Water sandals

Recreational Gear
- Binoculars and spotting scopes
- Camera
- Cribbage board
- Day pack
- Fishing rod and tackle
- Kayak, raft, or canoe
- Mountain bike and helmet
- Paddles and personal flotation devices
- Playing cards
- Trekking poles

fleece layer. Your pack should also be able to fit lunch, snacks, first-aid kit, sunscreen, bug juice, headlamp, and water. Consider the size of optional items you may enjoy, such as a camera and binoculars.

Good day packs will include small padded hip belts to keep the weight from pulling on your neck. The hip belts also work for attaching pepper spray holders for bears. Try day packs on for size in the store, as different brands work better for different body types. Air out packs after use and store them in a dry location.

Food and Cooking Gear

Cooking while camping can be as simple as

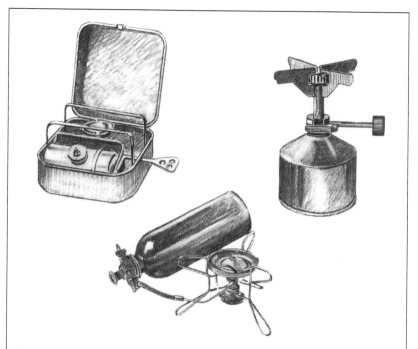

Stoves are available in many styles and burn a variety of fuels. These are three typical examples. Top left: **White gas stoves** are the most popular because they are inexpensive and easy to find; they do require priming and can be explosive. Top right: **Gas canister stoves** burn propane, butane, isobutane, and mixtures of the three. These are the easiest to use but have two disadvantages: 1) Because the fuel is bottled, determining how much fuel is left can be difficult. 2) The fuel is limited to above-freezing conditions. Bottom: **Liquid fuel stoves** burn Coleman fuel, denatured alcohol, kerosene, and even gasoline; these fuels are economical and have a high heat output, but most must be primed.

boiling water for quick instant freeze-dried meals or as involved as slow roasting on the fire. Your mode of travel will most likely dictate the type of cooking you choose to do. If backpacking, bicycling, kayaking, or canoeing, quick-cooking meals require less gas, they weigh less, and they need fewer pots. Slow roasting on the fire requires aluminum foil, aluminum pots, or Dutch ovens. Traveling by RV, car, or boat allows for more room to pack along meals that are entertaining to cook. Virtually any recipe can be adapted to cooking outdoors with a little ingenuity.

Stoves and cooking pots also come in a variety of sizes to suit different uses. Smaller versions are available for backpacking, kayaking, and canoeing, while larger, heavier options are only suitable for vehicle-assisted camping. Most stoves are heated with white gas and propane, both available across the Northern Rockies. Butane canisters are convenient, but replacement canisters may not be as easy to find, and they add to landfills. Most outdoor lightweight cooking pots are now available with nonstick surfaces.

In bear country, low-odor foods mean less scent to attract wildlife. Store all food, cooking gear, utensils, coolers, pet food, and garbage inside hard-sided vehicles when not in use or at night. For those traveling by foot, bicycle, or motorcycle, bear boxes are available at some campgrounds. Carry 30 feet of rope for hanging food and cooking gear in case bear boxes are not available. Hang food 20 feet from the ground and 10 feet from the trunk of a tree.

Water Treatment

While the water in developed campgrounds is usually safe to drink, most streams and lakes in the West run the risk of carrying giardia and cryptosporidium, the two most common cysts in the Northern Rockies. At campgrounds where potable water is not available, plan to purify or boil water to kill potential trouble causers.

Boiling water requires no extra equipment—just a stove and extra fuel. The Wilderness Medical Society recommends heating the water to a rapid boil for one minute to kill microorganisms.

Water filters and purifiers pump water by hand through filters that are rated to strain out certain sizes of critters. A 1.0-micron filter will remove giardia and cryptosporidium, but a 0.2-micron filter will also remove bacteria while a 0.0004-micron purifier will remove viruses, too.

Chemical treatments include the use of chlorine or iodine tablets, crystals, or liquid. Follow the manufacturer's instructions for their use, most of which require waiting 30 minutes before drinking. While many campers dislike the taste left from iodine, it can work as a backup in an emergency.

UV light is now available in a compact instrument about the size of an electric toothbrush for killing microorganisms. Immerse the light tube into the water for 60 seconds. Batteries are required.

What to Wear

LAYERS

Dress in layers to adapt to the quick-changing mountain conditions and weather. Mornings can start with blue skies and temperatures for T-shirts and shorts, but by afternoon, winds

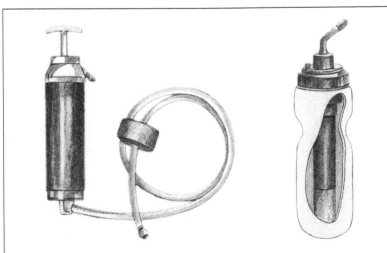

Water filters are a wise investment since all wilderness water should be considered contaminated. Make sure the filter can be easily cleaned or has a replaceable cartridge. The filter pores must be 0.4 micron or less to remove bacteria.

can usher in storm fronts delivering hail and even snow. The opposite can happen, too, with frosty mornings warming by afternoon. Layers allow adapting to the changing conditions by putting on additional clothing for protection from the elements or taking a layer off to cool down. Prepare for mountain extremes by packing a fleece or wool hat and gloves.

SUN PROTECTION
The sun's intensity increases at high elevations. With much of the Northern Rocky Mountains stretching above 6,000 feet in elevation, protection from the glaring sun is important for preventing blistering sunburns. Add white snowfields and glaciers to the elevation, and the sun's rays wax more intense. Ball caps or sun hats protect the face from the sun's scorching rays, and sunglasses will protect the eyes from burns and snowblindness.

RAIN GEAR
Breathable rain gear is essential camp clothing for the Northern Rockies. Breathable rain fabrics let you recreate outdoors without getting equally as wet beneath your jacket as outside. Both rain shells and pants are useful, especially when hiking in brushy meadows laden with moisture. Arm pit zippers let you adjust the ventilation of shells. Hoods allow for closing off the neck area to chilling, wet winds, and ankle zippers on pants allow for putting them on and taking them off without removing your hiking boots.

SHOES, SOCKS, AND FOOT CARE
Footwear needs to adapt to the recreation you plan to do while camping. Hikers need boots with a sturdy tread, which are available in lightweight, waterproof, and leather options. Ill-fitting shoes and incorrect socks cause blisters—preventable by shoe choice and fit. Squished toes and loose heels are the biggest culprits for blisters. To prevent toes from blistering by rubbing on each other, a shoe with a larger toe box is essential. If heels fit too loosely, two remedies can prevent blisters: Wearing one liner sock inside a heavier sock allows socks to rub against each other rather than against the heels, and footbeds, either custom or market-ready, will absorb excess space and provide more support for the foot.

Appropriate socks can also prevent blisters. Although cotton socks feel good, they aren't the best choice for hiking. Cotton absorbs water from the feet and holds it, providing a surface for friction. Synthetic, silk, or wool blend socks wick water away from the skin. Socks should fit smoothly over the feet with no added bunching. A comfortable fit, but not loose, is paramount for preventing blisters.

Those including water sports in their itineraries should also bring sturdy water sandals or shoes that will protect the feet on rough algae-slick rocks. Flip-flops do not protect the feet; use sandals or water shoes with a thick, solid tread. During spring and fall, booties will keep the feet warm in chilly waters.

SAFETY AND FIRST AID

Plants

POISON IVY
Montana, Wyoming, and Idaho have pockets of poison ivy. Recognize the below-knee-height plant by its three leaves, often tinged with red and clustering in river corridors. If your skin comes into contact with poison ivy, wash immediately with soap and water. Do not scratch infected areas as it can spread. Avoid contact with eyes, mouth, and open sores. If you have a reaction, an antihistamine can relieve symptoms. Seek medical help.

NETTLES AND COW PARSNIP
Lush, forested slopes of the Northern Rockies sprout with two irritating plants. Stinging nettles vary in height 2–4 feet. Recognize them by the serrated-edged leaves and minuscule

CAMPING IN BEAR COUNTRY

Most of the Northern Rocky Mountains of Montana, Wyoming, and Idaho comprise both prime grizzly bear habitat and black bear territory. Where bears are plentiful, campgrounds require strict food and garbage management practices. Even in areas with less frequent bear visitation, properly storing food and garbage prevents problems with other wildlife – deer, squirrels, jays, and rodents.

When not in immediate use, all food, meat, cooking appliances, utensils, pots, pans, canned foods, toiletries, and empty or full food storage containers should be kept in a closed, hard-sided vehicle during the day and at night. Coolers and beverage containers should also be stored inside vehicles, as should garbage.

For campers traveling on bicycles, motorcycles, or open vehicles, many campgrounds provide food lockers or bear boxes for storing food. Use these to store food, cooking gear, toiletries, and garbage, but do not leave the garbage in the bear box. Dispose of it properly in a bear-resistant trash container.

Store all pet items that may attract or provide a reward to wildlife inside vehicles. This includes pet food, empty food dishes, and toys. Stock feed should also be stowed in hard-sided vehicles.

When hiking or walking in the woods, make noise. To avoid surprising a bear, use your voice – sing loudly, hoot, holler, or clap your hands. Bears tend to recognize human sounds as ones to avoid and usually wander off if they hear people approaching. Consciously make loud noise in thick brushy areas, around blind corners, near babbling streams, and against the wind.

Hike with other people in broad daylight, avoiding early mornings, late evenings, and night. Avoid hiking alone. Keep children near.

flowers hanging on a drooping stem. If skin comes into contact with nettles, you can use sting-relief products such as those for mosquito bites. Calydene also provides relief.

Some people react to cow parsnip. Recognize the plants by their 10-inch-diameter heads of white flowers and gigantic leaves shaped like maple leaves. Reactions can vary from redness to blistering. For the latter, seek medical help.

Mosquitoes and Ticks

Bugs are irritants, but more importantly, they can carry diseases such as West Nile virus and Rocky Mountain spotted fever. Protect yourself by wearing long sleeves and pants as well as using bug repellents in spring and summer when mosquitoes and ticks are common. Also, avoid areas heavily trafficked by ungulates (deer, sheep, elk), which transport ticks. If a tick bites you, remove it and disinfect the bite; keep your eye on it for lesions or a rash, consulting a doctor if either appears.

Wildlife

BEARS

Safety in bear country starts from knowledge and behaving appropriately. With the exception of Alaska and Canada, the Northern Rockies harbor the highest density of grizzly bears, and black bears find likable habitat here, too. For safety while watching bears, maintain the distance of a football field between you.

Avoid bear-feeding areas. Since bears must gain weight before winter, feeding is their prime motive. Often, bears will pack in 20,000 calories in a day. In the early season, glacier lily bulbs attract grizzlies for their high nutritional value. By midseason, cow parsnip patches provide sustenance, in between high protein carrion. If you stumble across an animal carcass, leave the area immediately and notify a ranger. In August, huckleberry patches provide high amounts of sugar. Detour widely around feeding bears.

Never approach a bear. Watch the body language. A bear that stands on hind legs may just be trying to get a good smell or better viewpoint. On the other hand, head swaying, teeth clacking, laid-back ears, a lowered head, and huffing or woofing are signs of agitation: Clear out!

If you do surprise a bear, take care of yourself. Contrary to all inclinations, do not run! Instead, back away slowly, talking quietly and turning sideways or bending your knees to appear smaller and nonthreatening. Avoid direct eye contact, as the animal kingdom interprets eye contact as a challenge; instead, avert your eyes. Leave your pack on; it can protect you if the bear attacks.

In case of an attack by a bear you surprised, use pepper spray if you have it. Protect yourself and your vulnerable parts by assuming a fetal position on the ground with your hands around the back of your neck. Play dead. Only move again when you are sure the bear has vacated the area.

If a bear stalks you as food, which is rare, or attacks at night, fight back, using any means at hand – pepper spray, shouting, sticks, or rocks – to tell the bear you are not an easy food source. Try to escape up something, like a building or tree.

Hike safely by making noise on the trails with your voice. Do not rely on the bells sold in gift shops to alert bears to your presence. (Guides jokingly call them "dinner bells.") Bells are ineffective and may incur wrathful glares from fellow hikers who loathe them. To check the bells' effectiveness out hiking, see how close you are to oncoming hikers before you hear their ringing. Sometimes, it's too close! Bear bells are best as a souvenir, not as a substitution for human noise on the trail. Talk, sing, hoot, and holler. You'll feel silly at first, but after a while, you'll realize it's something everyone does.

Many hikers carry **pepper spray** to deter aggressive, attacking bears; however, they are not repellents like bug sprays to be sprayed on the human body, tents, or gear. Instead, spray the capsicum derivative directly into a bear's face, aiming for the eyes and nose. While pepper sprays have repelled some attacking bears, wind and rain may reduce effectiveness, as will the product's age. Small, purse-sized pepper sprays are not adequate for bears; carry an eight-ounce can, which can be purchased in most outdoor stores in the Northern Rockies, and practice how to use it. Pepper spray is not protection: Carrying it does not lessen the need for making noise in bear country. Pepper sprays are not allowed by airlines unless checked in luggage, and only brands with USEPA labels may cross through Canadian customs.

Bears are dangerous around food—be it a carcass a bruin may be guarding in the woods or a cooler left unwittingly in a campsite. Protecting bears and protecting yourself starts with being conscious of food—including wrappers and crumbs. Gorp tidbits dropped along the trail attract wildlife, as do "biodegradable" apple cores chucked into the forest. Pick up what you drop and pack out all garbage so you will not be leaving a Hansel and Gretel trail for bears.

MOUNTAIN LIONS

Mostly unseen because of their nocturnal wanderings, these large cats are a sight to behold in daylight. They rarely prey on humans, but they can—especially small kids. While hiking, make noise to avoid surprising a lion. Hike with others, and keep kids close. If you do stumble upon a lion, do not run. Be calm. Group together and look big, waving arms overhead. Look at the cat from peripheral vision rather than staring straight on as you back slowly away. If the lion attacks, fight back with everything: rocks, sticks, or kicking.

BISON, MOOSE, AND OTHER WILDLIFE

Bison can be as dangerous as bears. Gorings all too frequently occur despite the docile appearance of the animals. Moose also can be lethal with both antlers and hooves. For safety, maintain a distance of 25 yards from most wildlife and 100 yards from bears and wolves.

First Aid

DEHYDRATION

Many first-time visitors find the Northern Rockies to be surprisingly arid, despite the green appearance. Fight fluid loss by drinking plenty of water—especially when hiking. Altitude, sun overexposure, wind, and exercise can all lead to dehydration, which manifests in yellow urine (rather than clear), lightheadedness, headaches, dizziness, rapid breathing and heart rate, and fatigue. If you feel a headache coming on, try drinking water. If you hike with children, monitor their fluid intake. For mild dehydration, sports drinks on the market today can restore the balance of body fluids, electrolytes, and salt. Severe cases of dehydration may need intravenous fluids; treat these as a medical emergency and get to a hospital.

GIARDIA

Lakes and streams can carry parasites such as *Giardia lamblia,* which if ingested causes cramping, nausea, and severe diarrhea for an exceptionally long period of time. Tap water in the park campgrounds and picnic areas has been treated (you'll definitely taste the strong chlorine in some systems), but if you drink untreated water from streams and lakes, you run the risk of ingesting the cysts. Seek medical attention if you suspect a case of giardia.

WATER HAZARDS

Contrary to popular opinion, grizzly bears are not the number one cause of death and accidents in the Northern Rockies; drowning is. Be extremely cautious around lakes, streams, and especially waterfalls. Waters here are swift, frigid, plumb-full of submerged obstacles, and unforgiving. Be especially careful on rocks and logs around fast-moving streams; these often have moss and clear algae that makes the rocks slippery.

Yellowstone's gorgeous hydrothermic features can be deadly, too. In many, water bubbles above boiling, and what looks like solid ground may only be a thin crust that can give way with the weight of a human. Stay on designated boardwalks and trails. Toxic gases spew in some of the geyser basins. If you feel sick, leave the area immediately.

ALTITUDE

The Northern Rockies climb in elevation. Some visitors from coastal regions may feel the effects of altitude—a lightheadedness, headache, or shortness of breath—in high zones like Logan Pass in Glacier, the Yellowstone plateau, and the Beartooth Highway. In most cases, slowing down a hiking pace helps, along with drinking lots of fluids and giving the body time to acclimatize. If symptoms are more dramatic, descend in elevation as soon as possible.

Altitude also increases the effects of UV radiation. Above the tree line, you can actually feel cool but still redden with sunburn. Use a strong sunscreen to prevent burning. Sunglasses and a hat will also help protect you.

CREVASSES AND SNOWBRIDGES

While ice often looks solid to step on, it harbors unseen caverns beneath. Crevasses (large vertical cracks) are difficult to see, and snowbridges can collapse easily as a person crosses. Unless you have training in glacier travel, you're safer staying off the ice. Even Glacier's tiny icefields have caused fatalities. Snowfields also demand respect. Steep slopes can run out into rocks, trees, or over cliffs. If sliding for fun, choose a location with a safe runout. Do not travel across steep snowfields unless appropriately equipped with an ice axe and the knowledge to use it.

HYPOTHERMIA AND FROSTBITE

Because mountain weather can disintegrate rapidly from a summer balm to a winter snowstorm, hypothermia is a very real threat. At onset, the body's inner core loses heat, thus reducing mental and physical functions. It's insidious and progressively subtle: Watch for uncontrolled shivering, incoherence, poor judgment, fumbling, mumbling, and slurred speech. Exhausted, physically unprepared, and ill-clad hikers are most at risk. You can avoid becoming hypothermic by donning rain gear and warm layers. Don't let yourself get wet. Also, leave the cotton clothing back in the car; instead wear moisture-wicking layers that you can adjust to stay dry.

If someone in your party is hypothermic, get him or her sheltered and into dry clothing immediately. Warm liquid can help heat the body, but be sure it's nonalcoholic and noncaffeinated. Build a fire for warmth. If the victim cannot regain body warmth, get into a sleeping bag with the victim, with you and the victim stripped for skin-to-skin contact, and seek medical help.

Frostbite, which usually affects extremities when exposed to very cold temperatures, causes the tissues to freeze, resulting in hard, pale, and cold skin. As the area thaws, the flesh becomes red and painful. Prevent frostbite by watching the hands, feet, nose, and ears for discoloration and wearing appropriate clothing. Warm the hands in armpits, and cover the nose and ears with dry, gloved hands. If frostbitten, do not rub the affected skin, let thawed areas refreeze, or thaw frozen areas if a chance of refreezing exists. Seek medical help immediately.

BLISTERS

Blister prevention starts with recognition of "hot spots" or rubs. Before any blister forms, apply Moleskin or New Skin to the sensitive area. Both act as another layer of skin. Moleskin adheres to the skin, like a thick Band-Aid, with its fuzzy covering absorbing friction. New Skin, looking and smelling like fingernail polish, rubs off gradually, absorbing friction instead of the skin. Be aware that New Skin must be reapplied frequently and should not be used on open sores. In a pinch, duct tape can be slapped on potential trouble spots.

Once a blister occurs, apply Second Skin, a product developed for burns that cools the blister off and cushions it. Cover Second Skin with Moleskin, which absorbs future rubbing and holds the Second Skin in place. Also, marketed under several brand names, specialty blister bandages promote healing. Apply the adhesive bandage carefully with hand heat to mold it to the foot surface. Leave it in place until the blister begins to callus. Check placement often, as these bandages and moleskin tend to migrate away from the blister.

HANTAVIRUS

The hantavirus infection is contracted by inhaling the dust from deer mice urine and droppings. Once infected, you'll feel flu-like symptoms set in; seek medical attention immediately if you suspect contact with the virus. To protect yourself, avoid areas thick with rodents, their burrows, and woodpiles. Store all food in rodent-proof containers. If you find rodent dust in your gear or tent, spray with a mix of water and bleach (1.5 cups bleach to one gallon water).

GLACIER

© BECKY LOMAX

BEST CAMPGROUNDS

Looking like teeth gnawing at the heavens, Glacier

National Park's chiseled ramparts – some of the most ancient rocks in North America – scratch the sky. Ice-filled cirques glimmer above blooming blue, magenta, and neon-yellow wildflower meadows before plummeting into deep verdant green valleys speckled with turquoise lakes. Grizzly bears, mountain goats, bighorn sheep, and moose dine on the landscape, while wolves hunt down the weaker ungulates.

For visitors to Glacier, the best way to experience these Crown of the Continent's wonders is camping. You can wake to songbirds in early summer and see deer wander through campgrounds. The park, which is a National Heritage Site and UNESCO Biosphere Reserve, harbors 13 drive-to park service campgrounds within its boundaries – many of which fill by noon in midsummer and on holiday weekends. You can also boat to an additional handful of backcountry campgrounds. The surrounding national forests provide less-crowded campgrounds and primitive places to camp with access to trailheads. Three small towns dotting the park's perimeter offer RVers places to hook up to services.

Located a full day's drive north of Yellowstone, Glacier Park's one million acres split along a north-south line – the Continental Divide – that runs from the Canadian border to Marias Pass. Clad in thick evergreens, the western mountains tuck campgrounds into thick forests or at the toe of long lakes that feed into the Flathead River's Middle Fork and North Fork, which form the park's western and southwestern boundaries. On the eastern flanks, campgrounds cluster in a mix of grasslands and aspen groves, as the mountains tumble onto the Blackfeet Reservation's prairie. The border with Canada divides Glacier from its northern sister, Waterton Lakes National Park; together they formed the world's first international peace park, adding international camping to the mix.

Only one road bisects the core of Glacier Park. In a feat of ingenious 1920s engineering, Going-to-the-Sun Road slices through cliffs as it crawls on a narrow, precipitous path to Logan Pass. Tunnels, arches, and retaining walls give the road its unique character while leading cars into an alpine wonderland where marmot whistles ride air currents through top-of-the-world scenery. Five campgrounds flank its natural wonders, such as a pocket of rain forest harboring huge western red cedars up to 500 years old.

On the west side of the Continental Divide, several long, forested valleys spill from Glacier's peaks. The most popular houses the park's largest body of water – Lake McDonald – and three campgrounds, including two of the park's biggest. Forming the park's southern boundary, the Middle Fork of the Flathead River, which parallels Highway 2, runs from a canyon into West Glacier, the local capital for white-water rafting, fishing, float trips, and a string of private RV parks and campgrounds. To the north, long dirt roads cut through the bucolic backwoods of the North Fork of the Flathead River Valley to primitive river campsites or remote lake campgrounds that provide solitude.

On the east side of the Continental Divide, private campgrounds on the Blackfeet Reservation offer hookup services unavailable at the park's five campgrounds. St. Mary's private campgrounds garner views of Red Eagle Mountain's maroon slopes, with peaks rising straight up from the prairie. Of the east-side park service campgrounds, two are the most popular: Two Medicine on the southeast corner ranks as highest drive-to lake in the park, and Many Glacier in the Swiftcurrent Valley is a hub for well-traveled trails that lead to lakes floating with icebergs even in August.

Over 700 miles of trails crisscross Glacier, making it a hiker's playground. Paths climb to glaciers, duck under cascading waterfalls, tunnel through a mountain, lead to lookout perches with panoramic views, and reach lakes teeming with native westslope cutthroat trout. Two of the park's campgrounds sit at trailheads where you can stay for multiple days, hiking to a different place each day without traveling in your car.

For over a century, campers have come to Glacier to explore its rare country. With plenty of places to pitch a tent, plan to linger here for several days to a week.

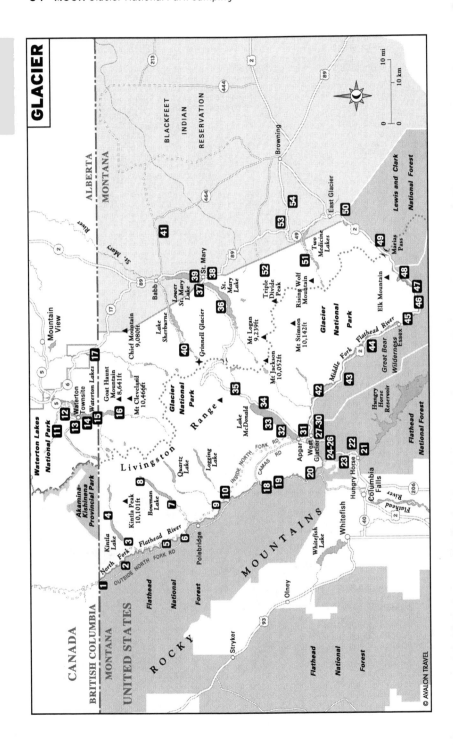

1 NORTH FORK BORDER PRIMITIVE

Scenic rating: 7

on the North Fork of the Flathead River in Flathead National Forest

The North Fork of the Flathead River enters the United States at the northwest corner of Glacier National Park. At the Border River Access for floating the river, a few dispersed tent-only campsites line the river near the parking lot. The campsites make a good base for rafting, canoeing, or fishing the river. The camp is also a 10-minute drive from the trailhead to climb 2,917 feet in five miles to Thoma Lookout for views that stretch across Glacier's entire northern panorama of peaks as well as down to the camp, across the border swath, and into Canada. While the border patrol still uses the station near the river, the crossing into Canada has been closed for over a decade after a flood washed out the Canadian road.

The primitive, partially shaded tent campsites with views of the river sit south of the parking lot. Since the bumpy, potholed drive to the border takes so long, the campsites are the most remote in the North Fork of the Flathead River Valley, guaranteeing privacy with only the sound of the river and the crackling campfire. Tucked under cottonwoods and firs, the campsites sit in their own cubbyholes, but within earshot of each other. During a midsummer day, the river access sees traffic, but at night there are only wolf howls.

Campsites, facilities: The river access has three primitive tent campsites. Facilities include rock fire rings and a vault toilet in the parking lot. (No fires are permitted in the parking lot.) Boil or purify river water before drinking. Pack out your trash. Camping is limited to three days. This is bear country: practice safe food storage. Leashed pets are permitted.

Reservations, fees: No reservations are accepted. Camping is free. Open year-round, although the last 0.1 mile is not plowed to the parking lot.

Directions: From Polebridge, drive north on the North Fork Road (Forest Road 486) for 22 miles to the U.S. border station. Turn right for 0.1 mile to the river access parking lot.

GPS Coordinates: N 49° 0.019' W 114° 28.538'

Contact: Flathead National Forest, Glacier View District, 10 Hungry Horse Dr., Hungry Horse, MT 59919, 406/387-3800, www.fs.fed.us/r1/flathead/.

2 NORTH FORK OF THE FLATHEAD RIVER PRIMITIVE

Scenic rating: 9

flanking Glacier National Park's west boundary in Flathead National Forest

With its headwaters in Canada, the North Fork of the Flathead River flows 59 miles from the border along the western boundary of Glacier National Park. Its route through the North Fork Valley flows through one of the most ecologically diverse areas of Montana, home to rare plants, woodpeckers and birds, and wildlife from the pygmy shrew to the wolf. The river, designated as Wild and Scenic, runs with Class II–III rapids, and the flow peaks in early June. Life jackets are required. Eight river accesses accommodate those rafting, kayaking, and canoeing: the border, Ford, Polebridge, Coal Creek, Big Creek, Great Northern Flats, Glacier Rim, and Blankenship. The river is best for rafting mid-May–early September.

Accessed only via rafts, canoes, or kayaks, primitive campsites flank the river's west bank. Camping on the east bank in Glacier is not permitted, except for Round Prairie (permit required). Most campsites tuck under cottonwoods and firs within view of the river, and most are not in sight of each other, which guarantees solitude. At night, you'll hear the sound of the river and moose walking through the water.

Campsites, facilities: About 15 primitive tent campsites that can accommodate 4–6 people line the river. Campers are required to take a groover for human waste and a fire pan to minimize burn scars. Purchase the *Three Forks of the Flathead River Floating Guide* from the Hungry Horse Ranger Station to aid in finding sites and avoiding private land. A permit is not required to camp overnight in the river corridor. Vault toilets are available at the eight river access sites. Pack out your trash. Pets are permitted. Practice safe food storage to deter bears.

Reservations, fees: No reservations are accepted. Camping is free. Open April–November.

Directions: From Columbia Falls, drive the potholed washboard North Fork Road (Forest Road 486) to the river access site of your choice. The border put-in is the farthest away at 53 miles. The other river access sites require turning east off the North Fork Road and driving less than 0.5 mile to reach launch sites. Each river access site is signed.

Contact: Flathead National Forest, Glacier View District, 10 Hungry Horse Dr., Hungry Horse, MT 59919, 406/387-3800, www.fs.fed.us/r1/flathead/.

3 KINTLA LAKE

Scenic rating: 8

on Kintla Lake in Glacier National Park

BEST (

Located at 4,015 feet in elevation between Starvation and Parke Ridges, Kintla Lake defines remote. Not only do you have to drive the bumpy, dusty miles of dirt road to reach the Polebridge entrance station to Glacier, but then you need to drive another hour of dirt road to reach the lake. Due to the cantankerous road, which is not recommended for large RVs and trailer combinations, and distance from pavement, the lake attracts few people; campers

who come here find the rewards of solitude. No motorboats or personal watercraft are permitted on the lake, leaving paddlers to ply its waters in quiet. Anglers—especially those who can get away from shore in a boat—can pull in native westslope cutthroat trout and bull trout. One trail departs the campground along the north shore and reaches the head of the lake in 6.2 miles. Backpackers continue on to Upper Kintla and over Boulder Pass to end at Goat Haunt at Waterton Lake (32 miles total) or Bowman Lake (37 miles total).

The tiny, quiet campground cuddles under big trees in one loop. Several of the campsites near Kintla Creek have their parking spot on the loop but their tent sites, tables, and campfires down an embankment below the road. Sites 10 and 12 sit closest to the lake; sites 1–3 sit the farthest away. Sites 4–10 border Kintla Creek. Little privacy remains due to stripped underbrush.

Campsites, facilities: The 13 RV and tent campsites can accommodate only small RVs, although the park service discourages RVs or trailer combinations. Facilities include picnic tables, fire rings with grills, hand pumps for potable water, vault toilets, garbage service, and a boat ramp. During primitive camping, when the water is turned off, boil or purify lake water. Strict food storage regulations are in effect for bears. Bring firewood; collecting is illegal. Leashed pets are permitted.

Reservations, fees: No reservations are accepted. Campsites cost $15 late May–mid-September. Cash, check, or credit card. Depending on snow, primitive camping ($10) is available mid-September–November and earlier in May.

Directions: From the Polebridge entrance station to Glacier National Park, drive 14.3 miles north on the Inside Road. The road terminates in the campground.

GPS Coordinates: N 48° 56.144' W 114° 20.743'

Contact: Glacier National Park, P.O. Box 128, West Glacier, MT 59936, 406/888-7800, www.nps.gov/glac.

4 HEAD OF KINTLA LAKE

Scenic rating: 8

on Kintla Lake in Glacier National Park

BEST (

Huddling between Starvation and Parke Ridges in Glacier's remote northwest corner, the six-mile-long Kintla Lake sees very few people at its upper end. Those who visit its campground at 4,100 feet in elevation enjoy solitude and watching bald eagles and bears. A 2.7-mile trail from the campground continues on to Upper Kintla Lake, where scenery unfolds with glaciers hanging off Kintla Peak and Kinnerly Peak rising straight from the lake. Take a brisk swim in the glacial waters before hiking back to the campground.

Reach the campground at the head of the lake by hiking 6.2 miles or paddling up the lake from Kintla Campground at the foot of the lake. At the head of the lake, the remote, quiet campground is built on a hillside with two communal cooking sites in the cedars near the shore and tent sites scattered on shaded terraces in the forest above. There are bears, so bring a rope for hanging food and cooking gear. In spring, high water floods some of the beach, but in summer as the water level drops, the smooth-stoned beach provides an easier place to pull boats out of the water. Tie up all boats at night in case winds arise!

Campsites, facilities: The campground has six designated tent campsites, and each holds up to four people each. Facilities include rock-rimmed fire pits, log benches, a food hanging cable, and a pit toilet. Boil or purify lake water for drinking. Pack out your trash. Pets are not permitted.

Reservations, fees: Backcountry permits are required. Advance reservations ($20) for three of the campsites are available starting April 15. Get permits for remaining sites in person 24 hours in advance at the Apgar Backcountry Office in Apgar. Permits cost $5 per adult per night and $2.50 for children 8–15. They are free for children 7 and under. Cash, check, or

credit card. Open June–November. With early snowmelt, the campground may be available by late May.

Directions: From the Polebridge entrance station to Glacier National Park, drive 14.3 miles north on the Inside Road to the Kintla Campground.

GPS Coordinates: N 48° 58.538' W 114° 15.186'

Contact: Glacier National Park, P.O. Box 128, West Glacier, MT 59936, 406/888-7800, www.nps.gov/glac.

5 ROUND PRAIRIE

Scenic rating: 7

on the North Fork of the Flathead River in Glacier National Park

At 3,850 feet in elevation, Round Prairie is the only campground on the North Fork of the Flathead River's east bank in Glacier National Park. It is one of four Palouse prairies in the North Fork Valley, blooming with wheatgrass, fescues, oatgrass, sagebrush, and rare plants. Due to Whitefish Mountain's rain shadow, Round Prairie sees only 20 inches of annual precipitation. Access the campground by floating the river or driving the bumpy, dirt Inside Road to walk through 0.5 mile of Round Prairie.

A mixed forest of firs and cottonwoods lines the river around the quiet, remote campground, which sits on the edge of Round Prairie. Bring a rope for hanging food and cooking gear. A large gravel bar allows boats to be beached. In the campground, a communal cooking site is available, and three tent sites are separated for privacy in the trees. The campground faces the sunset over the Whitefish Mountains.

Campsites, facilities: The walk-in or boat-in campground has three tent campsites, each holding up to four people. Facilities include a rock fire ring, log benches, a pit toilet, and food-hanging cable. Boil or purify river water for drinking. Pack out your trash. Permits for two of the three sites are reserved until 3 P.M. each day for river floaters. No pets are permitted.

Reservations, fees: Backcountry permits are required. Advance reservations ($20) for two of the campsites are available starting April 15. Get permits for other sites in person 24 hours in advance at the Apgar Backcountry Office in Apgar. Permits cost $5 per adult per night and $2.50 for children 8–15. They are free for children 7 and under. Cash, check, or credit card. Opens June–November. With early snowmelt, the campground may be available in late May.

Directions: For walking in, drive from the Polebridge park entrance station 7.6 miles north on the Inside Road to the trailhead on the left. For boating, drive north from the town of Polebridge on the dirt North Fork Road for 21 miles to the border or 10 miles to Ford to launch onto the river.

GPS Coordinates: N 48° 51.463' W 114° 21.985'

Contact: Glacier National Park, P.O. Box 128, West Glacier, MT 59936, 406/888-7800, www.nps.gov/glac.

6 SONDERSON MEADOW

Scenic rating: 9

on the North Fork of the Flathead River in Flathead National Forest

North of the town of Polebridge in the North Fork Valley, Sonderson Meadow sprawls into large open fields surrounded by fir forests and beaver ponds. The North Fork of the Flathead River runs around the perimeter of the meadow, making it popular for camping with those floating the river, but you can also drive to it. A skinny dirt road accesses the meadow, which used to harbor an old airstrip. Unmarked game trails good for morning and evening wildlife-watching hikes wander around the meadow. Call the Forest Service first to be sure the gate on the access road is open.

From campsites along the meadow and river, you get shots of the rugged, remote Livingston Range of Glacier National Park with the sunrise coming over the park. The primitive, quiet campsites sit along the river's bank with wide-open views of the night sky and the music of the river. The campsites are very spread out for privacy at the north and south ends of the meadows, accessed by two rough jeep trails.

Campsites, facilities: Sonderson Meadow has three RV or tent campsites, but the road is only suitable for small RVs—not trailers. Facilities include only rock fire rings, and fire pans are recommended instead. To use river water, boil or filter it first. Campers are required to use a self-contained system for solid waste and carry it out to an RV dump station. This is bear country, so practice safe food storage. Pack out your trash. Follow Leave No Trace principles in camping, using previous fire rings rather than making new ones and placing your tent on ground or rocks rather than sensitive vegetation. Leashed pets are permitted.

Reservations, fees: Reservations are not accepted. Camping is free. Open April–November.

Directions: Drive seven miles north from the town of Polebridge on the North Fork Road. Turn right at the sign for Schnauss Cabin onto Forest Road 10372 and follow the narrow road as it drops one mile down the steep hill to the river.

GPS Coordinates: N 48° 50.052' W 114° 20.407'

Contact: Flathead National Forest, Glacier View District, 10 Hungry Horse Dr., Hungry Horse, MT 59919, 406/387-3800, www.fs.fed.us/r1/flathead/.

7 BOWMAN LAKE

Scenic rating: 10

on Bowman Lake in Glacier National Park

BEST (

Sitting at 4,030 feet in elevation, Bowman Lake is one of two remote drive-to lakes in

© BECKY LOMAX

bear pole for hanging food at Head of Bowman Lake campground in Glacier

Glacier's northwest corner. Even though access to the campground requires miles of pot-holed dirt road driving—on either the Outside North Fork Road or the Inside North Fork Road, both equally nasty in dust—it is the most popular campground in the North Fork Valley. Trailheads lead to Numa Lookout (5.6 miles) for stunning views across to the Rainbow-Carter massif, Quartz Lake Loop (12.4 miles) for fishing, and the Bowman Lake Trail (7.1 miles) along the north shore. Motorboats of 10 horsepower or less are permitted, but not Jet Skiing and waterskiing. Canoeists and kayakers tour the shoreline to watch for bald eagles. The best fishing is from a boat; anglers go after westslope cutthroat and bull trout.

Sitting at the foot of Bowman Lake, the quiet campground winds one large loop through the brushy mixed forest. Filtered sunlight warms most of the campsites. A short road and trails connect to the beach and boat launch. Campsites are spread out for privacy,

but you will see a few other campsites through the trees. Sites on the east side of the loop sit closer to the beach, but none border the shoreline. Walk to the lakeshore after dark for a stunning look at the stars.

Campsites, facilities: The campground has 48 RV or tent campsites, which can fit small RVs. The park service does not recommend large RVs or trailer combinations on the rough, narrow access road. Facilities include picnic tables, fire rings with grills, pit toilets, drinking water, and garbage service. During primitive camping, the water is turned off, but you can boil or purify water from the lake. Leashed pets are permitted. Strict food storage regulations are in effect for bears. Bring firewood; collecting is illegal.

Reservations, fees: No reservations are accepted. Campsites cost $15. Cash, check, or credit card. Open late May–mid-September; however, primitive camping ($10) is possible mid-September–November and sometimes in early May depending on snow.

Directions: From the Polebridge entrance station to Glacier, drive 0.3 mile north to the Bowman Lake Road. Turn right and drive six miles to the campground on the left.
GPS Coordinates: N 48° 49.709' W 114° 12.087'

Contact: Glacier National Park, P.O. Box 128, West Glacier, MT 59936, 406/888-7800, www.nps.gov/glac.

8 HEAD OF BOWMAN LAKE

🚶 ⛴ 🛶 🚐 ⛵ ⛺

Scenic rating: 10

on Bowman Lake in Glacier National Park

BEST (

In Glacier Park's remote northwest corner, six-mile-long Bowman Lake cuts through a steep-walled valley between the hulks of Rainbow and Numa Peaks. Craggy Thunderbird Peak rises out of the lake's head. At an elevation of 4,100 feet at the lake's head, the backcountry campground is favored by canoeists, kayakers, boaters, and hikers for its rugged remote setting and very few people. Paddling to the campground takes about two hours; hiking the 7.1 miles along the northwest shore takes about 3 hours. A boat ramp at the foot of the lake assists launching, and a parking lot is available for overnight parking. Watch for winds; the half-mile-wide lake kicks up big whitecaps fast.

The quiet campground sprawls on both sides of a creek, with tent sites scattered in the trees for privacy and two communal cooking sites. Bring a rope for hanging food and cooking gear. In spring, high water floods some of the beach, but in summer as the water level drops, the smooth-stoned beach provides an easier place to pull boats out of the water. Beach all boats at night in case winds arise!

Campsites, facilities: The campground has six tent campsites, each holding up to four people. Facilities include rock fire pits, food hanging cables, and a pit toilet. Boil or purify lake water for drinking, and pack out your trash. Pets are not permitted.

Reservations, fees: Backcountry permits are required. Advance reservations ($20) for three of the campsites are available starting April 15. Get permits for remaining sites in person 24 hours in advance at the Apgar Backcountry Office in Apgar. Plan to be in the office as soon as it opens as the popular campground fills its sites fast. Permits cost $5 per adult per night and $2.50 for children 8–15. They are free for children 7 and under. Cash, check, or credit card. Opens mid-June–November. With early snowmelt, the campground may be available in late May and early June, too.

Directions: From the Polebridge entrance station to Glacier, drive 0.3 mile north on the Inside Road to the Bowman Lake Road. Turn right and drive six miles to the foot of Bowman Lake.

GPS Coordinates: N 48° 54.219' W 114° 7.264'

Contact: Glacier National Park, P.O. Box 128, West Glacier, MT 59936, 406/888-7800, www.nps.gov/glac.

9 QUARTZ CREEK

Scenic rating: 6

on the Inside North Fork Road in Glacier National Park

Located on the Inside North Fork Road through Glacier's western forests, tiny Quartz Creek Campground is used by campers looking for quiet and solitude. Its access requires driving miles of dirt road that is as notorious for its jarring potholes and bumpy washboards as it is for its clouds of dust. Adjacent to the campground, an infrequently maintained trail follows Quartz Creek for 6.8 miles to Lower Quartz Lake. Mountain bikers use this camp on North Fork tours, and anglers fish the creek and Quartz Lakes for native westslope cutthroat trout. Some camping supplies are available at the Polebridge Mercantile, 1.5 miles from the Polebridge entrance station; cookies and cinnamon rolls are freshly baked there daily.

The campground, which is tucked under a mix of large shade-producing firs and sunny brush, rarely fills up due to its remoteness. Sites 4, 5, and 6 border the creek. Bring bug juice as the riparian area tends to breed mosquitoes in droves. The small sites also have small dirt parking pads.

Campsites, facilities: The campground has seven RV and tent campsites that can accommodate small RVs. Large RVs and trailer combinations are not recommended on the Inside Road. Facilities include picnic tables, fire rings with grills, and a pit toilet. Water is available from the creek, but be sure to boil or purify it before use. Pack out your trash. Collecting of downed firewood is permitted on the Inside North Fork Road, but not in the campground. Leashed pets are permitted. Strict food storage regulations are in effect for bears.

Reservations, fees: No reservations are accepted. Campsites cost $10. Cash, check, or credit card. Open July–early November.

Directions: From the Polebridge entrance

station to Glacier National Park, drive 5.7 miles south on the Inside North Fork Road (Glacier Route 7). From Fish Creek Campground, drive 21.3 miles north on the Inside Road. The campground sits on the east side of the road.

GPS Coordinates: N 48° 43.297' W 114° 13.456'

Contact: Glacier National Park, P.O. Box 128, West Glacier, MT 59936, 406/888-7800, www.nps.gov/glac.

10 LOGGING CREEK

Scenic rating: 8

on the Inside North Fork Road in Glacier National Park

Located on Glacier's western forest slopes, Logging Creek sits on the Inside North Fork Road a long distance from pavement. Top speeds for driving the potholed, washboarded, curvy road reach about 20 mph. Sullivan Meadows, a few miles south of the campground, was home to the first pack of wolves that migrated from Canada in the 1980s. A nearby trail departs for Logging Lake, a 4.4-mile forested hike. The lake harbors westslope cutthroat trout, but fly-fishing requires wading away from the brushy shore. Many campers—including mountain bikers—use this remote campground for looping on a scenic tour through the North Fork Valley. Pack a birding field guide, for the area around the Logging Ranger Station and Logging Creek provides good bird-watching. Over 196 species of birds have been documented in the North Fork, including at least 112 that nest in the valley.

Logging Creek burbles adjacent to the campground, and across the road the idyllic Logging Ranger Station is staffed intermittently in summer. The quiet campground's one loop swings through large cedars and firs that admit filtered sunlight to the small campsites. Due to its remoteness, the campground rarely fills up. The damp vicinity also is a breeding ground for mosquitoes, so come prepared with repellent. Listen at night for wolf howls.

Campsites, facilities: The campground has seven RV and tent campsites that can accommodate small RVs. Large RVs and trailer combinations are not recommended on the Inside Road. Facilities include picnic tables, fire rings with grills, and a pit toilet. Water is available only from the creek, but be sure to boil or purify it before use. Pack out your trash. Collecting of downed firewood is permitted on the Inside North Fork Road, but not in the campground. Leashed pets are permitted. Strict food storage regulations are in effect for bears.

Reservations, fees: No reservations are accepted. Campsites cost $10. Cash, check, or credit card. Open July–early November.

Directions: From the Polebridge entrance station to Glacier Park, drive 8.3 miles south on the Inside North Fork Road, also called Glacier Route 7 on some maps. Or from the Fish Creek Campground, drive 18 miles north on the Inside Road. The campground sits on the east side of the road.

GPS Coordinates: N 48° 41.897' W 114° 11.535'

Contact: Glacier National Park, P.O. Box 128, West Glacier, MT 59936, 406/888-7800, www.nps.gov/glac.

11 CRANDELL MOUNTAIN

Scenic rating: 9

on Blakiston Creek in Waterton Lakes National Park, Canada

On the opposite side of Crandell Mountain from the Waterton Townsite, this campground tucks into a red-rock valley with outstanding wildlife-watching opportunities. Wildlife frequents its narrow paved access road—the Red Rocks Parkway. The campground nestles in the woods along Blakiston Creek, where you can see bears and moose. Bighorn sheep also graze on the slopes across the creek. An easy 3.1-mile round-trip walk to Crandell Lake departs from the campground, and a 10-minute drive leads to the end of Red Rocks Parkway, where trailheads depart to Blakiston Falls (0.6 mile), Goat Lake (3.9 miles), and Avion Ridge (14 miles). You can also mountain bike five miles to Snowshoe Cabin or around Crandell Mountain. Fishing is available in Blakiston Creek; Waterton Park and Alberta fishing licenses are both required.

With many campsites tucked deep in mixed forest, the campground's eight loops have a remote feel, with trees and brush providing some privacy between sites. A, B, C, and D loops sit in thicker trees; E, F, G, and H loops are more open with views of surrounding peaks. Tight loops and back-ins can cramp some RVs. Plan on arriving at the campsite office by noon in July and August to get a campsite.

Campsites, facilities: Crandell has 129 RV or tent campsites; some can accommodate midsized RVs. Facilities include picnic tables, fire rings, flush toilets, drinking water, kitchen shelters, firewood, a disposal station, interpretive programs, and bear-resistant food storage lockers. Strict food storage regulations are in effect. Leashed pets are permitted. A wheelchair-accessible toilet is available.

Reservations, fees: Reservations are not accepted. Campsites cost CDN$22. Add on CDN$8 for a burning permit for fires. Cash, check, or credit card. Open mid-May–early September.

Directions: Drive the 30-mile Chief Mountain International Highway across the border (open mid-May–September), turn west for 0.7 mile to the park entrance, then go 2.8 miles south on the park entrance road and turn west onto Red Rocks Parkway. Find the campground entrance on the left 3.8 miles up the parkway.

GPS Coordinates: N 49° 5.947' W 113° 56.758'

Contact: Waterton Lakes National Park, Box 200, 215 Mount View Rd., Waterton Park, AB T0K 2M0, Canada, 403/859-2224, www.pc.gc.ca/pn-np/ab/waterton.

12 PASS CREEK

Scenic rating: 9

on Blakiston Creek in Waterton Lakes National Park, Canada

Located 3.1 miles north of the Waterton Townsite, the Pass Creek Campground is a picnic area that converts to a campground in winter, when the town dwindles to a few hundred residents and offers only a few services. All of the park's campgrounds close by mid-October, except for Pass Creek. The campground is convenient for ducking in to town for a dinner out at Kilmorey Lodge—especially if the weather turns brutal. Heated washrooms and running water are available at the fire hall. The campground also provides excellent wildlife-watching in the shoulder seasons as animals, such as elk, move to lower ground. In spring, nearby Lower Waterton Lake and Maskinonge Lake attract scads of migrating birds. In winter, the cross-country skiers hit the two designated trails on the upper Akamina Parkway. Bertha Falls also provides a popular four-mile round-trip snowshoe destination. For those with avalanche gear, the park also has ski touring routes and ice climbing.

Located just south of Red Rocks Parkway and right on the Blakiston River, where you can fish, the campground has big views of the Waterton Valley. Be prepared, however, for winds, for the campground also hovers on the edge of the open prairie. A few cottonwood trees provide windbreaks, but the area is open, and the campsites are visible from the entrance road to the park.

Campsites, facilities: The campground has eight RV or tent campsites that can accommodate midsized RVs. Facilities include picnic tables, a kitchen shelter with a wood stove, and a pit toilet. Bring your own water, or if you plan on using creek water, purify or boil it first.

Leashed pets are permitted. Because of bears, strict food storage regulations are in effect.

Reservations, fees: No reservations are accepted. Camping is free. Open mid-October–mid-April.

Directions: From Highway 3 at Pincher Creek, drive 30 miles south on Highway 6 to the entrance to Waterton Lakes National Park. Turn south and drive 2.8 miles to the campground on the right. (Chief Mountain Highway is closed October–May.)

GPS Coordinates: N 49° 4.584' W 113° 52.901'

Contact: Waterton Lakes National Park, Box 200, 215 Mount View Rd., Waterton Park, AB T0K 2M0, Canada, 403/859-2224, www.pc.gc.ca/pn-np/ab/waterton.

13 WATERTON TOWNSITE

Scenic rating: 10

on Waterton Lake in Waterton National Park, Canada

Located in Waterton Townsite, the campground garners spectacular views and wildlife. It borders Waterton Lake, with large peaks rising to the north and east of town. Paved walking paths circle the campground, linking to restaurants in town, Cameron Falls, the beach, and the boat tours on the lake. Do not bicycle on the walking paths, only on the town roads or the several mountain-bike trails in the area. From the campground, the Waterton Lake hiking trail departs to roaring Bertha Falls (2 miles), Bertha Lake (3.5 miles), or Goat Haunt, U.S.A. (8.7 miles).

A paved road with paved parking pads circles through the mowed lawn campground, which is divided by Cameron Creek. The RV hookup sites line up in the open. A few trees shade some sites but offer no privacy. For lake views, go for unserviced spots in the G loop (sites 26–46), but be prepared for strong winds off the lake. For more sheltered scenery, go for the Cameron Creek E loop sites (even numbers 2–16). In July and August, arrive by noon to claim a site, or make reservations. In shoulder seasons without reservations, you'll have your pick of sites.

Campsites, facilities: The campground has 95 hookup campsites that can accommodate large RVs and 143 unserviced RV or tent campsites. Hookups include sewer, water, and electricity. Facilities include flush toilets, showers, a disposal station, drinking water, kitchen shelters, bear-resistant food storage lockers, and firewood. Fires are permitted only in kitchen shelters. Because of bears, strict food storage regulations are in effect. Leashed pets are permitted. A wheelchair-accessible toilet is available.

Reservations, fees: Reservations are available (877/737-3783, www.pccamping.ca). Hookups cost CDN$39. Unserviced sites cost CDN$23–28. A burning permit for fires costs $9. Cash, check, or credit card. Opens April–mid-October.

Directions: Drive the 30-mile Chief Mountain International Highway across the border (open mid-May–September), go west for 0.7 mile to the Waterton entrance, and then go five miles south to the Waterton Townsite. At the townsite, turn left on Mount View Drive for two blocks and right on Windflower Avenue for three blocks to the campground entrance.

GPS Coordinates: N 49° 2.917' W 113° 54.560'

Contact: Waterton Lakes National Park, Box 200, 215 Mount View Rd., Waterton Park, AB T0K 2M0, Canada, 403/859-2224, www.pc.gc.ca/pn-np/ab/waterton.

14 BERTHA BAY

Scenic rating: 9

on Waterton Lake in Waterton National Park, Canada

On the western shore of Upper Waterton Lake, Bertha Bay is accessible only by a 1.5-

mile hike or by boat. Boaters must scope the weather out carefully before launching trips because winds kick up fast on the lake, churning up monstrous whitecaps. The backcountry campsite does not have a boat ramp or dock; boats should be completely beached overnight. From the campground, a trail ascends 1.3 miles to Bertha Falls and then switchbacks up another 1.7 miles to Bertha Lake.

For protection from the wind, the campsites are set in the woods back from the rock and pebble shore. A designated cooking site separates food handling, storing, and eating from the tent platforms for sleeping. Keep all food in the cooking area to avoid attracting wildlife into the sleeping zone. Bring a gas stove for cooking and 30 feet of rope for hanging food at night.

Campsites, facilities: Bertha Bay has four tent platforms, which each can hold one tent. The campground can accommodate a total of 12 people, but only six are allowed per party. Facilities include a bear pole for hanging food and garbage, a pit toilet, and a fire pit. Bring your own drinking water, or purify or boil lake or stream water. Pack out your trash. Pets are not permitted.

Reservations, fees: Reservations for required wilderness passes are available by phone 90 days in advance beginning April 1 of each year. The park charges a nonrefundable CDN$12 reservation fee, plus a modification fee for any additional changes. April–mid-May, call the warden's office (403/859-5140); after then, call the visitors center (403/859-5133). Wilderness passes can also be picked up in person no sooner than 24 hours in advance of the starting date. Backcountry camping costs CDN$10 per person per night. Children 16 years old and under camp for free. Open May–November.

Directions: Hikers can locate the trailhead at the end of Evergreen Avenue on the west end of the Waterton Townsite. Kayakers and canoeists should launch from the Cameron Bay picnic area. Boat ramps for larger boats are available at Linnet Lake picnic area and the marina in the Townsite.

GPS Coordinates: N 49° 1.736' W 113° 54.530'

Contact: Waterton Lakes National Park, Box 200, 215 Mount View Rd., Waterton Park, AB T0K 2M0, Canada, 403/859-2224, www.pc.gc.ca/pn-np/ab/waterton.

15 BOUNDARY BAY

Scenic rating: 10

on Waterton Lake in Waterton National Park, Canada

BEST (

Boundary Bay sits near the international border between Canada and the United States on the western shore of Upper Waterton Lake. Reach the campground by hiking a 3.7-mile rolling trail or by boating. Boaters should check the weather forecast before departing because winds kick up fast into whitecaps. Since the campground does not have a boat ramp or dock, beach boats completely for overnighting. From the campground, the trail continues another 4.3 miles on to Goat Haunt. Bring your passport to go through customs at Goat Haunt.

Boundary Bay campground is set in a mixed forest of firs and cottonwoods back from the shore for protection from winds. A designated communal cooking site is separated from the tent platforms for sleeping. Keep all food in the cooking area to avoid attracting wildlife into the sleeping zone. Bring a gas stove for cooking and 30 feet of rope for hanging food.

Campsites, facilities: The campground has three tent sites, which allow one tent each. While the campground can accommodate nine campers total, only six are allowed per group. Facilities include a bear pole for hanging food and garbage, a pit toilet, and a fire pit. Bring your own drinking water, or if you plan to use lake or stream water, purify or boil it before drinking. Pack out your trash. Pets are not permitted.

Reservations, fees: Reservations for required wilderness passes are available by phone 90 days in advance beginning April 1 for a nonrefundable CDN$12 reservation fee, plus a modification fee for any additional changes. April–mid-May, call the warden's office (403/859-5140); after then, call the visitors center (403/859-5133). Wilderness passes can also be picked up in person no sooner than 24 hours in advance of the starting date. Backcountry camping costs CDN$10 per person per night. Kids 16 years old and under camp for free. Open May–November.

Directions: Hikers can locate the trailhead at the end of Evergreen Avenue on the west end of Waterton Townsite. Kayakers and canoeists should launch from the Cameron Bay picnic area. Boat ramps for larger boats are available at Linnet Lake picnic area and the marina in the Townsite.

GPS Coordinates: N 49° 0.002' W 113° 54.320'

Contact: Waterton Lakes National Park, Box 200, 215 Mount View Rd., Waterton Park, AB T0K 2M0, Canada, 403/859-2224, www.pc.gc.ca/pn-np/ab/waterton.

16 GOAT HAUNT

Scenic rating: 10

on Waterton Lake in Glacier National Park, U.S.A.

No roads reach Goat Haunt, which sits at the south end of Waterton Lake. Visitors must hike or boat. Backpackers hike to Goat Haunt in three- to five-day trips that start at six trailheads in Glacier. All others must travel through Canada and take either the tour cruise or a private boat from Waterton Townsite to reach Goat Haunt. Bring a passport. An 8.7-mile trail also leads from the townsite to Goat Haunt. When hiking or boating south on Waterton Lake, you cross the international boundary again back into Montana. Only those with U.S. or Canadian

© BECKY LOMAX

The Goat Haunt shelters sit behind the boat dock area and visitor center.

passports are allowed to stay overnight in Goat Haunt or hike past the International Peace Park Pavilion.

Sitting above the boat dock and the open-air visitors center, the campground comprises smaller shelters with cement floors bordered with two walls for privacy from other campers. (Bring a good pad for your back.) During the day, the area bursts with mayhem when the tour boat disgorges tourists, but nighttime brings quiet on your own private beach. Day hikes lead from Goat Haunt to Rainbow Falls (0.7 mile), an overlook (1 steep mile), and Kootenai Lakes (2.8 miles) to spot moose.

Campsites, facilities: The campground has seven designated campsites; each holds up to four people. A community cooking site sits behind the shelters with a bear pole for hanging food. Facilities include flush toilets and drinking water from the sinks. Campfires are permitted in the cooking site, but you'll need to gather your own wood. Pets are not permitted.

Reservations, fees: Backcountry permits are required. Advance reservations ($20) for four of the campsites are available starting April 15. Get permits for other sites in person 24 hours in advance at the Apgar Backcountry Office or St. Mary Visitor Center. Permits cost $5 per adult per night and $2.50 for children 8–15. They are free for children 7 and under. Cash, check, or credit card. Open mid-June–November, although the tour boat runs only through mid-September.

Directions: From Waterton, Alberta, take a private boat or the tour cruise boat across the lake to reach Goat Haunt, Montana. Contact Waterton Shoreline Cruises (403/859-2362, www.watertoncruise.com) for tour boat prices and departure times.

GPS Coordinates: N 48° 57.574' W 113° 53.277'

Contact: Glacier National Park, P.O. Box 128, West Glacier, MT 59936, 406/888-7800, www.nps.gov/glac.

17 BELLY RIVER

Scenic rating: 6

on Chief Mountain International Highway in Waterton Lakes National Park, Canada

For those who want to shoot back across the border from Canada first thing in the morning, the Belly River Campground sits five minutes north of Chief Mountain Customs. Trout anglers looking to fish here will need a Waterton Lakes National Park fishing license as well as an Alberta fishing license; you can get both at the visitors center in Waterton. A short trail, mostly used by anglers, leads up the Belly River but fizzles before the international boundary or any real destination. Some floaters also launch at the Belly River Campground to paddle the Class II river.

A mixed forest surrounds the campground, but the quaking aspen groves give it character. When breezes blow, the leaves chatter. That and the burbling of the Belly River are about the only noises you'll hear. The campsites are located in a mix of shady sites and open sites. Those that are open have forest views. The campground is also a good site for wildlife-watching and birding, particularly along the river. Look for moose, bears, and foxes.

Campsites, facilities: The campground has 24 RV or tent campsites that can accommodate midsized RVs. Facilities include picnic tables, fire rings, pit and flush toilets, kitchen shelters, group camping sites, firewood, a campground host, and bear-resistant food storage lockers. Bring your own drinking water, or boil or purify river water. Because of bears, strict food storage regulations are in effect. Leashed pets are permitted.

Reservations, fees: Reservations are not accepted. Campsites cost CDN$16. Burning permits for fires cost CDN$8. Group campsites are available by reservation only, with a minimum of 25 people; call the park for reservations. Cash or check. Open mid-May–early September.

Directions: Drive 19 miles up Chief Mountain International Highway, crossing the border (open mid-May–September). The campground is on the left about five minutes north of the border before you cross the Belly River. Coming from the north, look for the signed turnoff on the right as soon as you cross the Belly River Bridge.

GPS Coordinates: N 49° 2.840' W 113° 41.368'

Contact: Waterton Lakes National Park, Box 200, 215 Mount View Rd., Waterton Park, AB T0K 2M0, Canada, 403/859-2224, www.pc.gc.ca/pn-np/ab/waterton.

18 BIG CREEK
🏃 🛶 � ⚓ 🐕 🏕 ♿ 🚌 ⛺

Scenic rating: 9

on the North Fork of the Flathead River in Flathead National Forest

BEST (

Located on the North Fork of the Flathead River's west bank across from Glacier National Park, Big Creek nestles below Huckleberry Mountain, which blocks direct sun until late morning. Evidence of the 2001 Moose Fire still surrounds the campground, but the forest is regenerating with lodgepole pines and pink fireweed. The fire bypassed the campground, leaving its trees green. At 2.5 miles north of the campground, the Glacier View Trail climbs the steep 2.3 miles up to a ridgetop meadow that yields panoramic views of Glacier Park. Anglers fish both Big Creek and the North Fork of the Flathead River for westslope cutthroat and rainbow trout. The campground sits adjacent to a boat launch for rafting and kayaking.

Tall lodgepoles and firs shade most of the campsites, with a few cottonwoods sprinkled along the river. More than half of the campsites overlook the river or sit adjacent to it. Backing in to alcoves of trees on a gravel loop and spur road, the spacious campsites spread out for privacy, but you'll see neighboring tents through the trunks with no underbrush. Some

of the river campsites capture more sun along the meadows, and you'll only hear the sound of the river.

Campsites, facilities: The campground has 22 RV and tent campsites that can accommodate RVs up to 40 feet. The huge group campsite fits up to 200 people. Facilities include picnic tables, fire rings with grills, drinking water, vault toilets, a boat ramp, firewood for sale, and a campground host. Pack out your trash. Leashed pets are permitted. A wheelchair-accessible toilet is available.

Reservations, fees: Reservations are not accepted, except for the large group campsite ($25, 977/444-6777, www.recreation.gov). Campsites cost $13. Cash or check. Open mid-May–mid-October.

Directions: From Apgar, drive 11.5 miles north on the Camas Road. Turn left on the North Fork Road and drive 2.5 miles south to the campground entrance. From Columbia Falls, drive 20 miles north on the North Fork Road. Find the signed entrance road on the road's east side. When you drive in, bypass the road to the river launch site and the group campsite loop to reach the individual campsites.

GPS Coordinates: N 48° 36.126' W 114° 9.862'

Contact: Flathead National Forest, Glacier View District, 10 Hungry Horse Dr., Hungry Horse, MT 59919, 406/387-3800, www.fs.fed.us/r1/flathead/.

19 GREAT NORTHERN FLATS PRIMITIVE
🛶 � ⚓ 🏕 🚌 ⛺

Scenic rating: 7

on the North Fork of the Flathead River in Flathead National Forest

Along the North Fork of the Flathead River, Great Northern Flats has been revamped from a park-and-camp-anywhere place to designated campsites. The flats, a large river bar on the west bank opposite Glacier National Park, are also a river access for rafters, kayakers, and anglers to float the river. From the flats to Glacier Rim includes the Class II–III Fools Hen Rapids. Only hand-carried watercraft can be launched. From here downriver, motorboats with a 10-horsepower limit are also permitted. The flats huddle under the Apgar Mountains, which rise in steep semi-arid faces across the river. In 2001, the Moose Fire swept through here, part of a 73,000-acre fire that raged for two months. Despite the fire, Great Northern Flats is now fast regenerating with lodgepole pines and wildflowers.

Growing with grass, wildflowers, and tiny new lodgepoles, the arid, dusty, sunny flats are wide open with no shade and no privacy. The primitive back-in campsites tuck close together around a small gravel loop near the river. At night, after the daytime river traffic disappears, the campground goes quiet, with only the sound of the wind and the river. Tents are usually set up on the gravel parking pads, as no additional tent space is available.

Campsites, facilities: The campground has three RV or tent campsites that can accommodate only small RVs. Facilities include fire rings with grills and a vault toilet. Bring your own water, or boil or filter the water taken from the river. Camping is limited to three days. Leashed pets are permitted. A wheelchair-accessible toilet is available.

Reservations, fees: No reservations are accepted. Camping is free. Open late April–November.

Directions: From Apgar, drive 11.5 miles north on Camas Road. Turn left on North Fork Road and drive 5.8 miles to the campground. From Columbia Falls, drive 16 miles north on North Fork Road to the campground. Turn east into the river access site, marked only with a small sign saying "1070."

GPS Coordinates: N 48° 34.119' W 114° 7.861'

Contact: Flathead National Forest, Glacier View District, 10 Hungry Horse Dr., Hungry Horse, MT 59919, 406/387-3800, www.fs.fed.us/r1/flathead/.

20 GLACIER RIM PRIMITIVE

Scenic rating: 7

on the North Fork of the Flathead River in Flathead National Forest

Located on the North Fork of the Flathead River at 3,179 feet in elevation, the Glacier Rim River Access sits on the west bank opposite Glacier National Park. It's close to Columbia Falls (about 15 minutes south), so this is a popular place to camp, due to its access via pavement instead of dirt road. The area is also popular for local anglers, rafters, kayakers, and canoeists buzzing out for the evening after work to float to Blankenship Bridge. Motorboats with a 10-horsepower limit are also permitted on the river.

The two campsites are strikingly different. The RV site sits on a sloped gravel spur north of the parking lot. The site is sunny, visible from the cars driving in, and requires a five-minute walk to see the river. The idyllic tent site sits on the river adjacent to the boat ramp under heavy shade and filled with the sound of the river. Vehicles for the tent site must park up the hill 50 feet or in the parking lot. Plan to arrive early to claim a spot.

Campsites, facilities: Glacier Rim has two campsites. Facilities include rock fire rings, a boat launch, boat trailer parking, and a vault toilet. Bring your own water; if you plan to drink river water, purify or boil it first. A three-day maximum for camping is enforced. Leashed pets are permitted. A wheelchair-accessible toilet is available.

Reservations, fees: Reservations are not accepted. Camping is free. Open late April–November.

Directions: From Apgar, drive 11.5 miles north on Camas Road. Turn left on North Fork Road and drive 11.8 miles to Glacier Rim. From Columbia Falls, drive 10 miles north on North Fork Road to reach Glacier Rim. Look for the river access sign and turn off toward the east.

GPS Coordinates: N 48° 29.573' W 114° 7.588'

Contact: Flathead National Forest, Glacier View District, 10 Hungry Horse Dr., Hungry Horse, MT 59919, 406/387-3800, www.fs.fed.us/r1/flathead/.

21 TIMBER WOLF RESORT

Scenic rating: 7

on Highway 2 west of West Glacier

Timber Wolf Resort is the farthest west in the string of private RV campgrounds that line Highway 2 west of West Glacier. It sits about 10 minutes from Glacier National Park's west entrance station. The tiny town of Hungry Horse is 0.5 mile west. Less than two miles away, a frontage road parallels the dam-controlled section of the South Fork of the Flathead River, making for easy shoreline access to cast flies for rainbows and cutthroat. The resort's large group campfire serves as a place to meet other campers. A hiking trail loops around part of the campground, and a bike trail parallels the highway.

The campground, in 20 wooded acres on a terraced hillside, offers peek-a-boo views of Glacier's Apgar Range. Most of the narrow pull-through RV campsites have a tree for partial shade but garner plenty of sunshine views of the traffic. Tucked at the back of the campground, the tent sites have more shade and privacy from the road. You'll hear highway noise at this campground.

Campsites, facilities: The campground has 24 RV campsites that can accommodate RVs up to 40 feet, as well as five tent campsites. Hookups include sewer, water, and electricity up to 50 amps. Facilities include picnic tables, fire rings, pedestal charcoal grills (bring your own charcoal), flush toilets, showers, high-speed modem hookups, wireless Internet, a camp store, a playground, and firewood for sale. Leashed pets are permitted.

Reservations, fees: Reservations are accepted. Hookups cost $27–36. Tent sites cost $21 for one tent; each additional tent costs $5. Spring and fall rates run $5 less. Check the resort's website for specials. Rates cover two people, and up to six are permitted per campsite. Kids under age six camp for free, but additional adults are charged $3 per night. Pets are also charged $3 per day. The 7 percent Montana bed tax will be added on. Cash, check, or credit card. Open May–September.

Directions: From Hungry Horse, on Highway 2 drive eastward 0.25 mile past Hungry Horse Dam Road. From West Glacier, drive west on Highway 2 for 9 miles. Find the resort entrance on the south side of the highway.

GPS Coordinates: N 48° 23.217' W 114° 2.874'

Contact: Timber Wolf Resort, P.O. Box 190800, 9105 Hwy. 2 E., Hungry Horse, MT 59919, 406/387-9653, www.timberwolfresort.com.

22 MOUNTAIN MEADOWS

Scenic rating: 8

on Highway 2 west of West Glacier

Located nine miles west of Glacier National Park's west entrance, Mountain Meadows is one of the many private campgrounds lining the highway between West Glacier and Hungry Horse. Forty private acres behind the campground contain trails for walking in the forest. A paved walking-bicycle path leads 0.6 mile to the tiny town of Hungry Horse for browsing funky antique shops and huckleberry stores. About two miles east, the Coram Experimental Forest, which houses several 500-year-old larch trees, loops with trails through an area used by the Forest Service for research. You can also fish their private catch-and-release stocked rainbow trout pond. (No license needed.)

The campground sits on 77 natural forested

acres with views of Glacier's Apgar Range from its pond. Benches are available to watch the sun set over the peaks. Less railroad and highway noise filters into the campground than in others in the area. The back-in campsites gain partial shade and privacy from the tall forest of mixed trees. Big-rig sites are more open and sunny.

Campsites, facilities: The campground has 52 RV sites that can accommodate RVs up to 45 feet long with slide-outs and awnings. Hookups are available for water, sewer, and electricity up to 30 amps. Facilities include picnic tables, fire rings with grills, flush toilets, showers, a coin-operated launderette, a disposal station, a camp store, firewood for sale, and wireless Internet. Leashed pets are permitted.

Reservations, fees: Make midsummer reservations in winter to guarantee a spot. Hookups run $35–38. Check for Internet specials. Rates are based on two-person occupancy per site. Additional adults cost $4 and children $2. A 7 percent Montana bed tax will be added on. Cash, check, or credit card. Open May–September.

Directions: From Hungry Horse, drive east on Highway 2 up the hill 0.6 mile. From West Glacier, drive west on Highway 2 for nine miles. Find the park entrance on the highway's east side.

GPS Coordinates: N 48° 23.259' W 114° 2.749'

Contact: Mountain Meadows RV Park, P.O. Box 190442, 9125 Hwy. 2 E., Hungry Horse, MT 59919, 406/387-9125, www.mmrvpark. com.

23 CANYON RV AND CAMPGROUND

🚶 🚴 🛶 🐕 🎣 ♿ 🚐 ⛺

Scenic rating: 7

on Highway 2 west of West Glacier

Located between the tiny blips on Highway 2 of Coram and Martin City, Canyon RV and Campground is the only campground with river access. An eight-mile drive leads to the west entrance to Glacier National Park and West Glacier, with its rafting, golf, shopping, and restaurants. The campground neighbors Montana Fur Traders and sits across the highway from a paved walking-bicycling path that parallels the road. The campground sits on a treed plateau above the Flathead River, but its property runs right down to the river's bank. You can cast a line from the shore for rainbow or cutthroat trout, or just sit to watch rafts float by. A trail through the woods connects to the river.

A few sparse mature trees offer a wee bit of shade in the sunny campground. A narrow dusty gravel road loops through the grassy narrow pull-through and back-in campsites, which are lined up in RV parking lot fashion—close to the neighbors. Due to the proximity of the railroad tracks across the river and the highway, noise seeps into the campground.

Campsites, facilities: The campground has 50 RV and tent campsites that can accommodate RVs up to 45 feet. Hookups include water, sewer, and electricity up to 50 amps. Facilities include picnic tables, flush toilets, showers, a launderette available only by appointment, a disposal station, a camp store, a playground, and wireless Internet. Leashed pets are permitted. A wheelchair-accessible toilet and campsites are available.

Reservations, fees: Reservations are accepted. Hookups cost $33–36, but only $30 in May and September. Tent sites and RVs without hookups cost $24. Rates are based on two people; each extra person costs $3. Sometimes the park offers the seventh night free. A 7 percent Montana bed tax will be added to the bill. Cash, check, or credit card. Open May–September.

Directions: On Highway 2, from Hungry Horse, drive one mile east, or from West Glacier, drive eight miles west. Turn west into the campground entrance.

GPS Coordinates: N 48° 23.834' W 114° 2.500'

Contact: Glacier National Park, P.O. Box 7,

9540 Hwy. 2 E., Hungry Horse, MT 59919, 406/387-9393, www.montanacampground. com.

24 SUNDANCE CAMPGROUND AND RV PARK

Scenic rating: 5

on Highway 2 west of West Glacier

Sundance sits in the middle of the line of private RV parks and campgrounds strung along Highway 2 to the west of West Glacier. The entrance to Glacier National Park is 6.5 miles to the east. For those with pets, Sundance offers one amenity that other campgrounds do not: While you tour Glacier for the day, you can kennel Fido at the campground. For hikers, kenneling the dog allows you to explore the national park trails on which pets are not permitted. The neighboring Great Bear Adventure Park—a drive-through habitat with captive black bears—sits over the fence on the campground's east side.

A natural forest surrounds the campground, with little in the way of understory between the tall trees. Most campsites are grassy, and a dirt road loops through the campground for access to sites with gravel parking. The north-end sites are farthest from the highway but are closest to the railroad tracks. The east-side sites border the bear park. The campground also welcomes walk-ins after the office closes at 9 p.m.

Campsites, facilities: The campground has 22 RV sites that are pull-throughs with hookups for water and electricity up to 50 amps. Nine tent sites include water and fire rings. Facilities includes flush toilets, hot showers, a disposal station, truck pump service, a camp store, wireless Internet, a launderette, a day kennel, a playground, and a dishwashing station for tenters. Leashed pets are permitted. A wheelchair-accessible toilet is available.

Reservations, fees: Reservations are accepted.

Hookups cost $26; tent sites cost $18. Rates cover two people; additional campers over 10 years old cost $2 each. Inquire about pet kenneling costs. Add on 7 percent Montana bed tax. Cash, check, or credit card. Open May–October.

Directions: From West Glacier, drive six miles west on Highway 2. The campground is on the north side of the road between mileposts 147 and 148. Look for a red sign.
GPS Coordinates: N 48° 26.031' W 114° 2.589'

Contact: Sundance Campground and RV Park, P.O. Box 130037, 10545 Hwy. 2 E., Coram, MT 59913, 406/387-5016 or 866/782-2677.

25 NORTH AMERICAN RV PARK

Scenic rating: 5

on Highway 2 west of West Glacier

North American RV Park sits six miles west of West Glacier and its rafting, fishing, and horseback riding companies, plus the West Glacier Golf Course. It is also 6.5 miles west from the entrance to Glacier National Park. The gravel roads through the campground use names of famous places in Glacier Park.

Recent growth in the past decade put a fir tree barrier between the highway and the campground. Cabins and yurts also added to the wall. Growing trees are breaking up the parking lot feel and lending a bit of shade to some back-in sites. Most of the campsites, however, are sunny, open, and surrounded by mowed lawn. Big-rig drivers prefer this park because its fewer trees and pull-through sites allow for easier maneuvering, and satellites can often gain a clear shot at the sky. Campfires are not permitted in midsummer. Highway noise creeps into the campground, and trains run all night on the tracks on the opposite side of the highway. Sites 7–9 sit the farthest from the highway with the most privacy. Sites

43, 45, 47, 49, 51, 53, 54, and 55 also back up towards woods rather than other campers.

Campsites, facilities: The campground has 55 RV sites, which can fit RVs up to 45 feet, and 10 tent campsites. Hookups are available for sewer, water, and electricity up to 50 amps. Facilities include picnic tables, campfire rings, flush toilets, showers, a launderette, wireless Internet, a playground, and camp store. Leashed pets are permitted.

Reservations, fees: Reservations are highly recommended in midsummer. The office opens to begin taking reservations around mid-April. Hookups cost $33–38. Off-season (until mid-June, after September 1) rates are discounted by $5. Rates are for two people. Each additional person costs $5, but kids 12 years old and under camp for free. Add on 7 percent Montana bed tax. Cash, check, or credit card. Open mid-April–October.

Directions: From West Glacier, drive 5.5 miles west on Highway 2 to milepost 147.5. Turn south into the campground.

GPS Coordinates: N 48° 26.260' W 114° 2.495'

Contact: North American RV Park, P.O. Box 130449, 10784 Hwy. 2 E., Coram, MT 59913, 800/704-4266, www.northamericanrvpark. com.

26 DANCING BEAR CAMPGROUND

Scenic rating: 7

on Highway 2 west of West Glacier

Located four miles from the west entrance to Glacier National Park, Dancing Bear Campground provides something different in the string of private campgrounds between West Glacier and Hungry Horse. West Glacier's newest campground opened in 2008 for a test drive but is planning its big opening for 2010. The owners plan to develop the campground in an eco-friendly way with an emphasis on innovative green power and recycling. It is also aiming for the budget-conscious traveler, offering primitive camping in a natural setting. The owners, however, who have worked in Glacier Park for nearly two decades, are loaded with knowledge about where to hike, fish, raft, and see scenery.

A thick natural forest surrounds the campground; a few campsites have views of the mountains forming Bad Rock Canyon. A gravel road loops through the campground for access to sites. The large sites give a sense of privacy, as campers are not stacked right next to each other. The campsites—none of which have hookups—are suitable for tents, small RVs, truck campers, and small pop-up tent trailers, but not big RVs. Call to check on the current status of the campground.

Campsites, facilities: The campground has 20 RV or tent sites. Facilities include picnic tables, fire rings with grills, vault toilets, garbage service, drinking water, and a solar shower.

Reservations, fees: Reservations are accepted. Campsites cost $5 per person. Cash or check. Open mid-April–October.

Directions: From West Glacier, drive four miles west on Highway 2. Look for a sign tucked in the trees on the south side of the highway at about milepost 147.8. (The sign is easier seen coming from the west. From the east, by the time you see the sign, you've gone too far.) Turn south into the campground.

GPS Coordinates: N 48° 26.561' W 114° 2.297'

Contact: Dancing Bear Campground, 10780 Hwy. 2 E., Coram, MT 59913, 406/471-0640, www.dancingbearcampground.com.

27 LAKE FIVE RESORT

Scenic rating: 7

on Lake Five west of West Glacier

Lake Five Resort sets its cabins and campground on a 235-acre lake west of West Glacier. Due to the shallow lake depth, its waters are warmer than the chilly glacier-fed Lake McDonald five miles away in Glacier National Park—hence the tiny lake's attraction for waterskiing, canoeing, and swimming. Waterskiing lessons are available, and canoes can be rented. The lake buzzes with motorboats on hot summer days. Bicyclists can ride the local paved and dirt back roads to circle the lake or ride to the confluence of the Middle Fork and the North Fork of the Flathead River.

Unfortunately, most of the cabins claim the front spots on the lake, with the campground lining up most of it its tiny, cramped back-in sites close together behind them in a grassy, wooded setting that offers partial shade. Six campsites have beachfront, and the resort also has two tipis right on the shoreline for those who want the experience of camping in a Native American tradition. Set off Highway 2 on a side road, Lake Five Resort is quieter than some of the other area campgrounds, but like all in the area, it still picks up noise from the trains.

Campsites, facilities: The resort has 45 RV campsites that can fit RVs up to 40 feet. Hookups include sewer, water, and electricity up to 50 amps, but only 14 sites include sewer hookups. Facilities include fire rings, flush toilets, showers, a disposal station, a boat launch, a boat dock, a playground, and horseshoes. Tipis sleep up to six people. Leashed pets are permitted.

Reservations, fees: Reservations are highly recommended during midsummer. Campsites cost $40–45. The rate covers two people. Extra campers are charged $5 per night. Tipis rent for $50–60 per night. Dogs cost $5 per day. Add on 7 percent Montana bed tax. Cash, check, or credit card. Open May–October.

Directions: Drive 2.7 miles westward from West Glacier on Highway 2 and turn right onto the Lake Five Road. After driving 0.4 mile to Belton Stage Road, turn right and go 0.5 mile. Turn right into the campground. GPS Coordinates: N 48° 27.726' W 114° 1.104'

Contact: Lake Five Resort, P.O. Box 338, 540 Belton Stage Rd., West Glacier, MT 59936, 406/387-5601, www.lakefiveresort.com.

28 SAN-SUZ-ED RV PARK

Scenic rating: 4

on Highway 2 west of West Glacier

Located on Highway 2, this RV park is one of the closer private campgrounds to Glacier National Park's west entrance three miles to the east. It is also 2.5 miles from West Glacier activities: trail rides, white-water rafting, float trips, fishing, golf, and shopping. Instead of individual campfire rings at each site, the campground has one large community campfire every night. Bring your own marshmallows or hot dogs for roasting and glean news from fellow campers: where the fish are biting, where the bears are feeding, and where the huckleberries are ripe. The owners also bake homemade pies and, during the summer, serve a breakfast of Belgian waffles and sourdough hotcakes with homemade syrup.

Set in a mix of forest—with some sites shaded and others sunny—the campground sits between Highway 2 and the railroad tracks, which allows some noise to percolate through the trees. Light sleepers should bring earplugs. Part of the campground is paved, with paved pull-through and back-in parking pads, which eliminates dust. Wide sites allow for RV slide-outs and awnings. Each campsite has a different colored picnic table.

Campsites, facilities: The park contains 21 tent sites and 38 RV sites that can accommodate RVs up to 45 feet. Hookups include sewer, water, and electricity up to 50 amps. Facilities include picnic tables, flush toilets, showers, wireless Internet, a launderette, a convenience store, and three enclosed shelters without utilities. Leashed pets are permitted. A wheelchair-accessible toilet is available.

Reservations, fees: Reservations are

appreciated. Hookups cost $31–34. Tent campsites cost $27. Rates are for two people. Extra campers cost $5 per person, but kids under 10 years old stay free. The enclosed shelters cost $35 for up to four people. Add on the 7 percent Montana bed tax. Cash, check, or credit card. Open May–October.

Directions: On Highway 2, from West Glacier drive west for 2.5 miles, or from Hungry Horse drive east for 6.5 miles. The campground sits on the north side of the highway between mileposts 150 and 151.

GPS Coordinates: N 48° 27.753' W 114° 0.124'

Contact: San-Suz-Ed RV, P.O. Box 387, 11505 Hwy. 2 W., West Glacier, MT 59936, 406/387-5280 or 800/630-2623, www.sansuzedrvpark.com.

29 WEST GLACIER KOA

Scenic rating: 7

south of Highway 2 west of West Glacier

Located one mile south of the busy Highway 2 to the west of West Glacier, the KOA is 2.5 miles from Glacier National Park's west entrance. It is also two miles from West Glacier's rafting companies, horseback rides, golf, restaurants, and gift shops. The campground boasts the only swimming pool on the park's west side. While the heated outdoor pool is open June–mid-September, the two hot tubs steam all season long. The campground serves breakfast, ice cream, and an evening barbecue during summer months, and rotates a Tom Ulrich wildlife slide show with a Forest Service program and Glacier videos for evening entertainment.

Set in lodgepole pines, the campsites are separated from the pool area by a large grassy lawn, good for a game of Frisbee. Sites 121–152, which are grassy and more open, do not permit tents or campfires; the other sites have fire rings. Sites 113–125 sit at the back, away from the main camp hubbub but close to one restroom; tent sites 100–112 also gain privacy with larger spaces and picnic tables.

Campsites, facilities: The KOA has 139 RV sites that can accommodate 45-foot RVs. Fifty of the campsites are pull-throughs. Hookups include sewer, water, and electricity up to 50 amps. Facilities include picnic tables, fire rings, flush toilets, showers, a coin-operated launderette, a swimming pool, hot tubs, a playground, a game room, wireless Internet, a disposal station, and a dog-walk area. Leashed pets are permitted. Wheelchair-accessible facilities are available.

Reservations, fees: Reservations are accepted. Hookups run $46–49; no hookups and tent sites cost $29. Rates are based on two people. Extra adults cost $4.50 each, but kids 17 years old and under stay free. In shoulder seasons (May–early June, mid-September–October 1) campsite rates are discounted by $1–2. Add on 7 percent Montana bed tax. Cash, traveler's check, or credit card. Open May–September.

Directions: From West Glacier, drive west on Highway 2 for 2.5 miles. Turn south onto paved Half Moon Flats Road and drive one mile.

GPS Coordinates: N 48° 27.881' W 113° 58.874'

Contact: West Glacier KOA, 355 Half Moon Flats Rd., West Glacier, MT 59936, 406/387-5341 or 800/562-3313, www.westglacierkoa.com.

30 GLACIER CAMPGROUND

Scenic rating: 6

on Highway 2 west of West Glacier

Located one mile from the west entrance to the Glacier National Park, Glacier Campground is the closest private campground to the park in the long string of RV park campgrounds between West Glacier and Hungry Horse. Golf, restaurants, gift shops, an espresso stand, a post office, and the train depot sit 0.5 mile to the east. Four rafting companies that run white-water and float trips on the Middle Fork of the Flathead also have their offices within a five-minute drive. The park's historic red bus tours also will stop by the campground to pick up riders. For evening entertainment, the campground sponsors Forest Service presentations.

The family-owned campground is on 40 timbered acres set back a bit from the highway. The trees not only reduce the highway and railroad noise (you'll still hear it) but grant shade for hot days. Firs, birches, and copious underbrush verging on jungle help to maintain privacy for the campsites. Big rigs can get a few pull-through sites, but otherwise, parking requires a tight squeeze to back into the forest slot. Not all of the campsites have picnic tables and fire rings; ask specifically for these when you arrive or reserve a spot. The campground also has grassy sites for bicyclists and backpackers.

Campsites, facilities: The campground has 80 RV sites, with some pull-through sites that can accommodate RVs up to 40 feet, and 80 tent campsites. Hookups include water and electricity up to 30 amps. Facilities include flush toilets, showers, a pumper truck for sewer service ($10), a camp store, coin-operated launderette, wood-heated recreation room, a playground, and wireless Internet. Leashed pets are permitted.

Reservations, fees: Reservations are accepted. Hookups cost $24–29; no hookup and tent sites cost $19–20. For bikers and hikers, the campground charges $7 per person. Add on 7 percent Montana bed tax. Cash, check, or credit card. Open May–September.

Directions: On Highway 2, from West Glacier drive 0.5 mile west, or from Hungry Horse drive 8.5 miles east. Turn south off the highway at the signed entrance.

GPS Coordinates: N 48° 28.977' W 113° 59.806'

Contact: Glacier Campground, P.O. Box 447, 12070 Hwy. 2 W., West Glacier, MT 59936, 406/387-5689 or 888/387-5689, www.glaciercampground.com.

31 APGAR

Scenic rating: 9

on Lake McDonald on Going-to-the-Sun Road in Glacier National Park

At the foot of Lake McDonald on Glacier's west side, Apgar campground bustles with campers walking to Lake McDonald for a swim, bicycling to the Middle Fork of the Flathead River, or hopping shuttles up Going-to-the-Sun Road to Logan Pass. Adjacent to Apgar Village, the campground connects via paved trails to the Apgar Visitor Center, Eddy's Restaurant, a camp store, ice cream stand, and gift shops. Lake McDonald's only boat ramp

Boats are available for rent on Lake McDonald in Apgar.

© BECKY LOMAX

sits between the picnic area and the village. You can rent canoes, kayaks, or boats with small horsepower engines. Lower McDonald Creek sees heavy fishing and is a warm-day favorite for floating on kayaks, rafts, or tubes to Quarter Circle Bridge. Hikers drive 10 minutes to the trailhead to climb 2.8 miles to Apgar Lookout, which overlooks McDonald Valley and Glacier's jagged peaks.

None of the campsites sit right on Lake McDonald; however, the amphitheater where the park service holds evening programs does. Surrounded by birch and hemlocks, the campground is Glacier's largest, with open campsites beneath the trees and some road noise from Going-to-the-Sun Road. Vehicles over 21 feet must access this campground from West Glacier.

Campsites, facilities: The campground has 194 RV or tent campsites, including 25 that can accommodate RVs up to 40 feet and group sites for 9–24 people. Facilities include picnic tables, fire rings with grills, flush toilets, drinking water, raised gravel tent platforms, shared sites for hikers and bikers, garbage service, interpretive programs, and a disposal station. Bring firewood; collecting it is illegal. During the primitive camping season (April, mid-October–Nov) the campground has only pit toilets and no running water. In winter, camp at the picnic area—a plowed parking lot with a pit toilet. Leashed pets are permitted. A wheelchair-accessible toilet is available.

Reservations, fees: Reservations are not accepted. Sites cost $20 per night May–mid-October. Biker and hiker sites cost $5 per person. Primitive camping costs $10; winter camping is free. Cash, check, or credit card. Open year-round.

Directions: From the west entrance of Glacier National Park, drive northeast on Going-to-the-Sun Road one mile to the Apgar Junction. Turn right, driving for one mile, then turn left at the sign to Apgar Village and drive 0.3 mile to the campground entrance on the left.

GPS Coordinates: N 48° 31.592' W 113° 59.069'
Contact: Glacier National Park, P.O. Box 128, West Glacier, MT 59936, 406/888-7800, www.nps.gov/glac.

y Rec. gov

32 FISH CREEK

Scenic rating: 8

on Lake McDonald in Glacier National Park

Fish Creek Campground is located on Lake McDonald's north shore three miles from Apgar on Glacier's west side. While Fish Creek flows through the campground, the stream is closed to fishing. Anglers still fish nearby in Lake McDonald, especially where the creek runs into the lake. Built on a hillside in deep cedars, lodgepoles, and larches, the campground and picnic area border the shoreline with its multicolored perfect rock-skipping stones. As the water level drops throughout the summer, the beaches become larger and more appealing for sunbathing, swimming, and sunset-watching. The Lake McDonald Trail departs from loop C for a one-mile jaunt to Rocky Point—a rock bluff with views of Mount Edwards and Mount Brown. Hike farther up the lake to remote beaches, or loop back through the 2003 fire zone, which has interpretive signs. You can launch hand-carried watercraft from the picnic area, but no boat launch is available.

Loops C and D have the best sites for the quickest access to the lake. Some of their southern campsites have peek-a-boo water views, too. If privacy is valued, ask for one of the smaller campsites on the outer, uphill side of loop B. The shaded campground sits far enough away from the Apgar hubbub to be a peaceful, quiet place. Be prepared for mosquitoes.

Campsites, facilities: Fish Creek has 178 RV or tent campsites, including 18 campsites accommodating RVs up to 35 feet long and 62 sites fitting RVs up to 27 feet. Facilities include picnic tables, fire rings with grills, flush toilets, drinking water, shared hiker and biker campsites, garbage service, and a disposal station. Bring firewood; collecting it is illegal. Strict food storage regulations are in effect due to bears. Leashed pets are permitted. A wheelchair-accessible toilet is available.

Reservations, fees: Reservations are available (877/444-6777, www.reservations.gov). Campsites cost $23 per night; shared hiker or biker sites cost $5 per person. Cash, check, or credit card. Open June–early September.

Directions: From Glacier's west entrance, drive one mile northeast to the Apgar Junction. Turn left and drive 1.25 miles north on Camas Road and turn right at the campground sign, dropping one mile down past the picnic area to the staffed campground entrance station.

GPS Coordinates: N 48° 32.873' W 113° 59.139'

Contact: Glacier National Park, P.O. Box 128, West Glacier, MT 59936, 406/888-7800, www.nps.gov/glac.

33 LAKE MCDONALD

Scenic rating: 9

on Lake McDonald's north shore in Glacier National Park

At 10 miles long and 1.5 miles wide, Lake Mc-Donald is the largest lake in Glacier National Park. Its southern flank is bordered by Going-to-the-Sun Road, but its north side—where the Lake McDonald backcountry campground sits—is accessed only by hiking the Lake Mc-Donald Trail from Fish Creek Campground or by boating the lake. The Robert Fire in 2003 closed the campground, but the National Park Service opened it up again in 2009. From the shore near the camp, you get views of Mount Brown, Edwards, and Jackson Peak—mountains not visible from the Sun Road. The lake harbors kokanee salmon and lake trout. Paddling to the campground takes about 90 minutes from Apgar; traveling with a motorboat takes about

30 minutes. No dock is available; completely beach all boats at night in case winds arise.

The campground sits about halfway up the north side of the lake, with the communal cooking site and sleeping campsites set back in the trees from the lakeshore. In June, the rocky beach is minimal, but by August, it increases to a quiet spacious place to relax on the shore in the sun. The campground is prized for its quiet and solitude. Take 30 feet of rope for hanging food and cooking gear.

Campsites, facilities: The campground has two tent campsites; each holds up to four people. Facilities include a rock fire pit, food-hanging cables, communal cooking site with log benches, and a pit toilet. Boil or purify lake water for drinking. Pack out your trash. Pets are not permitted.

Reservations, fees: Backcountry permits are required. Advance reservations ($20) for one of the campsites is available starting April 15. Get permits for remaining sites in person 24 hours in advance at the Apgar Backcountry Office in Apgar. Permits cost $5 per adult per night and $2.50 for children 8–15. They are free for children 7 and under. Opens mid-May–November.

Directions: For boating, launch from the Apgar boat ramp. Parking for trailers is available across the street. For hiking, park at the Fish Creek picnic area.

GPS Coordinates: N 48° 35.610' W 113° 55.816'

Contact: Glacier National Park, P.O. Box 128, West Glacier, MT 59936, 406/888-7800, www.nps.gov/glac.

34 SPRAGUE CREEK

Scenic rating: 10

on Lake McDonald on Going-to-the-Sun Road in Glacier National Park

BEST(

Sitting at 3,200 feet on Lake McDonald's southeast shore, Sprague Creek is one of five campgrounds lining Going-to-the-Sun Road. It is the smallest drive-to campground on Lake McDonald and the first to fill up. Paths access the lake for launching canoes or kayaks, but large boats must go to Apgar for the boat ramp. Anglers fish the lake for lake trout and kokanee salmon. Squeezed in between Going-to-the-Sun Road and the lake, the campground sits one mile from historic Lake McDonald Lodge, restaurants, boat tours, red bus tours, a camp store, horseback riding, and the Sperry Trailhead. The trail ascends to Snyder Lake (4.4 miles), historic Sperry Chalet (6.4 miles), Sperry Glacier (10.4 miles), and Mount Brown Lookout (5.8 steep miles), with its dizzying view down to Lake McDonald. A shuttle stop at the campground connects with 17 places on Going-to-the-Sun Road, including Logan Pass.

Shaded by large cedars, the campsites cluster tight in the forest with little to no underbrush between them to add privacy. Strung around a narrow, curvy, paved road, sites 1, 2, 5, 7, 8, 10, 12, 13, 15, and 16 overlook the lake. The backs of sites 17, 20, 21, 22, and 24 flank the busy Going-to-the-Sun Road, but traffic quiets after dark. Due to the campground's popularity, plan on arriving around 11 A.M. in midsummer.

Campsites, facilities: The campground has 25 RV or tent campsites that can accommodate RVs up to 21 feet. No towed units are allowed. Facilities include picnic tables, fire rings with grills, raised gravel tent platforms, drinking water, and garbage service. Bring firewood; collecting is illegal. Strict food storage regulations—stapled to the picnic tables—are in effect for bears. Leashed pets are permitted. A wheelchair-accessible toilet is available.

Reservations, fees: No reservations are accepted. Campsites cost $20. Shared sites for hikers and bikers cost $5 per person. Cash, check, or credit card. Open mid-May–mid-September.

Directions: From the west entrance to Glacier National Park, drive 9.5 miles east on Going-to-the-Sun Road. From the St. Mary entrance,

drive 40.5 miles west over Logan Pass. Find the campground entrance on the lake side of the road.

GPS Coordinates: N 48° 36.371' W 113° 53.082'

Contact: Glacier National Park, P.O. Box 128, West Glacier, MT 59936, 406/888-7800, www.nps.gov/glac.

35 AVALANCHE

Scenic rating: 9

in McDonald Valley on Going-to-the-Sun Road in Glacier National Park

Tucked into a narrow canyon between massive peaks, Avalanche Campground sits at 3,550 feet on Going-to-the-Sun Road in Glacier National Park. This is the closest west-side campground to Logan Pass, 16 miles east. Named for the nearby avalanches that rip down Mount Cannon's slopes, the campground sits in a pocket of rain forest preserved from fire. The 0.7-mile, wheelchair-accessible, paved and boardwalk Trail of the Cedars loops from the campground through ancient cedars and past red-rocked Avalanche Gorge. A spur trail climbs two miles up to Avalanche Lake, where giant waterfalls plummet from a hanging valley. In midsummer, the trail sees a constant stream foot traffic heading to the lake for swimming, fishing, or gazing at mountain goats on the cliffs. The free Going-to-the-Sun Road shuttles stop at the campground. Vehicles over 21 feet are not permitted farther east on Going-to-the-Sun Road past this campground.

Driving into the shady campground is akin to driving into a jungle. Grandfather cedar trees and thick underbrush crowd into campsites, and boggy places can produce prodigious numbers of mosquitoes. Avalanche Creek runs adjacent to the campground. You'll be able to see a couple other campsites, but the campground goes silent after dark. Due to the campground's popularity, plan on arriving before 3 P.M. during midsummer and before noon on Saturday. Vehicles over 21 feet must access this campground from West Glacier, not St. Mary.

Campsites, facilities: The campground has 87 RV or tent campsites that can accommodate RVs up to 26 feet. Facilities include picnic tables, fire rings with a grills, drinking water, flush toilets, garbage service, shared hiker and biker campsites, and an amphitheater for evening interpretive programs. Strict food storage regulations are in effect because of bears. Bring firewood; collecting is illegal. Leashed pets are permitted. A wheelchair-accessible toilet is available.

Reservations, fees: No reservations are accepted. Campsites cost $20. Shared sites for hikers and bikers cost $5 per person. Cash, check, or credit card. Open early June–early September.

Directions: From the west entrance to Glacier National Park, drive 15.7 miles up Going-to-the-Sun Road. From the St. Mary entrance, drive 34 miles west over Logan Pass. The entrance is on the south side of the road.

GPS Coordinates: N 48° 40.791' W 113° 49.152'

Contact: Glacier National Park, P.O. Box 128, West Glacier, MT 59936, 406/888-7800, www.nps.gov/glac.

36 RISING SUN

🚶 🚲 ⛵ 🏊 🛶 🎣 🐕 ♿ 🚐 ⛺

Scenic rating: 10

In St. Mary Valley on Going-to-the-Sun Road in Glacier National Park

BEST (

Below Otokomi and Goat Mountains north of St. Mary Lake, Rising Sun is one of two east-side campgrounds on Going-to-the-Sun Road. As daylight shifts, streaks of red argillite douse peaks, offset by the lake's turquoise water. The Rising Sun complex includes cabins, a restaurant, a camp store, a boat ramp, boat tours, a picnic area, shuttle stop, and trailhead. Walk across the road to swim in the lake, or hop a boat tour around Wild Goose Island. If boating or fishing, watch the winds; in minutes, fierce winds can kick up huge whitecaps on St. Mary Lake. On Going-to-the-Sun Road a five-minute drive west, photographers will want to shoot Wild Goose Island in early morning light. From the campground, hike five miles up to Otokomi Lake to watch mountain goats climb on the cliffs, or hop a free shuttle up to other popular trailheads around Logan Pass. Vehicles over 21 feet must access the campground from St. Mary, not West Glacier.

The campground's two loops feature different types of sites. Many are set under firs and cottonwoods for shade, but some are grassy, with wide-open views of peaks and the night sky—particularly those on the west loop's southwest side. Rising Sun bustles during the day but quiets after dark when traffic diminishes on Going-to-the-Sun Road.

Campsites, facilities: The campground has 83 RV or tent campsites. Only 10 campsites can accommodate RVs or trailer combinations up to 25 feet long. Facilities include picnic tables, fire rings with grills, drinking water, flush toilets, a disposal station, shared hiker and biker campsites, and an amphitheater for interpretive programs. Purchase tokens from the camp store for showers at the adjacent motel. Leashed pets are permitted. A wheelchair-accessible toilet is available.

Reservations, fees: No reservations are accepted. Campsites cost $20. Shared sites for hikers and bikers cost $5 per person. Cash, check, or credit card. Open late May–mid-September.

Directions: From the St. Mary entrance to Glacier, drive six miles west up Going-to-the-Sun Road. From the west entrance to Glacier National Park, drive 43.5 miles over Logan Pass. The campground entrance is on the north side of the road.

GPS Coordinates: N 48° 41.638' W 113° 31.278'

Contact: Glacier National Park, P.O. Box 128,

West Glacier, MT 59936, 406/888-7800, www.nps.gov/glac.

37 ST. MARY

Res. Accepted
Rec.gov

Scenic rating: 9

in St. Mary Valley on Going-to-the-Sun Road in Glacier National Park

St. Mary marks the east entrance to Glacier National Park, in a place where the mountains sweep up right out of the lakes. The campground, which sits just inside the park entrance, requires a half-mile walk to reach the visitors center, where interpretive programs are held and free shuttles depart up Going-to-the-Sun Road for trailheads and Logan Pass. A 2.5-mile drive toward the 1913 ranger station ends at a trailhead that departs for Red Eagle Lake, where a state record 16-pound native westslope cutthroat was caught. The 7.5-mile trail to the lake passes through broad, colorful wildflower meadows blooming with lupines and crosses the outlet river twice on Indiana Jones–type suspension bridges. A one-mile walk or drive from the campground takes you outside the park to the town of St. Mary, with its restaurants, gift shops, launderette, and gas station. Vehicles over 21 feet must access this campground from Highway 89, not Going-to-the-Sun Road from West Glacier.

The campground circles around a wideopen prairie comprising grasses, currant bushes, and ground squirrel holes, but with views of Divide and Red Eagle Mountains, particularly in the C loop. Some of the small campsites are tucked into aspen groves that afford some shade, but most are hot, windy, or within sight of each other. From the campground, a rough game trail with downed trees climbs four miles along the park boundary to the top of Napi Point, named for the creator of Blackfeet legends. Traffic on Going-to-the-Sun Road quiets after dark.

Campsites, facilities: The campground has 148 RV or tent campsites. Only 25 of the sites can accommodate RVs or trailer combinations up to 35 feet long. Facilities include picnic tables, fire rings with grills, flush toilets, drinking water, a disposal station, large group sites, and shared hiker and biker campsites. During winter and primitive camping (April–mid-May, late September–November) periods, there are only pit toilets, and no potable water is available. Leashed pets are permitted.

Reservations, fees: Reservations are accepted (877/444-6777, www.recreation.gov). Campsites cost $23 late May–mid-September. Shared sites for hikers and bikers cost $5 per person. Primitive camping (April–mid-May and late September–November) costs $10. Winter camping is free. Cash, check, or credit card.

Directions: From the St. Mary entrance station to Glacier, drive 0.5 mile on Going-to-the-Sun Road. Turn right into the campground. GPS Coordinates: N 48° 45.053' W 113° 26.811'

Contact: Glacier National Park, P.O. Box 128, West Glacier, MT 59936, 406/888-7800, www.nps.gov/glac.

38 JOHNSON'S OF ST. MARY

Scenic rating: 9

in St. Mary on the Blackfeet Reservation

Johnson's of St. Mary is located on a knoll above the tiny seasonal town of St. Mary at the east entrance station to Going-to-the-Sun Road in Glacier National Park. The town—with its restaurants, gift shops, lodges, cabins, and grocery store—packs out with visitors in summer. Since vehicles over 21 feet are not permitted past Sun Point on Going-to-the-Sun Road, those with big RVs can catch park tours from the campground on the historic red jammer buses or Native American Sun Tours. Cyclists on Highway

89 use the campground for its convenience, and a five-minute drive leads to trailheads for a 0.1-mile stroll to the historic ranger station or a 7.5-mile hike to Red Eagle Lake. Fishing is also available at St. Mary Lake and on the St. Mary River.

For many of the RV sites, the knoll affords spectacular views of the St. Mary Valley and sunsets over Glacier's peaks. From the campground, views include Napi Point to the north. The rocky outcrop was named for the creator in Blackfeet legends. A dirt road, which can be dusty in late summer, winds through the campground to get to the tent sites—all in grassy open meadows for sun or aspen groves for shade. The RV sites here are notoriously narrow, cramping the use of awnings and slide-outs. The grassy tenting area has an old cinder-block restroom and shower house, but campers can hike down the hill to the newer RV restroom and showers.

Campsites, facilities: Johnson's has 82 RV sites with pull-throughs that can fit large RVs, plus over 50 tent sites. Hookups include water, sewer, and electricity up to 30 amps. Facilities include picnic tables, fire rings, flush toilets, showers, coin-operated launderette, wireless Internet, a disposal station, propane, restaurant, and small camp store. Johnson's also has overnight facilities for horses. Leashed pets are permitted.

Reservations, fees: Reservations are accepted. Hookups run $33–40. RVs using no hookups cost $26; tents cost $23. Fees include two adults, two kids, and two vehicles per site. Extra people and vehicles cost $5 each. Add on 7 percent Montana bed tax. Cash, check, or credit card. Open late April–late September.

Directions: In St. Mary, drive 0.5 mile north of the Going-to-the-Sun and Highway 89 intersection. Turn right up the hill at the sign for the campground.

GPS Coordinates: N 48° 45.005' W 113° 25.569'

Contact: Johnson's of St. Mary, HC 72-10, Star Route, St. Mary, MT 59417-9701, 406/732-4207, www.johnsonsofstmary.com.

39 ST. MARY KOA

Scenic rating: 9

In St. Mary on the Blackfeet Reservation

Located east of the town of St. Mary, the KOA sits on the west end of St. Mary Lake bordering the St. Mary River. The east entrance to Glacier Park and Going-to-the-Sun Road sits less than two miles away, with restaurants, groceries, and gas in the town one mile west. At the KOA, you can rent a kayak or canoe to paddle the lake, hone golf skills on the campground's putting green, and tour back roads on a mountain bike. With a Blackfeet fishing license available on site, anglers can fish the lake or river. Elk frequent the campground, and the riparian habitat along the water attracts scads of birds, including eagles. Since vehicles over 21 feet are not permitted past Sun Point on Going-to-the-Sun Road, you can catch the Blackfeet-led Sun Tours from here.

Pull-through RV sites line up parking-lot style on gravel, with dramatic views of Singleshot Mountain. Tent sites are scattered in grassy sunny meadows or among the aspens and firs for partial shade. The complex centers around an outdoor pool and a 22-person hot tub, both with views of Glacier's peaks and stars at night. Campground views include, to the north, Napi Point, named for the creator in Blackfeet legends. Several tent sites in the L and K loops border the river.

Campsites, facilities: The campground has 100 RV sites (65 full hookups and 35 partial hookups) and 59 tent campsites. Hookups include water, sewer, and electricity up to 50 amps. Facilities include picnic tables, fire rings with grills, flush toilets, showers, wireless Internet, a pool, a hot tub, a disposal station, a playground, a camp store, and a café that serves breakfast and dinner in the summer. Leashed pets are permitted. A wheelchair-accessible toilet is available.

Reservations, fees: Reservations are accepted.

Hookups cost $25–50. Tents cost $25–31. Rates cover two people. Additional adults cost $7. Kids 17 and under camp free. Add on 7 percent Montana bed tax. Cash, check, or credit card. Open May–September.

Directions: From Babb, drive 8.7 miles south on Highway 89 and turn right heading north on W. Shore Road. From St. Mary Resort gas station, drive 0.4 mile north on Highway 89 and turn left on W. Shore Road. The campground is 0.9 mile north from the turnoff.

GPS Coordinates: N 48° 45.487' W 113° 26.156'

Contact: St. Mary KOA, 106 W. Shore, St. Mary, MT 59417, 406/732-4122 or 800/562-1504, www.goglacier.com.

40 MANY GLACIER

Scenic rating: 10

in Swiftcurrent Valley in Glacier National Park

BEST (

Park the car for days at this most coveted campground on the Continental Divide's east side in Glacier National Park! Located below Grinnell Point, the campground sits at a hub of trails. Hike 4.5 miles to Iceberg Lake to swim with icebergs in August. Ascend the 5.5 miles to see Grinnell Glacier melting fast into a turquoise pool. Grunt up the 5.2 miles to the Ptarmigan Tunnel for views of the Belly River drainage. Slog 8 miles of switchbacks to the top of the Continental Divide at Swiftcurrent Lookout. Shorter walks lead to waterfalls, wildflowers meadows, and blue lakes with moose feeding. Launch canoes, kayaks, and small motorboats onto Swiftcurrent Lake for paddling or fishing. Boats are also available for rent.

Set in firs and aspens, the small, shaded campsites pack in tight next to the busy Swiftcurrent parking lot and the ranger station. Across the Swiftcurrent parking lot you'll find a restaurant, a camp store, and showers (buy tokens in the store), and often the park service erects telescopes for viewing bighorn sheep and grizzly bears on the surrounding slopes. A few campsites get peek-a-boo views of Grinnell Point, especially those on the south side of the southern loop and

A 5.5-mile hike leads to Grinnell Glacier, perched below the Continental Divide.

© BECKY LOMAX

the northwest corner of the northwest loop. Due to the campground's extreme popularity, claim a site before 11 A.M. during July and August.

Campsites, facilities: The campground has 110 RV or tent campsites. Only 13 sites can accommodate RVs up to 35 feet long. Facilities include picnic tables, fire rings with grills, flush toilets, drinking water, a disposal station, large group sites, bear boxes, shared hiker and biker campsites, garbage service, and campground hosts. Primitive camping (late September–October) offers only pit toilets and no potable water. Due to bears, strict food storage regulations are in effect. Leashed pets are permitted. A wheelchair-accessible toilet is available.

Reservations, fees: No reservations are accepted. Campsites cost $20 late May–mid-September. Primitive camping costs $10. Shared sites for hikers and bikers cost $5 per person. Cash, check, or credit card. Open late May–October.

Directions: From Babb, drive 12 miles on Many Glacier Road (Glacier Route 3). Turn left at the ranger station sign and veer right into the campground.

GPS Coordinates: N 48° 47.831' W 113° 40.452'

Contact: Glacier National Park, P.O. Box 128, West Glacier, MT 59936, 406/888-7800, www.nps.gov/glac.

41 DUCK LAKE LODGE

Scenic rating: 7

west of Duck Lake on the Blackfeet Reservation

At 5,015 feet in elevation, Duck Lake on the Blackfeet Reservation is renowned for its fishing, including ice fishing in winter. From Duck Lake, Glacier's peaks spread across the horizon, with Chief Mountain taking prominence to the northwest, and the east entrance to Glacier's Going-to-the-Sun Road is 10 minutes to the west. The lake harbors rainbow and brown trout averaging 8 pounds, but a few lucky anglers pluck out 15-pounders. Float tubes or boats work best in the lake for fishing, rather than casting from shoreline, and motorized boats are restricted to a 10 mph speed limit. Anglers are required to purchase a tribal fishing license and recreation tags for boats. The lodge sells both.

Duck Lake Lodge with its small campground sits two miles west of Duck Lake. Ponds border the gravel access road leading to Duck Lake Lodge, and aspens surround the campground. Tents fit on an open grassy field with no privacy, catching the full sun and wind, and the RV campsites stack very close together along the edge of the aspens. The campground mostly attracts anglers and hunters coming to experience the reservation. The lodge draws on a collection of reliable Blackfeet outfitters for guided fishing or hunting trips on the reservation. The small lodge also has a restaurant and bar.

Campsites, facilities: The campground has five RV sites that can fit midsized RVs, plus room for five tents in a grassy meadow. Hookups include electricity, water, and sewer. Facilities include flush toilets, showers, a launderette, and wireless Internet in the lodge. Leashed pets are permitted.

Reservations, fees: Reservations are recommended. Hookups cost $40. Tent camping costs $10. Cash, check, or credit card. The lodge is open year-round, but camping runs May–October.

Directions: From St. Mary, drive eight miles south on Highway 89 and turn right onto Highway 464. Drive 1.3 miles to milepost 29. At the lodge sign, turn right onto the gravel entrance road.

GPS Coordinates: N 48° 50.314' W 113° 23.562'

Contact: Duck Lake Lodge, P.O. Box 210, 3215 Hwy. 464, Babb, MT 59411, 406/338-5770, www.montanaducklakelodge.com.

42 MIDDLE FORK OF THE FLATHEAD

Scenic rating: 9

on the Middle Fork of the Flathead River in Flathead National Forest

The Middle Fork of the Flathead River churns with white water for some of its 87 miles. The Wild and Scenic River, which springs from headwaters deep within the Bob Marshall Wilderness Complex, races through John F. Stevens Canyon en route to its confluence with the North Fork of the Flathead River near Coram. From Bear Creek, the river flows along the southeast boundary of Glacier National Park, where scenic float sections alternate with Class II–IV white water. Rapids such as Jaws, Bonecrusher, and Screaming Right Hand Turn require technical finesse to navigate. Seven river accesses (Bear Creek, Essex, Paola, Cascadilla, Moccasin Creek, West Glacier, and Blankenship) allow boaters to vary the length of the trips. Most overnight trips take 2–3 days and can add on hiking adventures in the park or the national forest. Most of the white water packs into the section between Moccasin Creek and West Glacier, and notorious logjams litter the Cascadilla to Moccasin Creek float. During high water in late May, some rapids can reach Class IV. Life jackets are required.

The campsites all sit on the south shore of the river on rocky river bars, on willow and grass flats, or in cottonwood, cedar, and fir forests. You can hear the highway at some, but views at all of them look across the river to Glacier.

Campsites, facilities: No camping is permitted between Bear Creek and Essex, but below Essex, you'll find at least 10 tent campsites. Campers are required to take a groover for human waste and a fire pan to minimize burn scars. Camping is only permitted on the south shore in Flathead National Forest; no camping is permitted on the Glacier Park side to the

north. Get a copy of *Three Forks of the Flathead Floating Guide* from the Forest Service to help with campsite selection; the national forest side also has private property to avoid. The river accesses all have vault toilets. Pets are permitted.

Reservations, fees: Reservations are not available. No permit is needed; camping is free. The rafting and kayaking season runs mid-May–early September.

Directions: From West Glacier, drive east on Highway 2 to reach the various signed river accesses.

GPS Coordinates: N 48° 14.035' W 113° 33.929'

Contact: Flathead National Forest, Hungry Horse District, 10 Hungry Horse Dr., Hungry Horse, MT 59919, 406/387-3800, www.fs.fed.us/r1/flathead/.

43 STANTON CREEK LODGE

Scenic rating: 4

on Highway 2 in Flathead National Forest

At 3,550 feet in Flathead National Forest across from the southwestern boundary to Glacier National Park, Stanton Creek Lodge is one of the old fixtures on the Highway 2 corridor. The lodge, campsites, and cabins sit right next to the highway, with the railroad tracks across the street. (Bring earplugs for a good night's sleep here.) A one-mile trail climbs to Stanton Lake in the Great Bear Wilderness. Anglers drop lines into the lake for native westslope cutthroat trout. Those looking for bigger views of glaciers and ridgetop walking continue climbing the Grant Ridge Loop, which returns to the lodge in 10.2 miles. A half mile west of the lodge at Coal Creek, a 10-minute trail cuts down to the Middle Fork of the Flathead River, also for fishing.

Hailing from 1932, the lodge itself was one of a string of wild bars dotting the Marias Pass route within a day's horse ride of each other.

Drunken visitors rode horses through the bar, and bullets flew at passing trains. You can still see bullet holes in the original floor inside the bar. Because of the adjacent highway and railroad tracks, the camping experience here is not quiet wilderness. The tight, small RV campsites sit in the sun between the cabins; tent campsites are shaded under firs. Views are of the forest, highway, and a snippet of Glacier's southern peaks.

Campsites, facilities: The campground has four tent campsites and eight RV campsites that can accommodate midsized RVs. Hookups are available for sewer, water, and electricity up to 30 amps. Facilities include picnic tables, a community fire pit, flush toilets, showers, a restaurant, and bar.

Reservations, fees: Reservations are accepted. RV hookups cost $25; tent sites cost $15. Prices are for two people. Extra campers pay $5 each. Children camp for free. Cash, check, Canadian currency, or credit card. Open late May–mid-September.

Directions: From West Glacier, drive 16 miles east on Highway 2. From East Glacier, drive 44 miles west on Highway 2. The lodge and campground are at milepost 170 on the south side of the highway.

GPS Coordinates: N 48° 24.139' W 113° 42.971'

Contact: Stanton Creek Lodge, HC 36 Box 2C, Essex, MT 59916, 406/888-5040 or 866/883-5040, www.stantoncreeklodge. com.

44 GLACIER HAVEN RV

Scenic rating: 7

on Highway 2 west of Essex surrounded by Flathead National Forest

Located west of Essex on Highway 2, the Glacier Haven RV and Campground opened in summer 2009. It sits in the Middle Fork of the Flathead River corridor across from Glacier National Park. For RVs over 21 feet long that are not permitted to drive over Going-to-the-Sun Road, the campground added one more RV campground on Highway 2. A five-minute drive east to Essex or west to Paola leads to fishing accesses, also places to launch rafts and kayaks to float the Middle Fork of the Flathead River. Also within a five-minute drive, Dickey Lake Road turns south to reach trailheads into Great Bear Wilderness. Marion Lake requires an elevation change of 1,810 feet over 1.7 miles, and 2.4-mile Dickey Lake trail climbs up a steep, brushy headwall to reach into a hanging valley. The campground is five minutes from the historical Izaak Walton Inn, with bike trails in summer.

Glacier Haven added the new campground adjacent to its hotel and a small restaurant, which serves home-style meals. The campground does not permit smoking, even outdoors. The forested campground with one gravel loop squeezes in between the highway and the railroad tracks; bring earplugs to help with sleeping as trains rumble by at night. Most of the RV spots are gravel back-ins. One open area is available for tents with undesignated sites. Views include the forest, highway, and railroad tracks.

Campsites, facilities: The campground has 19 RV campsites, including three that can accommodate large RVs on pull-through gravel parking pads, and room for five tents in a large camping zone. Hookups include water, sewer, and electricity. Facilities include flush toilets, showers, a launderette, and restaurant. Leashed pets are permitted.

Reservations, fees: Reservations are accepted. RV sites cost $35. Tent sites cost $25. Rates are for two people; additional people are charged $5 each. Children ages nine and under camp for free. The pet fee is $2.

Directions: On Highway 2 west of Essex, look for milepost markers 173 and 174. Turn south into the campground on the gravel road west of the Glacier Haven Inn.

GPS Coordinates: N 48° 21.830' W 113° 39.752'

Contact: Glacier Haven, 14297 Hwy. 2 E., Essex, MT 59916, 406/888-9987 or 406/888-5720, www.glacierhavenrv-campground. com.

45 ESSEX PRIMITIVE
🧍 🚲 🛶 🚤 ⛵ 🐴 🚐 ⛺

Scenic rating: 6

on the Middle Fork of the Flathead River in Flathead National Forest

Walton picnic area marks the southernmost tip of Glacier National Park, and across the Middle Fork of the Flathead River sits the tiny community of Essex. The Essex river access site provides a place to launch onto the river for floating or fishing; it is also a location along the river where you can camp right on the bank. Essex also houses the historical Izaak Walton Inn, which offers summer mountain biking, and the Half-Way House convenience store and restaurant. From Walton picnic area, a trail climbs 4.7 miles to Scalplock Lookout for a dramatic view of Mount St. Nicholas. From the Dickey Lake Road (Highway 2, milepost 178.7), you can access two trailheads in Flathead National Forest. A popular, steep trail climbs 1.7 miles to Marion Lake, and a 2.4-mile trail leads up to Dickey Lake in a hanging valley.

The Essex river access site sits on a sandy bar, which increases in size as the river level drops during the season. Primitive camping is permitted on the bar, but it is without privacy. A few cottonwoods provide some shade for the campsites. A bridge above the site crosses the river, blocking the view of Scalplock Mountain. Traffic dwindles at night, but between the road, the river, and the railroad track above, this is not a place for quiet.

Campsites, facilities: The campground has three primitive RV or tent campsites, which can fit midsized RVs. Facilities include rock fire rings and a portable toilet June–August. Boil or filter water taken from the river. Pack out your trash. This is bear country, so practice safe food storage. Camping is limited to three days. Leashed pets are permitted.

Reservations, fees: No reservations are accepted. Camping is free. It's open May–November, but during late May and early June high water can flood the sandbar.

Directions: On Highway 2 between Essex and Walton, turn north at milepost 180. The unsigned exit sits on the west side of the bridge over the river and swings under the bridge to reach the sandbar.

GPS Coordinates: N 48° 16.492' W 113° 36.301'

Contact: Flathead National Forest, Hungry Horse District, 10 Hungry Horse Dr., Hungry Horse, MT 59919, 406/387-3800, www.fs.fed. us/r1/flathead/.

46 BEAR CREEK PRIMITIVE
🧍 🛶 🚤 🐴 🚐 ⛺

Scenic rating: 7

on the Middle Fork of the Flathead River in Flathead National Forest

At the confluence of Bear Creek and the Middle Fork of the Flathead River, Bear Creek river access site sits where the Middle Fork of the Flathead River plunges from the Bob Marshall Wilderness Area to then form Glacier National Park's southern boundary. It is a large site used for launching onto the river to float for day-long or overnight float trips and for hikers and horse-packers heading into the Bob Marshall Wilderness. Day hikers also use the trail heading up the Middle Fork, which spurs off up Edna Creek for a 3.5-mile steep grunt up to scenic Tranquil Basin Overlook, and a 0.5-mile climb farther to summit 7,394-foot Mount Furlong yields views of Glacier's peaks.

The area roars equally with churning rapids and noise from the highway and railroad. Those camping here may want to bring earplugs. The wide-open, giant dusty parking lot yields big views of the surrounding mountains—the Great Bear Wilderness and Glacier—but at a cost to privacy. The area is not designed with designated campsites, but the big parking lot permits plenty of room for primitive camping for those needing campsites while traveling over Marias Pass.

Campsites, facilities: The area has room for three RVs or tent campsites. Facilities include a wheelchair-accessible vault toilet. Boil or filter water taken from the river. Pack out your trash. Camping is limited to three days. Because of bears, practice safe food storage. Leashed pets are permitted.

Reservations, fees: No reservations are accepted. Camping is free. Open May–November.

Directions: On Highway 2, between Essex and Marias Pass, find Bear Creek River Access at milepost 185 on the south side of the highway.

GPS Coordinates: N 48° 14.032' W 113° 33.942'

Contact: Flathead National Forest, Hungry Horse District, 10 Hungry Horse Dr., Hungry Horse, MT 59919, 406/387-3800, www.fs.fed.us/r1/flathead/.

47 DEVIL CREEK

Scenic rating: 6

on Highway 2 in Flathead National Forest

At 4,450 feet in elevation along Highway 2, Devil Creek is close to both river recreation and hiking trails in the Great Bear Wilderness, which surrounds it, and trails across the narrow valley in Glacier National Park. Across the highway from the campground, Bear Creek harbors brook trout and westslope cutthroat trout. Five miles to the west, the creek collides with the Middle Fork of the Flathead River as it roars out of the Bob Marshall Wilderness Area, and a 3.5-mile trail climbs to Tranquil Basin. At the Bear Creek river access site, rafters and anglers launch to float a portion or all of the 44 miles to the North Fork of the Flathead River. Hikers drive two miles east to catch the trail up Elk Mountain in Glacier National Park. The 3.5-mile trail slogs up 3,355 feet for top-of-the-world views. From the campground, a trail also leads to Elk Lake (5.9 miles) and Moose Lake (8.2 miles).

hiking down from Elk Mountain on Glacier's southern end

The small campground tucks into the forest adjacent to Devil Creek. One loop holds all the campsites, with those at the top of the loop being farthest from the highway. All of the sites are shaded under firs and lodgepole pines. The small sites are spread out, but you can still see neighboring campers. You'll hear both highway and railroad noise in the campground. Due to the limited campgrounds along Highway 2, plan on arriving before 3 P.M. during midsummer to claim a campsite.

Campsites, facilities: The campground has 14 RV or tent campsites that can fit RVs up to 40 feet. Facilities include picnic tables, fire rings with grills, drinking water, vault toilets, and campground hosts. Pack out your trash. Firewood is not provided, but you're free to scour the surrounding forest for downed limbs. Leashed pets are permitted. A wheelchair-accessible toilet is available.

Reservations, fees: No reservations are accepted. Campsites cost $10. Cash or check. Open late May–mid-September.

Directions: On Highway 2 between Essex and Marias Pass, turn south at milepost 190 into the campground.

GPS Coordinates: N 48° 15.103' W 113° 27.919'

Contact: Flathead National Forest, Hungry Horse District, 10 Hungry Horse Dr., Hungry Horse, MT 59919, 406/387-3800, www.fs.fed.us/r1/flathead/.

48 GLACIER MEADOW RV PARK

Scenic rating: 7

on Highway 2 in Flathead National Forest

Located at 4,450 feet in elevation on Highway 2, Glacier Meadow RV Park has Flathead National Forest on its south boundary and Glacier National Park a mile to the north. From the campground, river rafters and anglers head seven miles to the west to the Middle Fork of the Flathead River. Hikers drive less than 0.5 mile to reach the Elk Mountain Trailhead and its strenuous 3,355-foot, 3.5-mile climb to an old lookout site with views into Glacier National Park. For those traveling with RVs over 21 feet long that are not permitted over Going-to-the-Sun Road, the red buses stop at Glacier Meadow to pick up riders for the 8.5-hour tour that loops over Logan Pass. Nearby Skyland Road is also available for ATV riding.

The campground, which sits on 58 acres, adjoins a large meadow that attracts elk in May and June. A gravel road connects the campsites, and for large RVs, the campground's wide-open large grassy field makes for easy parking. Sites in the open have full views of the surrounding peaks. Some sites along the campground's east side receive morning shade from a mixed forest of firs and lodgepoles. The 25 pull-through sites have electric and water hookups; 16 sites along the woods have electricity only. Only some of the sites have picnic tables.

Campsites, facilities: The campground has 41 RV campsites, which can fit RVs up to 40 feet, and 16 tent campsites. Facilities include picnic tables, drinking water, flush toilets, showers, a launderette, a shuffleboard floor, horseshoe pits, wireless Internet, a playground, and a disposal station. The management can also provide horse boarding. Leashed pets are permitted. A wheelchair-accessible toilet is available.

Reservations, fees: Reservations are accepted. Hookups cost $30–32. Tent sites cost $20. Rates include two people; each additional person is charged $5. Kids 10 years old and under camp for free. The Montana bed tax of 7 percent will be added to the bill. Cash or credit card. Open mid-May–mid-September.

Directions: From East Glacier, drive 16 miles west on Highway 2. From West Glacier, drive 44 miles east on Highway 2. Turn south between mileposts 191 and 192.

GPS Coordinates: N 48° 15.981' W 113° 26.605'

Contact: Glacier Meadow RV Park, P.O. Box 124, East Glacier, MT 59936, 406/226-4479, www.glaciermeadowrvpark.com.

49 SUMMIT

Scenic rating: 7

at Marias Pass in Lewis and Clark National Forest

Of all the passes crossing the Rocky Mountains, Marias Pass is the lowest at 5,220 feet. It sits in Lewis and Clark National Forest across from Glacier National Park. Ironically, the pass eluded Lewis and Clark. John F. Stevens discovered it in 1889 while looking for a route for the Great Northern Railway to cut through the mountains. The pass also marks the Continental Divide, the split where waters flow to the Atlantic and Pacific, and the place where geologists first discovered the Lewis Overthrust Fault, where 1.6 billion-year-old rocks buried younger layers from the dinosaur age. Departing across the highway, the Continental Divide Trail enters Glacier Park and passes Three Bears Lake in 0.6 mile—a good place to fish, spot moose, and go bird-watching. At 1.1 miles, the trail intersects with Autumn Creek Trail, which parallels the front range of peaks.

The small forested campground tucks into the lodgepole pines for partial shade on the east side of the Marias Pass rest area. Both the highway and the railroad tracks pass in front of the campground, admitting noise all night long, especially from the railway. Bring earplugs for a good night's sleep. A few sites on the north side of the loop have peek-a-boo views of Glacier's peaks. Because campgrounds are limited along Highway 2, plan on arriving before 3 p.m. during midsummer to claim a campsite.

Campsites, facilities: The campground has 17 RV or tent campsites that can fit midsized RVs. Facilities include picnic tables, fire rings with grills, vault toilets, and potable water. Pack out your trash. Firewood is not provided, but you're free to scour the surrounding national forest for downed limbs. Leashed pets are permitted. A wheelchair-accessible toilet is available.

Reservations, fees: No reservations are accepted. Camping costs $10. Cash or check. Open early June–mid-September.

Directions: From East Glacier, drive Highway 2 west for 11.3 miles to Marias Pass at milepost 198. From West Glacier, drive 48.9 miles east. On the east side of the Marias Pass rest area, locate the campground entrance.

GPS Coordinates: N 48° 19.121' W 113° 21.109'

Contact: Lewis and Clark National Forest, Rocky Mountain Ranger District, 1102 N. Main Ave., P.O. Box 340, Choteau, MT 59422, 406/466-5341, fax 406/466-2237, www.fs.fed.us/r1/lewisclark.

50 Y LAZY R RV PARK

Scenic rating: 7

in East Glacier on the Blackfeet Reservation

South of the main road through East Glacier, this campground appears at first to be little more than a large grassy field, but the views of Glacier's peaks, from the Calf Robe to Dancing Lady—especially at sunset—make up for the setting. From the campground, a quick two-block walk puts you in tiny East Glacier, where you'll find groceries, a few gift shops, three restaurants, and a post office. Walk under the railroad overpass to see the historic East Glacier Park Hotel, with its monstrous Douglas firs in the lobby. The lodge's golf course (its nine holes are named for former Blackfeet chiefs) has the oldest grass greens in Montana. Drive 12 miles north to Two Medicine Lake for picnicking, hiking, fishing, boating, and sightseeing. Two hiking trails depart from the north side of town; pick up Blackfeet Tribal recreation licenses before hiking these.

The campground covers three acres, most of which is mowed grass with only a couple of trees for shade. The campsites with the trees tend to get snagged early. Sites on the south end at the edge of the bluff overlook Midvale Creek and grab views of the mountains, too. A gravel road accesses the tight sites, and while the overall campground is level, the individual sites can present a challenge for leveling an RV. You can hear both the highway and the railroad tracks from the campground. Be aware that East Glacier's water supply often requires boiling for purification. Ask when you check in about the current water quality and any "boil orders."

Campsites, facilities: The campground has 30 RV campsites that can fit large RVs, plus 10 tent sites. Hookups are available for sewer, water, and electricity. Facilities include picnic tables, flush toilets, coin-operated showers, a playground, a disposal station, and a huge coin-operated launderette with 17 commercial washers.

Reservations, fees: Reservations are accepted. Hookups cost $20–23. Tent sites cost $18. The Montana bed tax is included in the price. Cash or check. Open June–mid-September.

Directions: In East Glacier, coming from the east on Highway 2, turn left at the fourth street. From the west on Highway 2, take the first right in town. Then, drive two blocks south to Washington Street and turn right to reach Lindhe Avenue. Turn left for 1.5 blocks.

The campground sits west of the junction of Lindhe Avenue and Meade Street.

GPS Coordinates: N 48° 26.405' W 113° 12.958'

Contact: Lazy R RV Park, P.O. Box 146, East Glacier, MT 59936, 406/226-5505.

51 TWO MEDICINE

Scenic rating: 10

on Pray Lake in the southeast corner of Glacier National Park

BEST (

Huddling below the massive hulk of Rising Wolf Mountain, Two Medicine Campground sits on Pray Lake, a small outlet pond for the much larger Two Medicine Lake. Sitting a mile high, the campground offers hikers, sightseers, boaters, and anglers a taste of Glacier's less-crowded realm. From the campground, the 18.8-mile Dawson-Pitamakin Trail loops around Rising Wolf, along the Continental Divide. A mile up the road, the Scenic Point Trail climbs 3.1 miles to a bluff overlooking

Two Medicine Campground surrounds Pray Lake in Glacier.

© BECKY LOMAX

the lakes and staring out onto the plains. The *Sinopah* tours the lake several times daily for sightseers, and rental canoes, kayaks, and motorboats are available near the boat dock. The historical dining hall from the park's early days now houses a camp store, and the staffed ranger station keeps track of bear sightings on a large map.

Set in stunted subalpine firs, the quiet campground curls around Pray Lake, a good fishing and swimming outlet pool from Two Medicine Lake. At least half of the campsites at Two Medicine have stunning views—most of Rising Wolf. You can sit in your campsite with a pair of binoculars and watch mountain goats or grizzly bears crawl around the slopes. Find these sites in loops A and C. Sites 92–100 yield closer views of the slopes. Due to the campground's popularity, plan on arriving before noon during July and August.

Campsites, facilities: The campground has 99 RV or tent campsites. Only 13 sites can accommodate RVs or trailer combinations up to 35 feet. Facilities include picnic tables, fire rings with grills, flush toilets, drinking water, a disposal station, large group campsites, interpretive programs, shared hiker and biker campsites, and campground hosts. Primitive camping (late September–October) offers only pit toilets, and there's no potable water. Leashed pets are permitted. A wheelchair-accessible toilet is available.

Reservations, fees: No reservations are accepted. Campsites cost $20 late May–mid-September. Primitive camping costs $10. Hikers and bikers pay $5 per person. Cash, check, or credit card.

Directions: From East Glacier, drive four miles north on Highway 49 and then swing left onto Two Medicine Road for 7.5 miles. Turn right at the ranger station to enter the campground.

GPS Coordinates: N 48° 29.301' W 113° 22.045'

Contact: Glacier National Park, P.O. Box 128, West Glacier, MT 59936, 406/888-7800, www.nps.gov/glac.

52 CUT BANK

Scenic rating: 7

in Cut Bank Valley on the east side of Glacier National Park

At 5,200 feet in a rugged, remote valley on Glacier's east side, Cut Bank sits between East Glacier and St. Mary. Two barriers deter RVs from going to Cut Bank—the narrow curvy Highway 89 and the five miles of potholed dirt road leading to the campground. The campground is a favorite for tenters, who relish the quiet and the campground's real rusticity. A 7.2-mile trail departs up-valley from here towards Triple Divide Pass, so named for the peak above that feeds water to the Atlantic, Pacific, and Hudson Bay drainages. A less strenuous hike ends in six miles at Medicine Grizzly Lake, a lure for anglers and bears alike because of its 12-inch rainbow trout. Frequently, the lake closes because of bear sightings. Another spur leads to Atlantic Creek Falls at 4.1 miles; add on another 2.5 miles to reach Morning Star Lake, in a small cirque below cliffs that hold a golden eagle nest and mountain goat paths.

Tucked under a deep shaded forest, the ultra-quiet campground stays cool even on hot August days. Atlantic Creek burbles adjacent to the campground. Unfortunately, most of the undergrowth beneath the canopy is gone, leaving little privacy between sites. The sites are small but do have room for tents. Those with small RVs may find it a challenge to level them.

Campsites, facilities: The campground has 14 RV and tent campsites that can fit only small RVs. The park service discourages RVs and trailers from using this campground. Facilities include picnic tables, fire rings with grills, and pit toilets. Bring your own water, or boil or filter water taken from the creek for drinking. Bring firewood, as gathering even downed limbs is prohibited in the park. Pack out your trash. Leashed pets are permitted.

Reservations, fees: No reservations are accepted. The fee is $10 per night. Cash, check, or credit card. Open late May–mid-September.

Directions: From St. Mary, drive 14.5 miles south on Highway 89. From East Glacier, drive 13.5 miles north on Highway 49 and 5.5 miles north on Highway 89. At the campground sign on Highway 89, turn west onto the dirt road for five miles.

GPS Coordinates: N 48° 36.116' W 113° 23.020'

Contact: Glacier National Park, P.O. Box 128, West Glacier, MT 59936, 406/888-7800, www.nps.gov/glac.

53 ASPENWOOD RESORT

Scenic rating: 8

west of Browning on the Blackfeet Reservation

Located west of Browning below Glacier's eastern front range, the campground and resort sit on the Blackfeet Reservation, where just about the only sound is the incessant wind. On the prairie to the east, Browning has a little over 1,000 residents. The small Museum of the Plains Indians provides the best look at the tribe's history, with dioramas and clothing made with phenomenal beadwork. The Blackfeet Heritage Center and Gallery also provides a venue for locals to market their art. Recently, the tribe built the Glacier Peaks Casino, a 33,000-square-foot gaming facility with more than 300 slot machines. For four days each year, the annual North American Indian Days festival brings out dancing, singing, storytelling, and a rodeo during the second weekend in July, at the powwow grounds behind the museum. Two beaver ponds offer fishing, paddleboating, wildlife-watching, and hiking. The resort also arranges for Native American guided fishing trips, tours, and horseback riding.

The resort includes a small lodge with rooms, a restaurant, and a campground. The resort's restaurant—the Outlaw Grill—serves breakfast, lunch, and dinner, and does takeout orders if you prefer to eat at your campsite. The RV sites are gravel pull-throughs surrounded by grass with no trees; however, the open venue allows for views of Glacier's peaks. Tent sites are tucked in between the aspen groves for shade and wind protection.

Campsites, facilities: The campground has 10 RV campsites and eight tent campsites. The pull-through RV sites can fit large rigs; eight of the RV spaces have hookups, with two for dry camping. Hookups are available for electricity and water only. Facilities include picnic tables, fire pits, flush toilets, showers, a disposal station, firewood, a game and exercise room, and paddleboats. Leashed pets are permitted. Horse boarding is also available.

Reservations, fees: Reservations are accepted and are highly recommended for powwow weekends—the second weekends of July and August. Hookups cost $30–35. Tent sites cost $18. Cash, check, or credit card. Open mid-May–mid-October.

Directions: From the junction of Highway 2 and Highway 89 in Browning, drive west on Highway 89 for 9.5 miles. From Kiowa Junction, drive 2.3 miles east on Highway 89. The resort sits on the north side of the road.

GPS Coordinates: N 48° 32.467' W 113° 13.514'

Contact: Aspenwood Resort, HC-72, Box 5150, Hwy. 89, Browning, MT 59417, 406/338-3009, www.aspenwoodresort.com.

54 LODGEPOLE TIPI VILLAGE

Scenic rating: 9

west of Browning on the Blackfeet Reservation

Located on the Blackfeet Reservation below Glacier's eastern front range, the Lodgepole

Tipi Village offers a different type of camping—camping in a tipi with cultural insight into the traditional life of the Blackfeet. The tipi village sprawls across 200 acres of wildflower prairie with a spring-fed lake and unobstructed views of Glacier's southern ramparts. A small herd of Spanish mustangs runs wild on the property. The village also contracts with Blackfeet guides to offer horseback riding trips on the rolling foothills below Glacier's peaks and fly fishing for rainbow trout on the reservation's renowned lakes. The owner also leads cultural history tours to historical buffalo jumps, tipi rings, and medicine lodges.

Camping in the tipi village is expensive, but you're paying for the cultural experience provided by its Blackfeet owner, Darrell Norman. Tour his small gallery, or add on an art workshop to make a drum or parfleche. Breakfast and a Blackfeet wild game dinner are also available by reservation. With a campfire in the tipi, it glows under the night sky. The sun brightens the inside early when the sunrise hits the prairie. Wind and the hooves of the Spanish mustangs are the only sounds you'll hear.

Campsites, facilities: Camping is permitted only in tipis here—not RVs nor tents. The seven double-walled lodgepole tipis remain cool in the summer heat but retain warmth in cooler months. Each tipi centers around a rock-ringed fire pit (firewood provided). Facilities include picnic tables, flush toilets, and showers. A large communal campfire is sheltered from wind by a wooden arbor built to resemble a traditional Blackfeet ceremonial lodge. Bring your own sleeping bag and pad as well as a flashlight. Tipis have no floors, so your sleeping pad will go on the ground.

Reservations, fees: Reservations are wise—especially for Browning powwow weekends during the second weekends of July and August. The first person in the tipi is charged $50 per night, and for each additional person its $15. Children under 12 years old are charged $8. Check or credit card. Open May–September.

Directions: From Browning, drive 2.5 miles west on Highway 89. Locate the entrance on the south side of the road.

GPS Coordinates: N 48° 33.261' W 113° 4.492'

Contact: Lodgepole Tipi Village, P.O. Box 1832, Browning, MT 59417, 406/338-2787, www.blackfeetculturecamp.com.

NORTHWEST MONTANA

© BECKY LOMAX

BEST CAMPGROUNDS

【 Boat-in Camping
Elk Island, page 110.

【 Hiking
Little Therriault Lake, page 88.
Holland Lake, page 124.

【 Hot Springs
Cascade, page 123.

【 Lake Camping
Big Arm State Park, page 113.

【 Montana
Big Therriault Lake, page 89.
Spotted Bear, page 60.

【 River Camping
Bull River, page 97.

【 Wildlife-Watching
Swan Lake, page 119.

Ice carved out the jagged, snowcapped north-

west Montana mountains, leaving wet thumbprints of ponds, lakes, and alpine tarns. As the ice receded, water etched valleys, frothing white in rocky drops and smoothing placidly into clear, blue-green glass through the flats. Campgrounds line the rivers and lakes, from high alpine passes to the lowest elevation in Montana.

In contrast with other states where luxury homes and posh resorts take up every inch of shore along rivers and lakes, in Montana the public maintains access to miles of water. Plus, the region teems with wildlife: grizzly bears, wolves, mountain lions, elk, moose, mountain goats, and bighorn sheep. Accessibility and wildlife lure campers, but the area has even more attributes.

More than five million acres of public, accessible forests envelop northwest Montana. That's comparable to the size of New Jersey. The region also holds more state parks than any other area of Montana. Seven mountain ranges, five wilderness areas, four national forests, and two special hiking areas gain the region a reputation as a camping mecca. Add more than 500 lakes, three major rivers, three huge reservoirs, and 3,000 miles of streams, and the options for camping multiply far beyond what you can visit in months of travel.

But, while many campgrounds are accessible by paved two-lane roads, a substantial number are accessed only by dirt roads that crawl deep into the forest. To camp at Spotted Bear — the springboard into the Bob Marshall Wilderness — you must drive almost 60 dusty miles of washboards.

The most popular camping areas cluster around lakes, where waters buzz with water-skiers, anglers, sailors, sea kayakers, and canoeists. Flathead Lake, the largest freshwater lake west of the Mississippi River, attracts the most boaters; its five state parks have campgrounds rimming its shoreline. The sheer size of the lake — almost 30 miles long — makes it seem more on par with an inland sea, and its whitecaps attest to winds that can whip up several-foot-high waves. The lake's 50-pound mackinaw trout attract sport anglers, and its Wild Horse Island — a day-use park —

lures hikers for its wild horses, bighorn sheep, wildflowers, and views of the peak-rimmed lake from its summit.

Two other large reservoirs also attract boaters, but in far fewer numbers than at Flathead Lake. East of Flathead Lake, Hungry Horse Reservoir squeezes between two mountain ranges with 14 campgrounds. Anglers especially relish its fishery, which harbors westslope cutthroat trout. Several islands dot the 35-mile-long reservoir – two contain campgrounds. Northwest of Flathead Lake, Lake Koocanusa sprawls 90 miles, crossing the border into Canada. Its name combines the Kootenai River plus the names of its two countries. Campgrounds rim the lake, which offers boating and fishing for kamloops trout.

Those who enjoy camping at smaller lakes head to Tally Lake, Montana's deepest lake, which plummets to nearly 500 feet. Other lake getaways include two valleys lining lakes up in strings. Southeast of Flathead Lake, the narrow Highway 83 corridor cradles seven large lakes between the Mission and Swan Mountains. You can watch bald eagles fishing and wake up to the call of loons. These lakes attract not only boaters and anglers, but hikers as well, as trails lead both east and west into wilderness areas. West of Flathead Lake, the Thompson Chain of Lakes along Highway 2 links up another seven large lakes with a handful of smaller ponds – all loaded with state-run and national forest campgrounds.

Campers looking for special places to hike will find campgrounds at the base of mountains that climb from cedar canopies to wildflower meadows. Ten Lakes Scenic Area, with its two campgrounds, weaves hiking trails along ridges right on the border with Canada; views encompass tiny subalpine lakes, the northern Whitefish Range, and Glacier Park in the distance. The Cabinet Mountain Wilderness – topped by glaciers on Snowshoe Peak – offers lakes, huckleberry picking, and high passes as destinations for hikers. Jewel Basin, with its 27 alpine lakes, has trails with views of Flathead Lake and the wild interior of the Great Bear Wilderness.

For campers, northwest Montana is one vast playground. Rarely do campgrounds swell to over 50 campsites, and many are small free sites with room for only a few tents.

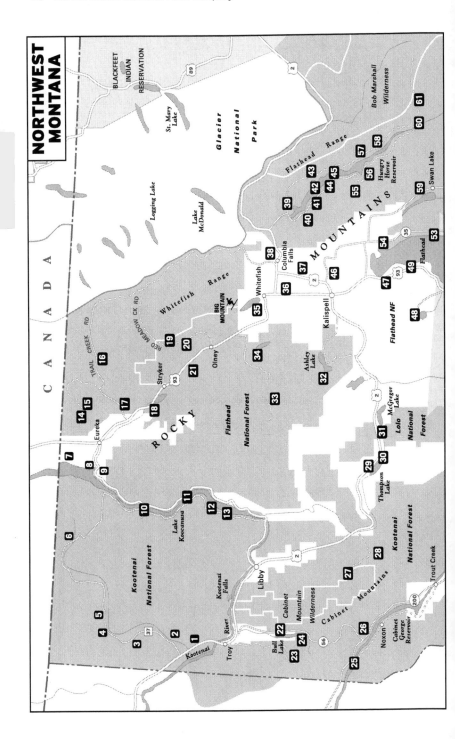

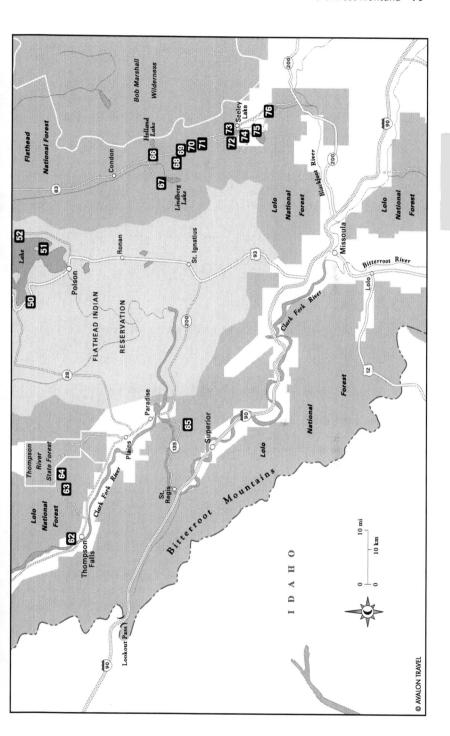

© AVALON TRAVEL

1 YAAK RIVER

Scenic rating: 8

on the Yaak River in the Purcell Mountains in Kootenai National Forest

At 1,900 feet at the confluence of the Kootenai and Yaak Rivers, the campground is the only developed Forest Service campground right on the highway between the Idaho border and Libby. It also has the fame of being the lowest in Montana and frequently fills up, particularly on weekends. The 53-mile Yaak River, which drains the remote Purcell Mountains, holds rainbow trout, mountain whitefish, and brook trout. The fishing is best from the bank or by wading. The color of the river changes from crystal clear most of the year to cloudy gray during the May and June runoff. With only a few riffles, the lower Kootenai River is also a favorite with locals for floating rafts and fishing in drift boats. Put in at the Troy Bridge to float about nine miles to the campground. A primitive boat ramp works for launching canoes and small boats.

The campground, which has two paved loops, sits on both sides of the Yaak River, with turnoffs north and south of the Yaak River Bridge. Shaded by tall larches and cedars, both loops have access to both the Yaak and Kootenai Rivers, although the north loop has a larger sandy beach. Campsites are spaced out for privacy, with tall brush between sites. You'll hear some trucks at night on the highway above. Eight sites offer pull-through paved parking pads, and several parking pads are double-wide.

Campsites, facilities: The campground has 44 RV or tent campsites. RVs are limited to 32 feet. Facilities include picnic tables, fire rings with grills, vault toilets, garbage service, campground hosts, and drinking water. You can collect downed limbs for firewood from the surrounding national forest. Leashed pets are permitted. A wheelchair-accessible toilet is available.

Reservations, fees: Reservations are not available. Campsites cost $10. Cash or check. Open year-round, with limited services September–May.

Directions: From Troy, drive on Highway 2 northwest for seven miles. Turn west off the highway into the campground. Entrances flank the Yaak River Bridge; however, the fee station and campground hosts are on the south side before crossing the river. From the Idaho border, drive about seven miles southeast. GPS Coordinates: N 48° 33.662' W 115° 58.335'

Contact: Kootenai National Forest, Three Rivers Ranger District, Troy Ranger Station, 12858 Hwy. 2, Troy, MT 59935-8750, 406/295-4693, www.fs.fed.us/r1/kootenai/.

2 YAAK FALLS

Scenic rating: 7

on the Yaak River in the Purcell Mountains in Kootenai National Forest

Sitting at 2,400 feet on the Yaak River in the Purcell Mountains, the campground is named for the nearby falls 0.3 mile to the north. The falls, named after the Yaak Indians who once populated the area, cascade through some of the oldest rock in the world. Due to the eastward shift of the Pacific plate, rocks 800 million to 1.5 billion years old shoved up to the surface. The 53-mile Yaak River cuts through these slabs, which you can sit on to view the two falls. During high water in late May and early June, they roar. The river harbors westslope cutthroat and rainbow trout. Above the falls, pools work for fly-fishing and the access is easy due to the road's proximity. Larger rainbows hang out below the falls. White-water rafters and kayakers also float the Yaak. Below the falls, the canyon holds expert Class IV–V drops. Above the falls in the four-mile stretch from Seventeen Mile Bridge, the rapids rank more around Class II–III; experience in navigating boulders is a must.

The campground receives filtered sunlight through larch and cedar trees. Underbrush alternates with open rocky areas, granting some sites privacy. You can hear the roar of the river in the campground.

Campsites, facilities: The campground has seven RV or tent campsites. RVs are limited to 32 feet. Facilities include picnic tables, fire rings, and a vault toilet, but no drinking water. Bring water with you, or haul it from the fishing access. If you plan to use the river water, purify or boil it before drinking. Sometimes firewood is available, but you can also collect downed limbs for firewood from the surrounding national forest. Pack out your trash. Leashed pets are permitted.

Reservations, fees: Reservations are not available. Campsites are free. Open year-round, but services are limited September–May.

Directions: On Highway 2, drive 10 miles west from Troy or four miles east from the Idaho-Montana border. Turn north onto Highway 508, a paved road, and drive for seven miles. Turn right into the campground.

GPS Coordinates: N 48° 38.656' W 115° 53.229'

Contact: Kootenai National Forest, Three Rivers Ranger District, Troy Ranger Station, 12858 Hwy. 2, Troy, MT 59935-8750, 406/295-4693, www.fs.fed.us/r1/kootenai/.

3 RED TOP

Scenic rating: 6

in the Purcell Mountains in Kootenai National Forest

Sitting at 2,920 feet in the Purcell Mountains, Red Top Campground is used mostly by those touring the Yaak River drainage. However, the campground does not sit on the river, but rather across the road on Red Top Creek. Fishing is available in Red Top Creek, but most of the Yaak

River adjacent to the campground is flanked by private land, although fishing accesses are available both north and south on the river. The campground is named for the 6,226-foot summit of Red Top Mountain to the west.

Dense conifers shade the tiny campground, which is bordered on the north side by the creek. Its location on the road to Yaak allows for road noise to enter the campground, but at night, traffic quiets so you can hear the creek. The dirt campground road is narrow, affording limited maneuvering space for trailers.

Campsites, facilities: The campground has five RV or tent campsites. RVs are limited to 32 feet. Facilities include picnic tables, fire rings with grills, and a vault toilet, but no drinking water. Bring water with you, or haul it from Red Top Creek. If you plan to use the creek water, purify or boil it before drinking. Pack out your trash. You can collect downed limbs for firewood from the surrounding national forest. Leashed pets are permitted.

Reservations, fees: Reservations are not available. Campsites are free. Open year-round, but services are limited September–May.

Directions: On Highway 2, drive 10 miles west from Troy or five miles east from the Idaho-Montana border to Highway 508. Turn north onto the paved road and drive for 16 miles. Turn west into the campground.

GPS Coordinates: N 48° 45.660' W 115° 55.070'

Contact: Kootenai National Forest, Three Rivers Ranger District, Troy Ranger Station, 12858 Hwy. 2, Troy, MT 59935-8750, 406/295-4693, www.fs.fed.us/r1/kootenai/.

4 WHITETAIL

Scenic rating: 7

on the Yaak River in the Purcell Mountains in Kootenai National Forest

Sitting at 3,080 feet in the heavily forested Purcell Mountains, Whitetail is one of four campgrounds accessed by pavement along the lower Yaak River. The river, which is slow-flowing in this area, is good for floating from the Yaak Bridge in the town of Yaak to the campground. The distance is about six miles, and the river stretches wide enough for canoes, inflatable kayaks, small rafts, and drift boats. Larger rafts are better only in the last half from Pete Creek to the campground. The river has occasional logjams, so keep alert. A primitive boat ramp in the campground allows for launching or loading canoes and small boats. The river also harbors rainbow and brook trout. Forest Road 4354 leads to a trailhead into the Northwest Peak Scenic Area, and mountain bikers can ride to Mount Baldy Lookout.

A loose coniferous forest lends partial shade to the campground, which tucks between the road and the river. Thick, lush brush and grass envelops the shoreline, but trails weave through it to reach the water. Sites are spread out for privacy, and a few of them overlook the river. Some also back into the hillside against the road. At night, the road noise dwindles, and the sound of the river is pervasive, especially in early summer. A paved road loops through the campground, which is a good place for sighting moose.

Campsites, facilities: The campground has 12 RV or tent campsites. RVs are limited to 32 feet. Facilities include picnic tables, fire rings with grills, a vault toilet, drinking water, campground hosts, a boat ramp, and limited firewood for sale. Leashed pets are permitted. A wheelchair-accessible toilet is available.

Reservations, fees: Reservations are not available. Campsites cost $7. Cash or check. Open year-round, with limited services September–May.

Directions: On Highway 2, drive 10 miles west from Troy or four miles east from the Idaho-Montana border. Turn north onto the paved Highway 508 and drive for 24 miles to the campground, located on the south side of the road. From Yaak, the campground is 5.5 miles to the west.

GPS Coordinates: N 48° 49.667' W 115° 49.035'

Contact: Kootenai National Forest, Three Rivers Ranger District, Troy Ranger Station, 12858 Hwy. 2, Troy, MT 59935-8750, 406/295-4693, www.fs.fed.us/r1/kootenai/.

5 PETE CREEK

Scenic rating: 8

on the Yaak River in the Purcell Mountains in Kootenai National Forest

Pete Creek sits at 3,120 feet along the Yaak River in the Purcell Mountains. A primitive boat launch in the campground works for rafts, kayaks, and canoes. You can float from the Yaak Bridge 2.6 miles east or three miles from the campground to Whitetail Campground, but larger rafts should stick to the section below Pete Creek. Floaters must be on the lookout for logjams. The Yaak River also harbors rainbow and brook trout. To explore the 19,100-acre Northwest Peak Scenic Area, drive 19 miles north on Forest Road 338. From the trailhead, a 2.3-mile path leads to the top of 7,705-foot-high Northwest Peak for views in Canada and glimpses of the Cabinet Mountains toward the southwest. Plenty of Forest Service roads are also available for mountain biking, hunting, and winter snowmobiling. The campground is also the closest to Yaak, a tiny, remote year-round community.

Dense, tall conifers and lush undergrowth lend both shade and privacy to this intimate campground tucked between the road, Pete Creek, and Yaak River. With both the creek and the river, the sound of flowing water is heard at most of the campsites. Rock walls provide bouldering right in the campground. Three sites overlook Pete Creek, and two small, private walk-in campsites are best for tenters.

Campsites, facilities: The campground has 11 RV or tent campsites, plus two walk-in campsites for tents. RVs are limited to 32 feet. Facilities include picnic tables, fire rings, a vault toilet, drinking water, campground hosts, firewood for sale, and a boat ramp. Leashed pets are permitted. A wheelchair-accessible toilet is available.

Reservations, fees: Reservations are not available. Campsites cost $7. Cash or check. Open year-round, with limited services September–May.

Directions: On Highway 2, drive 10 miles west from Troy or four miles east from the Idaho-Montana border. Turn north onto the paved Highway 508 and drive for 27 miles to the campground, which is on the south side of the road. From Yaak, the campground is 2.5 miles to the west.

GPS Coordinates: N 48° 49.867' W 115° 45.960'

Contact: Kootenai National Forest, Three Rivers Ranger District, Troy Ranger Station, 12858 Hwy. 2, Troy, MT 59935-8750, 406/295-4693, www.fs.fed.us/r1/kootenai/.

6 CARIBOU

Scenic rating: 8

in the Purcell Mountains in Kootenai National Forest

At an elevation of 3,700 feet in the Purcell Mountains, Caribou Campground requires a long drive from everywhere. Caribou Creek runs adjacent to Caribou Campground, which sits only 3.5 miles from the Canadian border. Fishing is available in the creek. The campground works as a base camp for exploring the remote northern Yaak. Upper Yaak Falls is about 10 miles west of the campground, and much of the area along the road provides good wildlife-watching. The Caribou Trail (#56), which begins about 0.5 mile northwest of the campground, traverses Caribou Mountain and peters out near the border. The Vinal–Mount Henry–Boulder National Recreation Trail sits in the mountains south of the campground. Trails 7 and 17 lead to Mount Henry Lakes and the summit of Mount Henry, while connecting with the trail.

The tiny secluded campground is the epitome of quiet. Located miles from pavement in both directions, the forest road passing the campground produces minimal traffic and none at night. The creek, which flows on the west side of the campground, is the only sound you'll hear beside wildlife: owls, coyotes, and ravens. The campsites rim a meadow surrounded by a loose forest of conifers.

Campsites, facilities: The campground has three RV or tent campsites. RVs are limited to 32 feet. Facilities include picnic tables, fire rings, and a vault toilet. No drinking water is available. Bring your own, or if you plan to use creek water, then filter or boil it before drinking. Leashed pets are permitted.

Reservations, fees: Reservations are not available. Campsites are free. Open mid-April–mid-November, but services are limited until May and after early September.

Directions: On Highway 2, drive 10 miles west from Troy or four miles east from the Idaho-Montana border. Turn north onto the Highway 508 and drive for 30 miles to Yaak, where the road becomes dirt and changes to Forest Road 92. Drive 19 more miles and turn north into the campground. From the Eureka area, cross the Lake Koocanusa Bridge and drive six miles north on Forest Road 92 and turn left after crossing Sullivan Creek, driving about 19 miles west on Forest Road 92.

GPS Coordinates: N 48° 56.900' W 115° 30.226'

Contact: Kootenai National Forest, Three Rivers Ranger District, Troy Ranger Station, 12858 Hwy. 2, Troy, MT 59935-8750, 406/295-4693, www.fs.fed.us/r1/kootenai/.

7 SWISHER LAKE

Scenic rating: 8

northwest of Eureka in Kootenai National Forest

Located at 2,480 feet, Swisher Lake is one of several small ponds sitting northwest of Eureka. The tiny grassland- and forest-surrounded nine-acre lake is also within two miles of Lake Koocanusa and two miles from the Canadian border. A 0.3-mile foot and horse trail leads to the campsites on the northwest shore of the lake. The trailhead for horses sits 0.2 mile past the campground gate, but no equine loading ramp is available. The campground includes a primitive boat ramp with a dock, and the lake harbors brook and westslope cutthroat trout, but also is stocked regularly with rainbow trout. The campground sits about one mile from the Murray Spring Fish Hatchery, where you can take tours. The lake works for hand-carried watercraft, such as small rafts and canoes.

Swisher Lake is a walk-in campground for tents only. Parking is available for only four vehicles at the trailhead. The quiet campground sits on the grassy shore of the lake in a mixed open forest—a good location to spot wildlife.

Campsites, facilities: The tent-only campground has only four campsites. Facilities include picnic tables, fire rings, a vault toilet, and boat ramp. You can collect downed limbs for firewood from the surrounding national forest. No drinking water is available. Bring your own, or if you plan to use lake water, then filter or boil it before drinking. Pack out your trash. Leashed pets are permitted.

Reservations, fees: Reservations are not available. Campsites are free. Open year-round.

Directions: From just north of Eureka, turn west on Highway 37 and drive 2.5 miles to the junction with the Sophie Lake and Tetrault Lake Road. Turn north and drive five miles to the gate at the Swisher Lake entrance and the tiny parking lot. (The pavement ends about 0.5 mile before the gate.)

GPS Coordinates: N 48° 58.128' W 115° 8.020'

Contact: Kootenai National Forest, Rexford Ranger District, Eureka Ranger Station, 949 Hwy. 93 N., Eureka, MT 59917-9550, 406/296-2536, www.fs.fed.us/r1/kootenai/.

8 REXFORD BENCH COMPLEX

Scenic rating: 8

on Lake Koocanusa in Kootenai National Forest

Contrary to many of Kootenai National Forest's quiet remote campgrounds, the Rexford Bench Complex is not wilderness. The campground sits at 2,470 feet on Lake Koocanusa, a 90-mile-long reservoir spanning the international boundary. (Hence, the invented name that combines KOOtenai, CANada, and USA.) The Libby Dam formed the lake when it was completed in 1974. The huge lake garners plenty of recreational boaters around bays, but the main lake always seems empty. During droughts, late summer draw-downs drop the lake very low, sometimes prohibiting launching boats. The complex includes a boat launch with low- and high-water concrete ramps, docks, fish-cleaning stations, trailer parking, and a buoyed swimming beach. The campground sits on a narrow, sheltered side bay that is popular for waterskiing, canoeing, and fishing for kokanee salmon.

A paved road loops through the campground, which is shaded by firs. The campsites have no views of the lake, and the open understory permits visibility of neighboring campers. Vehicle noise from the highway floats through the campground. Six campsites have pull-through parking pads.

Campsites, facilities: The campground has 34 RV or tent campsites and 20 campsites for tents only. RVs are limited to 32 feet. Facilities include picnic tables, fire rings with grills, flush toilets, drinking water, garbage service, campground hosts, a disposal station ($2), a boat ramp, a swimming beach, and overflow overnight parking for RVs, but no hookups. Without designated parking spaces, the Kamloops Terrace overflow area fits about 25 RVs and has flush toilets, drinking water, tables, and fire rings. Leashed pets are permitted. A wheelchair-accessible toilet is available.

Reservations, fees: Reservations are available (877/444-6677, www.recreation.gov). Campsites cost $12. Cash or check. Open mid-May–early September, but the swimming beach doesn't open until June and the boat launch is available whenever reservoir water levels allow launching. Kamloops Terrace overflow camping costs $9 and has services only mid-June–mid-September.

Directions: From Highway 93 north of Eureka, drive five miles west on Highway 37 to reach Rexford. Turn north off the highway into the campground. From the Lake Koocanusa Bridge, drive eight miles northeast. GPS Coordinates: N 48° 53.908' W 115° 9.480'

Contact: Kootenai National Forest, Rexford Ranger District, Eureka Ranger Station, 949 Hwy. 93 N., Eureka, MT 59917-9550, 406/296-2536, www.fs.fed.us/r1/kootenai/.

9 CAMP 32

Scenic rating: 5

east of Lake Koocanusa in Kootenai National Forest

The turnoff to Camp 32 sits 1.5 miles northwest of the Lake Koocanusa Bridge, the longest and tallest bridge in Montana. The bridge, built in 1970, is 2,437 feet long. You can park in the lot just south of the bridge and walk across the half-mile span. To get to the campground, the road follows Pinkham Creek, which draws anglers going after rainbow trout. Few people come here because of the narrow, rough access road, which also offers a few large secluded dispersed camping sites along the creek.

Since the campground is off the main Lake Koocanusa highway, the campground is ultra quiet. The campground circles around one loop under Douglas firs, with small vine maples and wild rosebushes forming privacy barriers between campsites. All of the sites are pull-ins, and some of the tables are in disrepair. The campsites are also fairly small. A large field parallels the entrance to the campground. Two campsites with less privacy back up to the dirt entrance road rather than the creek.

Campsites, facilities: The campground has eight RV or tent campsites. The sites can accommodate a maximum RV size of 20 feet, and trailers are not recommended. Facilities include picnic tables, rough rock fire rings, vault toilets, drinking water from a hand pump, and limited firewood. Leashed pets are permitted. A wheelchair-accessible toilet is available.

Reservations, fees: Reservations are not accepted. Campsites are free. Open year-round, but serviced only mid-May–early September.

Directions: From Highway 93 north of Eureka, drive 12 miles southwest on Highway 37. Turn east onto the dirt Rondo Road (Forest Road 7182). Drive 2.5 miles on the single-lane, narrow, potholed road to the campground. From the Lake Koocanusa Bridge, the signed turnoff sits 1.5 miles northeast. GPS Coordinates: N 48° 50.238' W 115° 11.458'

Contact: Kootenai National Forest, Rexford Ranger District, Eureka Ranger Station, 949 Hwy. 93 N., Eureka, MT 59917-9550, 406/296-2536, www.fs.fed.us/r1/kootenai/.

10 PECK GULCH

Scenic rating: 9

on Lake Koocanusa in Kootenai National Forest

Peck Gulch is a unique campground. People either love it or hate it, depending on tastes. At 2,470 feet, the campground sits on a flat, wide, treeless sandbar jutting several hundred feet out into Lake Koocanusa's east shore. The rocky cliffs, broken with open grassy areas between Peck Gulch and the Lake Koocanusa Bridge, provide excellent habitat for bighorn sheep, and the cliffs also attract rock climbers. From the campground, a steep 0.5-mile trail climbs to Peck Gulch. Two boat ramps—one for high water and one for low water—allow for launching when the reservoir water reaches different levels during the season. An adjacent paved parking lot provides a place to drop the trailer before claiming a campsite.

Raised grassy areas circle the campground around four large, round gravel parking lots with no designated parking strips or campsite boundaries. No vegetation—no trees, no bushes—grows on the sandbar, so campsites have no privacy and no wind blocks. Sidle up to a place that looks good and claim it. Many of the campsites sit right on the edge of the bar, with unobstructed views of the reservoir and the Purcell Mountains rising from the opposite shore. More-protected sites tuck up against the firs and ponderosas along the hillsides.

Campsites, facilities: The campground has undesignated campsites on a flat, open, dirt, table-like sandbar with room for 22 RV or tent camping units. Vehicles over 32 feet are not permitted. Facilities include picnic tables, rock fire rings with grills, vault toilets, drinking water, and a campground host. Firewood is available. Leashed pets are permitted. A wheelchair-accessible toilet is available.

Reservations, fees: Reservations are not accepted. Campsites cost $9. Cash or check. Open mid-April–September but serviced only mid-May–early September.

Directions: From Highway 93 north of Eureka, drive 21 miles southwest on Highway 37, or from Libby, drive 48 miles northeast on Highway 37. Turn west off the highway at the sign, which leads to a narrow, steep, paved single-lane road that drops to the campground.

GPS Coordinates: N 48° 43.456' W 115° 18.459'

Contact: Kootenai National Forest, Rexford Ranger District, Eureka Ranger Station, 949 Hwy. 93 N., Eureka, MT 59917-9550, 406/296-2536, www.fs.fed.us/r1/kootenai/.

11 ROCKY GORGE

Scenic rating: 8

on Lake Koocanusa in Kootenai National Forest

Located at 2,470 feet on the east shore of 90-mile-long Lake Koocanusa, Rocky Gorge Campground sits at one of the narrowest stretches of the reservoir. A cement boat launch allows for getting out on the reservoir. At low pool (when water level is at its lowest seasonal levels), plenty of beach opens up with its combination of clay sand and rocks. Watch for bald eagle nests and ospreys fishing along this side of the reservoir.

Islands of bushes and trees divide up the campground, but the rough-paved, parking lot effect is evident. No designated parking spaces denote campsites. Just roll in and claim a spot that looks good. The campground sits under ponderosa pines, but with the open parking, little privacy is available. Sites along the west perimeter have peek-a-boo views of the reservoir and work better for those with tents. Two walk-in tent sites sit right on the bluff with broad views of the reservoir. Recent thinning added more views, too. Spring brings on blooms of yellow arrowleaf balsamroot in the campground.

Campsites, facilities: The campground has undesignated campsites with room for 60 RV or tent camping units. The maximum vehicle length is 32 feet. Facilities include picnic tables, rock fire rings with grills, vault toilets, drinking water, and a campground host. While you can collect firewood in the surrounding forest, the downed limbs have mostly been plucked up. Pack out your trash. Leashed pets are permitted. A wheelchair-accessible toilet is available.

Reservations, fees: Reservations are not accepted. Campsites cost $9. Cash or check. Open year-round, but serviced only mid-May–early September.

Directions: From Highway 93 north of Eureka, drive 31 miles southwest on Highway 37, or from Libby, drive 40 miles northeast on Highway 37. Turn west off the highway into the campground entrance at milepost 41.4.

GPS Coordinates: N 48° 39.132' W 115° 18.683'

Contact: Kootenai National Forest, Rexford Ranger District, Eureka Ranger Station, 949 Hwy. 93 N., Eureka, MT 59917-9550, 406/296-2536, www.fs.fed.us/r1/kootenai/.

12 BARRON FLATS

Scenic rating: 7

on Lake Koocanusa in Kootenai National Forest

On Lake Koocanusa, known for its kokanee salmon fishery, Barron Flats sits at 2,500 feet on the reservoir's west side. A snowmobile destination in winter and a quiet getaway in summer, the campground serves as a west-side stop on the Koocanusa Scenic Byway, which loops 67 miles around the reservoir via the Lake Koocanusa Bridge on the north and Libby Dam on the south. The west-side road, which is closed in winter, usually melts out by April and receives snow again in November. Take binoculars, for the region provides habitat for bighorn sheep, black bears, and bald eagles. A concrete boat launch allows launching of powerboats, kayaks, and canoes.

The quiet campground sits above the reservoir in a large, grassy field with two loops through the west side of the meadow. The sites are undesignated; just pull over next to a patch of grass. Camping on the open west sides of the loops grants views of the surrounding terrain, but no privacy; for tidbits of shade and a semblance of privacy, camp along the

south and east perimeters adjacent to the forest. Three rock fire rings are tucked along the southwest perimeter in the trees.

Campsites, facilities: The campground has dispersed RV or tent camping with no designated campsites or picnic tables, but space to accommodate 15 rigs. The maximum vehicle length is 32 feet. Facilities include a few rock fire rings and vault toilets. No drinking water is provided. Plan on bringing your own; lake water must be filtered or boiled before drinking. Pack out your trash. Leashed pets are permitted. A wheelchair-accessible toilet is available.

Reservations, fees: Reservations are not accepted. Campsites are free. Open year-round, but serviced only mid-May–early September.

Directions: Approach the campground from the north via the Koocanusa Bridge, about an hour's drive on the curvy but paved Forest Road 228. At milepost 12.5, turn east onto the paved road to the boat launch and turn right onto a dirt road dropping into the campground's huge meadow. From the south, turn off Highway 37 one mile northeast of the Canoe Gulch Ranger Station and drive 13 miles north.

GPS Coordinates: N 48° 30.960' W 115° 17.638'

Contact: Kootenai National Forest, Libby Ranger District, Canoe Gulch Ranger Station, 12557 Hwy. 37, Libby, MT 59923-8212, 406/293-7773, www.fs.fed.us/r1/kootenai/.

13 MCGILLIVRAY

Scenic rating: 7

on Lake Koocanusa in Kootenai National Forest

On Lake Koocanusa, McGillivray is the closest designated Forest Service campground to Libby Dam. It sits on the reservoir's west side and is a snowmobile destination in winter on the snow-covered west-side road. The Libby Dam Visitor Center is located on the same side of the dam as the campground. Between Memorial Day and Labor Day, four dam tours depart daily for 90-minute guided walks through the dam and powerhouse. The 422-foot-tall dam retains 90 miles of water in Lake Koocanusa, with 48 of the lake's miles in the United States and the other miles over the international border in Canada. Near the dam, the Souse Gulch picnic area is home to nesting bald eagles. The two boat ramps accommodate both high and low reservoir levels, plus a dock and boat trailer parking. Set back in the firs above the reservoir—a kokanee salmon fishery—the campground connects to the swimming and boating beaches via either roads or trails. Trails also loop around the bluffs for views of the reservoir and Salish Mountains. The swimming beach is formed by a narrow inlet at high pool (when water level is at its highest seasonal levels).

The two campground loops sit under thick ponderosas and firs with no views. Recent thinning has opened up some of the campground to filtered sunlight, but most of the campsites are shaded. Campsites are spread apart for privacy, and the campground is ultra-quiet.

Campsites, facilities: The campground has 22 RV or tent campsites. The maximum vehicle length is 32 feet. Facilities include picnic tables, fire rings with grills, vault and flush toilets, drinking water, campground hosts, a boat ramp, a covered picnic shelter, and a swimming beach. Limited firewood is available. Leashed pets are permitted. A wheelchair-accessible toilet is available.

Reservations, fees: Reservations are not accepted. Campsites cost $10. Cash or check. Open year-round, but serviced only mid-May–early September.

Directions: From north side of the Lake Koocanusa Bridge, drive south on the curvy, paved Forest Road 228 for about an hour to milepost 10.1. Turn east into the campground. From the south, turn north onto Forest Road 228

one mile northeast of Canoe Gulch Ranger Station and drive 10 miles north.

GPS Coordinates: N 48° 29.174' W 115° 18.277'

Contact: Kootenai National Forest, Libby Ranger District, Canoe Gulch Ranger Station, 12557 Hwy. 37, Libby, MT 59923-8212, 406/293-7773, www.fs.fed.us/r1/kootenai/.

14 LITTLE THERRIAULT LAKE

Scenic rating: 9

in Ten Lakes Scenic Area in Kootenai National Forest

BEST (

Tucked under Ten Lakes Scenic Area at 5,650 feet, idyllic Little Therriault Lake provides a convenient base camp for exploring proposed alpine wilderness area in the north end of the Whitefish Range. Less than 0.5 mile from the campground, the nearest trailhead (#83) leads 1.5 miles up to a pair of subalpine lakes. Surrounded by wildflower meadows, Paradise and Bluebird Lakes make the best kid-friendly destinations, but the trail also connects with the longer Galton Range Trail (#88), which runs along the crest of Ten Lakes toward Poorman Peak, the site of an old lookout at 7,832 feet. Starting from the horse camp above the campground, an 11-mile loop trail with both lakes and ridge walking links the Wolverine Lakes with the Bluebird Basin on trails #82, 84, 88, and 83. Plan for a long, dusty, dirt-road drive to get here. A rough ramp provides for launching boats for fishing or canoeing; powerboats are not permitted, and the trout-filled lake is best for smaller boats and canoes. Snowmobilers ride here in winter.

The small, secluded one-acre campground sits right on the lake. Bring the bug spray, for the area sometimes breeds voracious mosquitoes. Campsites are spread out for privacy and shaded. Due to the proximity of the campsites on the lakeshore, they often fill first before those just around the corner at Big Therriault Lake.

Campsites, facilities: The campground has six RV or tent campsites. RVs are limited to 32 feet in length. Facilities include picnic tables, fire rings, a vault toilet, and drinking water (July–early September). Leashed pets are permitted. A wheelchair-accessible toilet is available.

Reservations, fees: No reservations are accepted. A campsite costs $5. Cash or check. Open year-round, but snowbound November–mid-June.

Directions: From Eureka, drive eight miles south on Highway 93 to Graves Creek Road and turn east. Follow the road, which turns from pavement into the dirt Forest Road 114, for 12 miles as it heads east and circles north. Where Trail Creek Road (Forest Road 114) veers east, drive north for 16 miles on Forest Road 319. Turn right at the sign for the campground.

GPS Coordinates: N 48° 56.633' W 144° 53.3660'

Contact: Kootenai National Forest, Fortine Ranger District, Murphy Lake Ranger Station, P.O. Box 116, 12797 Hwy. 93 S., Fortine, MT 59918-0116, 406/882-4451, www.fs.fed.us/r1/kootenai/.

15 BIG THERRIAULT LAKE
🚶 🏊 🛶 🛥 🎣 🎿 🏠 ♿ 🚐 ⛺

Scenic rating: 9

in Ten Lakes Scenic Area in Kootenai National Forest

BEST (

On the edge of Ten Lakes Scenic Area at 5,650 feet in elevation, Big Therriault Lake provides a convenient base camp for exploring proposed alpine wilderness area in the north end of the Whitefish Range. Departing from the lake, a trail climbs 1.5 miles up to Therriault Pass, which in itself isn't much of a destination in the trees, but it links to several other trails. The Galton Range Trail (#88)

walks north across the entire Ten Lakes Scenic Area just under the ridge toward Poorman Peak, the highest mountain in the area. From the pass, a trail also leads 1.75 miles farther to Stahl Lookout at 7,392 feet. The lookout provides views of the northern Whitefish Range, plus Glacier Park's peaks in the distance. A one-mile, often muddy trail also loops around the lakeshore, climbing through boulders and meandering near shoreline so you can stare into the clear water at the multicolored sedimentary rocks. A rough ramp provides for launching boats for fishing or canoeing; no power boating is permitted on the lake. The campground is a snowmobile destination in winter.

The dusty dirt-and-gravel drive to get to the campground goes on forever. The campground sprawls its few campsites into private locations tucked into five acres of thick Douglas and subalpine firs, with heavy vegetation between most of the sites.

Campsites, facilities: This campground has 10 RV or tent campsites. RVs are limited to 32 feet in length. Facilities include picnic tables, fire rings, a vault toilet, and drinking water (July–early September). Leashed pets are permitted. A wheelchair-accessible toilet is available.

Reservations, fees: No reservations are accepted. A campsite costs $5. Cash or check. Open year-round, but snowbound November–June.

Directions: From Eureka, drive eight miles south on Highway 93 to Grave Creek Road and turn east. Follow the road, which turns from pavement into the dirt Forest Road 114, for 12 miles as it heads east and circles north. Where Trail Creek Road (Forest Road 114) veers east, drive north for 16 miles on Forest Road 319. Turn right at the sign for the campground. The lake sits at the end of the road.

GPS Coordinates: N 48° 56.200' W 114.G> 52.650'

Contact: Kootenai National Forest, Fortine Ranger District, Murphy Lake Ranger Station, P.O. Box 116, 12797 Hwy. 93 S., Fortine, MT

59918-0116, 406/882-4451, www.fs.fed.us/r1/kootenai/.

16 TUCHUCK

Scenic rating: 6

east of Eureka in the Whitefish Range in
Flathead National Forest

A night or two at Tuchuck lets you explore some of the remote trails at the north end of Flathead National Forest. Thoma Lookout, in particular, is worth the grunt up its 1,900 vertical feet in three miles because of its panoramic view of Glacier's Kintla-Kinnerly peaks. Miles below, on the Flathead Valley floor, the international boundary swath cuts through the forest, and north of it sit the peaks of Canada's Akamina-Kishenena Provincial Park. Locate the trailhead about 6.6 miles east of the campground and up Forest Road 114a, where the road dead-ends. A faint trail also connects to Mount Hefty from the Thoma trail. The forested campground is near the confluence of the Yakinikak and Tuchuck Creeks at 4,500 feet in elevation at the confluence of Trail Creek. Fishing is available in the creeks.

Regardless of the approach road, accessing this two-acre campground requires driving long, bumpy, dusty gravel and dirt roads. Its quiet location miles from highways gives it appeal. Sites are spread out for privacy in a forested loop.

Campsites, facilities: The small, two-acre campground has seven RV or tent campsites. RVs are limited to 22 feet. Facilities include picnic tables, fire rings, and a vault toilet. Drinking water is not available; filter or boil any water dipped from the creeks. Pack out your trash. Collecting firewood from the surrounding forest is permitted. Leashed pets are permitted. A wheelchair-accessible toilet is available.

Reservations, fees: Reservations are not accepted. Campsites are free. Open mid-May–September.

Directions: From Polebridge, drive 15 miles north on the North Fork Road to Trail Creek Road (Forest Road 114) and turn west for nine miles. Turn south into the campground. From Eureka, drive eight miles south on Highway 93 to Graves Creek Road and drive east, north, and then east for 20 miles to the campground. Note: Graves Creek Road turns from pavement into the dirt Forest Road #114, which becomes Trail Creek Road.
GPS Coordinates: N 48° 55.406' W 114° 36.034'
Contact: Flathead National Forest, Glacier View District, 10 Hungry Horse Dr., Hungry Horse, MT 59919, 406/387-3800, www.fs.fed.us/r1/flathead/.

17 GRAVE CREEK

Scenic rating: 6

south of Eureka in Kootenai National Forest

At 3,000 feet on the east edge of the Tobacco Valley in the north end of the Whitefish Range, Grave Creek Campground provides a base camp for exploring trails in Ten Lakes Scenic Area. A 12-mile drive ends at the south trailhead to Stahl Peak Lookout. A four-mile climb on trail #81 leads to the lookout, which sits at 7,435 feet in elevation with views of Therriault Pass, Gibralter Ridge, and tidbits of Glacier Park in the distance. The nearest trailhead, however, departs from two miles away to climb Gibralter Ridge (#335) for views down into the Tobacco Valley. While the trail continues farther, it tops out at 7,131 feet on Mount Gibralter after a five-mile ascent. With the campground set on Grave Creek at the site of a historical dam, anglers who prefer stream fishing should drop in a line.

An open mixed forest of birches, cottonwoods, and firs dominates the narrow canyon that houses the campground. The first campsite, which looks like a huge parking area, sits across from the dam. The first two campsites view less of the road across the creek than the last two. The campsites, which line up along the creek, are run-down. The third site is missing a picnic table.

Campsites, facilities: The campground has four RV or tent campsites. The maximum vehicle length is 20 feet, and trailers must be 12 feet or less. Facilities include picnic tables, fire rings, and a vault toilet. The campground has no water, so plan on purifying creek water or boiling it. Pack out your trash. Leashed pets are permitted. A wheelchair-accessible toilet is available.

Reservations, fees: No reservations are accepted, and the campsites are free. Open year-round, but serviced only mid-May–early September and snow-covered in winter.

Directions: From Eureka, drive Highway 93 eight miles south to Grave Creek Road 114. Turn east and drive three miles before turning right onto dirt Stoken Road 7019. Cross the bridge, continue for 0.5 mile, and make a left turn, dropping down the steep, narrow gravel road into the campground.

GPS Coordinates: N 48° 47.885' W 114° 57.102'

Contact: Kootenai National Forest, Fortine Ranger District, Murphy Lake Ranger Station, P.O. Box 116, 12797 Hwy. 93 S., Fortine, MT 59918-0116, 406/882-4451, www.fs.fed.us/r1/kootenai/.

18 NORTH DICKEY LAKE

🏃 🚴 ⛱ 🛶 🚤 ⛵ ❄ 🏕 ♿ 🚐 ⛺

Scenic rating: 8

south of Eureka on the west flank of the Whitefish Range in Kootenai National Forest

Located adjacent to Highway 93 at 3,200 feet, North Dickey Lake Campground is a cinch to reach compared to many of the other Kootenai National Forest campgrounds. Its day-use area includes a boat ramp, dock, roped-off swimming area, and grassy beach. The 800-acre lake lures anglers looking to hook kokanee salmon and rainbow trout. It is also a popular for waterskiing, with room in the day-use parking lot for boat trailers. The Mount Marston Trailhead sits on the east side of Highway 93 just opposite the entrance road. The nine-mile climb slogs up to the lookout, sitting at 7,343 feet, for views of the Whitefish Range. Paddlers find both raptors and songbirds at the lake as well as waterfowl. In the spring and early summer, listen for the sound of the loon as a morning wake-up call. From the campground, a short wheelchair-accessible trail leads to a platform for viewing the lake, and a descent down the hill on a footpath is required to reach the lake. Cyclists can tour the bucolic paved roads to Trego.

The shady hillside campground is tucked back from the shoreline in the lodgepole pine and larch forest, with low brush as ground cover, allowing visibility of other campsites. With a paved loop through the trees, the campground has a secluded feel, but you can still hear commercial trucks on the two-lane highway and see the highway from the beach.

Campsites, facilities: The campground has 25 RV or tent campsites. RVs are limited to 32 feet. Facilities include picnic tables, fire rings with grills, vault toilets, tent pads, garbage service, drinking water, and a disposal station. Leashed pets are permitted. A wheelchair-accessible toilet is available.

Reservations, fees: Reservations are accepted (877/444-6777, www.recreation.gov). Campsites cost $10. Cash or check. Open mid-April–November, but serviced only mid-May–early September.

Directions: On Highway 93, drive 14.8 miles south from Eureka or 35.3 miles north from Whitefish to the signed Trego turnoff. Turn west and drive 0.2 mile to a left turn into the campground.

GPS Coordinates: N 48° 43.128' W 114° 49.908'

© BECKY LOMAX

North Dickey Lake swimming beach and dock in Kootenai National Forest

Contact: Kootenai National Forest, Fortine Ranger District, Murphy Lake Ranger Station, P.O. Box 116, 12797 Hwy. 93 S., Fortine, MT 59918-0116, 406/882-4451, www.fs.fed.us/r1/kootenai/.

19 RED MEADOW LAKE

Scenic rating: 10

in the Whitefish Range of Flathead National Forest

Red Meadow Lake perches like a jewel at 5,500 feet atop the Whitefish Divide on the midway crossover from the Flathead Valley to the North Fork Valley. Mountain bikers ride the route, but many drivers are deterred by the miles of bumpy, dusty, jarring road. About 0.5 mile south of the lake, the Ralph Thayer Memorial Trail ascends to the Whitefish Divide crest and traverses 17 miles south to Werner Peak Lookout, with big views of the Whitefish Range and Glacier Park; turn around at Diamond Peak for a 10-mile day.

Other trails within a 10-minute drive from the lake climb to Chain Lakes (a very steep 2 miles), Link Lake (1.5 miles), or Nasukoin Mountain (5.8 miles), the highest peak in the Whitefish Range. Small hand-carried boats, canoes, and kayaks can be launched from the shoreline for paddling or fishing.

The small campground is quite open with exceptional views, but at the cost of privacy. Winter avalanches keep much of the mature timber pruned out around the lake. A couple of the campsites sit right on the lakeshore only inches off the road; others are across the road from the lake. Despite the road slicing right through the campground, this is a quiet location, with the rough dirt miles deterring lots of traffic.

Campsites, facilities: The campground has six RV or tent campsites. RVs are limited to 32 feet. Facilities include picnic tables, fire rings, and a vault toilet. Drinking water is not available; bring water, or plan on purifying or boiling lake water. Pack out your trash. Leashed pets are permitted. A wheelchair-accessible toilet is available.

Reservations, fees: No reservations are

accepted. Camping is free. Open mid-May–September.

Directions: From the North Fork Road five miles north of the Polebridge junction, drive 11 miles west on Red Meadows Road (#115). From Highway 93 north of Whitefish, turn east onto the Olney Crossover Road across the highway from Olney and drive 8.5 miles to a signed three-way junction. Turn left and continue another 11 miles, staying on the main road and climbing steeply in the last two miles.

GPS Coordinates: N 48° 45.234' W 114° 33.787'

Contact: Flathead National Forest, Glacier View District, 10 Hungry Horse Dr., Hungry Horse, MT 59919, 406/387-3800, www.fs.fed.us/r1/flathead/.

20 UPPER WHITEFISH LAKE

Scenic rating: 9

north of Whitefish in Stillwater State Forest in the Whitefish Range

A favorite with anglers in summer and hunters in fall, the 80-acre Upper Whitefish Lake sits at 4,549 feet in elevation at the base of the Whitefish Divide. While fly-fishing and spin-casting can work from shore, a boat helps to catch the bigger native westslope cutthroat. (A dirt launch is available.) Canoeists enjoy paddling the placid lake in the morning and evening calm because the waterfowl, songbirds, and raptors make for good bird-watching. Most of the hiking trails in the area depart from trailheads in the vicinity of Red Meadows Lake, about six miles up the road. The trail to three destinations—Link Lake (1.5 miles), Lake Mountain (3.5 miles), and Nasukoin Mountain (5.8 miles)—departs off a spur road, Road 589. Look for the Link Lake sign and drive 1.3 miles to the trailhead. The forest road is a favorite for mountain bikers.

Sitting on the southeastern corner of the lake, the six-acre quiet campground clusters around both sides of the road north of the bridge that crosses the outlet stream. A few sites are accessed via a spur road to the left just before the lake comes into view. Foliage and mature trees maintain privacy between the sites. Most of the campsites rest in the trees along the lake, with short trails running down to the shore, but a couple are on the opposite side of the road with more open views of the surrounding mountains.

Campsites, facilities: The campground has 13 RV or tent campsites. RVs are limited to 32 feet. Facilities include picnic tables, fire rings with grills, vault toilets, and a boat launch. No drinking water is available; bring your own, or purify or boil the lake water. Pack out your trash. Leashed pets are permitted. A wheelchair-accessible toilet is available.

Reservations, fees: No reservations are accepted, and campsites are free. The campground is open June–October.

Directions: From Highway 93 north of Whitefish, turn east onto the Olney Crossover Road across the highway from Olney and drive 8.5 miles to a signed three-way junction. Turn left and continue another five miles to the campground, which sits on both sides of the creek and road.

GPS Coordinates: N 48° 41.068' W 114° 34.441'

Contact: Stillwater State Forest, P.O. Box 164, Olney, MT 59919, 406/881-2371, http://dnrc.mt.gov.

21 STILLWATER LAKE

Scenic rating: 7

north of Whitefish on Upper Stillwater Lake in Flathead National Forest

Located at 3,250 feet on Upper Stillwater Lake, this tiny campground is favored by anglers year-round; there's ice fishing in winter, and stream fishing in the slow-moving Still-water River nearby can land a 20- to 30-pound pike. Canoeists enjoy the lake but should be wary of logjams when floating the river. A boat ramp works for launching small watercraft. Mountain bikers hit the forest roads around the lake. For hikers, a nearby 1.5-mile trail tours the LeBeau Natural Area through old-growth larches and ancient Belt Sea formation rocks to large bluffs above Finger Lake. A spur trail cuts off to Hole-in-the-Wall Lake. Hunters also use the campground in fall.

Sitting right on the Stillwater lakeshore in sparse tall trees, the campsites may have you waking up to the slap of beavertails on the water. The small campground with four sites received an overhaul in 2008 with new picnic tables, fire rings, leveled gravel parking pads, and a bench for viewing the lake and the beaver lodge just offshore. Watch here for moose, otter, and songbirds. Campsites 1, 2, and 4 overlook the lake.

Campsites, facilities: The campground has four RV or tent campsites. Trailers are limited to 12 feet. Facilities include picnic tables, fire rings with grills, and a vault toilet. Drinking water is not available; bring water, or plan on purifying or boiling lake water. Pack out your own garbage. A bear pole is available for hanging food. Leashed pets are permitted. A wheelchair-accessible toilet is available.

Reservations, fees: Reservations are not accepted, and camping is free. Open late April–November.

Directions: From Whitefish, drive 21 miles north on Highway 93 and turn west at the Stillwater Lake Campground sign at milepost 151.5. Follow the signs two miles to the campground. The dirt road snakes left, then right, before crossing the railroad tracks and turning left to climb over a hill.

GPS Coordinates: N 48° 36.224' W 114° 39.370'

Contact: Flathead National Forest, Talley Lake Ranger District, 650 Wolfpack Way, Kalispell, MT 59901, 406/758-5204, www.fs.fed.us/r1/flathead/.

22 DORR SKEELS

Scenic rating: 9

on Bull Lake in Kootenai National Forest

Bull Lake, which sits at 2,350 feet in elevation, tucked between the Cabinet Mountains and Scotchman Peaks, runs 4.5 miles in length—the largest lake on Bull River—and harbors rainbow trout, kokanee salmon, and largemouth bass. While the lake borders public land on its west shore, the east shore contains private land and homes. The campground sits on the north end of the lake, with a warm, sunny, south-facing swimming beach. The day-use area sees heavy weekend visitation from locals. At the campground, a concrete ramp and dock aid those launching boats, kayaks, and canoes, and several boat tie-up anchors are available near the campsites. A buoyed sand-and-pebble swimming beach separates swimmers from boaters. The Ross Creek Scenic Area, with its giant cedars, requires a seven-mile drive from Dorr Skeels Campground. If you're pulling a trailer and planning to visit Ross Creek Cedars, leave the trailer in the designated parking area because the curvy road and parking area at the trailhead do not accommodate larger RVs.

Sitting on a forested bluff under cedars and firs, the shaded tent campsites have peek-a-boo views of the lake. Sites 6 and 7 offer the most privacy. Some of the flat sleeping spaces will accommodate only two-person tents. The self-contained RV campsites consist of a parking lot with no privacy.

Campsites, facilities: The campground has seven walk-in tent campsites and two RV campsites that can fit trailer combinations up to 32 feet. Facilities include picnic tables and fire rings with grills at tent sites only, vault toilets, campground hosts, drinking water, garbage service, a boat launch, and swimming beach. Leashed pets are permitted. A wheelchair-accessible toilet is available.

Reservations, fees: Reservations are not

© BECKY LOMAX

China Rapids on the Kootenai River between Libby and Troy, Montana

accepted. Campsites are free. Open year-round, but serviced mid-May–early September.
Directions: On Highway 2, from Libby drive 15.2 miles west, or from Troy drive three miles east. Turn south onto Highway 56 and drive 13 miles. Turn west onto the 0.5-mile road that leads to the campground. From Highway 200, drive 21.6 miles north on Highway 53 to the campground turnoff on the left.
GPS Coordinates: N 48° 16.024' W 115° 51.209'
Contact: Kootenai National Forest, Three Rivers Ranger District, Troy Ranger Station, 12858 Hwy. 2, Troy, MT 59935-8750, 406/295-4693, www.fs.fed.us/r1/kootenai/.

23 SPAR LAKE

Scenic rating: 7

in Scotchman Peaks in Kootenai National Forest

At 3,300 feet in the Scotchman Peaks, the 383-acre Spar Lake is so popular with locals

that the Forest Service expanded the campground in 2009. The small lake with a dirt boat ramp is good for small motorboats, canoes, and kayaks. Fish species include kokanee salmon, brook trout, and lake trout. Two hiking trails in the Scotchman Peaks—a proposed wilderness area—sit about three miles south of the campground, starting from the same trailhead. Gaining 2,300 feet in elevation over three miles, the Little Spar Lake Trail (#143) ascends along Spar Creek through lush forest to the small lake, which harbors native westslope cutthroat trout. With 3,000 feet of elevation gain, the Spar Peak Trail (#324) climbs a steep 3.2-mile path along Cub Creek through bear grass meadows to the summit. At 6,585 feet in elevation and waltzing above tree line, the peak grants a 360-degree view of both the Scotchman Peaks and Cabinet Mountains.

The ultra-quiet campground is tucked in tall firs above the lake at the head of a west side bay. The expansion added a new toilet and four more campsites, but the campground is so far removed from roads and towns that it guarantees solitude. Campsites are spread out for privacy.

Campsites, facilities: The campground has 12 RV or tent campsites. Sites can fit RVs and trailer combinations up to 32 feet long. Facilities include picnic tables, fire rings with grills, vault toilets, and drinking water. You can collect downed limbs for firewood from the surrounding national forest. Pack out your trash. Leashed pets are permitted.

Reservations, fees: Reservations are not accepted. Campsites are free. Open May–November, but serviced late May–early September.

Directions: From two miles east of Troy on Highway 2, drive 19 miles south on Lake Creek Road (Forest Road 384). The paved road passes by small ranches for 10 miles before turning to dirt. It crosses Lake Creek, enters the national forest, and climbs to the lake.

GPS Coordinates: N 48° 16.268' W 115° 57.382'

Contact: Kootenai National Forest, Three Rivers Ranger District, Troy Ranger Station, 12858 Hwy. 2, Troy, MT 59935-8750, 406/295-4693, www.fs.fed.us/r1/kootenai/.

24 BAD MEDICINE

🥾 🏊 🛶 🚣 ⛵ 🐕 ♿ 🚗 ⛺

Scenic rating: 8

on Bull Lake in Kootenai National Forest

At an elevation of 2,350 feet on the southwest corner of 4.5-mile-long Bull Lake, below Scotchman Peaks and the Cabinet Mountains, Bad Medicine is the closest campground for those hiking the one-mile Ross Creek Cedars interpretive trail. Located four miles from the campground, the 100-acre ancient grove of western red cedar trees—some that were saplings when Columbus landed in the New World—survived the ravages of floods, fires, and insects. Great-grandfather trees span eight feet in diameter and stand over 175 feet tall. The campground also has a boat ramp, dock, and small swimming beach. Paddling the lake early or late in the day yields calmer waters with big views of the surrounding mountains.

A paved road loops through the campground, parts of which are reminiscent of dark, coastal cedar rain forests dripping with moss. Dense vegetation and thick trees close off the views from the campsites but also provide seclusion and cool shade for hot days. Sites 3, 4, and 9–12 are especially private. Sites 1 and 2 sit closest to the lake. For views, head to the beach for beautiful reflections of the Cabinet Mountains on calm days. Prepare for mosquitoes.

Campsites, facilities: The campground has 17 RV or tent campsites. RVs are limited to 32 feet. Facilities include picnic tables, fire rings or grates, vault toilets, campground hosts, drinking water, garbage service, a boat launch, and swimming beach. You can collect downed limbs for firewood from the surrounding national forest. Leashed pets are permitted. A wheelchair-accessible toilet is available.

Reservations, fees: Reservations are not accepted. Campsites cost $10. Cash or check. Open April–November, but managed mid-May–early September.

Directions: From Libby drive 15 miles west, or from Troy drive three miles east to Highway 56. Turn south and drive 21 miles to Ross Creek Cedars Road (Forest Road 398), between mileposts 16 and 17. From Highway 200, drive 13.5 miles north on Highway 53 to the Ross Creek Cedars turnoff on the left. On Forest Road 398, drive two paved miles to the campground, passing the turnoff to Ross Creek Cedars about halfway.

GPS Coordinates: N 48° 13.236' W 115° 51.425'

Contact: Kootenai National Forest, Three Rivers Ranger District, Troy Ranger Station, 12858 Hwy. 2, Troy, MT 59935-8750, 406/295-4693, www.fs.fed.us/r1/kootenai/.

25 BIG EDDY

Scenic rating: 7

on Cabinet Gorge Reservoir in Kootenai National Forest

At an elevation of 2,200 feet, eight miles east of the Montana-Idaho border, Big Eddy Campground sits on the north shore of Cabinet Gorge Reservoir, closest to the dam. The dam's viewing platform (open spring–fall) affords a bird's-eye view of the spillway and is an interpretive site for the new Ice Age Floods National Geologic Trail, created by Congress in 2009. The site marks the location of an ice dam that formed Glacial Lake Missoula 14,000 years ago and repeatedly failed, flooding Idaho, Washington, and Oregon. One of the best hikes is to the west in the proposed Scotchman Peak Wilderness Area, on a beargrass-flanked trail to Scotchman Peak. The trail requires only a 3.5-mile climb up switchbacks, but with 3,700 feet of elevation gain, it's a grunt to get to the views of the Clark Fork River and Lake Pend Oreille. The boat ramp at the campground accesses the Cabinet Gorge Reservoir for fishing, waterskiing, paddling, and bird-watching.

The tiny campground has small campsites and short parking pads. A narrow dirt road loops through the old-growth forest of hemlock and cedar, which admits filtered sunlight. An overnight parking area with undesignated campsites provides overflow camping. Noise from trucks and trains seeps into the campground.

Campsites, facilities: The campground has three RV or tent campsites. RVs are limited to 20 feet. Facilities include picnic tables, fire grates, a vault toilet, and a boat ramp, but no drinking water. Bring water with you, or if you plan to use the reservoir water, filter or boil it before drinking. Leashed pets are permitted. A wheelchair-accessible toilet is available.

Reservations, fees: Reservations are not accepted. Campsites are free. Open year-round, but serviced only mid-May–early September.

Directions: From Noxon, drive eight miles west on Highway 200. From Libby, drive 55 miles, heading west on Highway 2 and then south on Highway 56. Turn west on Highway 200 for three miles. From Sandpoint, Idaho, drive 41 miles east on Highway 200. The campground sits on the south side of the highway at milepost 7.

GPS Coordinates: N 48° 4.016' W 115° 55.144'

Contact: Kootenai National Forest, Cabinet Ranger District, Trout Creek Ranger Station, 2693 Hwy. 200, Trout Creek, MT 59874-9503, 406/827-3533, www.fs.fed.us/r1/kootenai/.

26 BULL RIVER

Scenic rating: 8

on Bull River in Kootenai National Forest

BEST (

Located in the Bull River Recreation Area at 2,200 feet on the south flank of the Cabinet Mountains, the campground sits at the confluence of the Bull River and the eight-mile-long Cabinet Gorge Reservoir. On the east shore of a narrow, sheltered north bay, the campground is one of the most popular in the area due to its diverse activities. The boat ramp sits right at the entrance to the campground, allowing boaters, water-skiers, anglers, and paddlers to launch on the bay. Paddlers can tour the bay to look for wildlife, while anglers head out on the reservoir to fish for bass, trout, and large northern pike. The campground also makes a good base camp for exploring trails on the west side of the Cabinet Mountain Wilderness, and mountain bikers ride the Old Bull River Road.

Set in thick, green conifers, the campground loops with paved roads linking to paved parking pads. Sites 12, 13, and 15–18 overlook the water, but the upper loop campsites have more privacy—especially site 6. From the campsite loops, two sets of stairs drop down the bank to the water. Campsites are spread out for privacy, but you will see neighbors. You can also hear a few commercial trucks on the highway and trains across the water at night. Only two of the campsites are pull-throughs. Claim a site early in high season.

Campsites, facilities: The campground has 26 RV or tent campsites. RVs are limited to 32 feet. Facilities include picnic tables, fire grates, vault and flush toilets, drinking water, campground hosts, and a boat ramp. Firewood is available during the serviced season. Leashed pets are permitted. A wheelchair-accessible toilet is available.

Reservations, fees: Reservations are not accepted. Campsites cost $10. Cash or check. Open mid-April–November, but serviced only mid-May–early September.

Directions: From Noxon drive four miles west on Highway 200, or from Libby drive 55 miles, heading west on Highway 2, south on Highway 56, and then east on Highway 200 for 0.5 mile. Turn north into the campground. GPS Coordinates: N 48° 1.806' W 115° 50.597'

Contact: Kootenai National Forest, Cabinet Ranger District, Trout Creek Ranger Station, 2693 Hwy. 200, Trout Creek, MT 59874-9503, 406/827-3533, www.fs.fed.us/r1/kootenai/.

27 HOWARD LAKE

Scenic rating: 8

In the Cabinet Mountains in Kootenai National Forest

Tiny Howard Lake, which is popular with Libby locals for fishing, sits serene in a deep pocket amid a thick, mature forest. At 4,100 feet in elevation, the lake is only 33 acres in size, making it best for canoeing and fishing from small boats. It is stocked with rainbow

trout. The Gold Panning Recreation Area is one mile from the lake, and nearby hiking trails climb up creek drainages into the Cabinet Mountain Wilderness. Unfortunately, the most popular hiking trail requires a long drive back out to the highway and a nine-mile drive up Bear Creek Road to the Leigh Lake Trailhead. The 1.5-mile trail climbs a steep ascent, gaining 1,000 feet past Leigh Falls and following rock cairns to find the easiest route into the alpine bowl where Leigh Lake clings.

The ultra-quiet campground sits half under big shade-producing conifers and half on the open edge of the forest adjacent to the lake. The campground's one road loops between the campsites and the lake, with a boat ramp that doubles as a swimming beach. Because it has little underbrush and several open sites, you will see neighbors.

Campsites, facilities: The campground has nine RV or tent campsites. Three of them accommodate small RVs up to 20 feet in pull-through sites; five are tent sites that will not fit RVs. Facilities include picnic tables, fire grates, a vault toilet, garbage service, and drinking water. Leashed pets are permitted. A wheelchair-accessible toilet is available.

Reservations, fees: Reservations are not accepted. Campsites cost $8. Cash or check. Open late May–September.

Directions: On Highway 2, drive 13 miles east from Libby or 75 miles west from Kalispell to the junction of Libby Creek Road (Forest Road 231). Turn south onto this road, which turns into dirt, and drive 14 miles to the campground sign. As you drive, stay on the well-traveled route, veering left at all junctions. At the junction with the campground sign, go right, climbing up the hill and driving about one mile. The campground entrance sits on the left. GPS Coordinates: N 48° 6.001' W 115° 31.838'

Contact: Kootenai National Forest, Libby Ranger District, Canoe Gulch Ranger Station, 12557 Hwy. 37, Libby, MT 59923-8212, 406/293-7773, www.fs.fed.us/r1/kootenai/.

© BECKY LOMAX

Leigh Lake, a steep 1.5-mile hike, in the Cabinet Mountains of Kootenai National Forest

28 LAKE CREEK

Scenic rating: 8

in the Cabinet Mountains in Kootenai National Forest

At 3,360 feet on the east flank of the Cabinet Mountains, Lake Creek Campground sits at the confluence of Lake and Bramlet Creeks. For stream anglers going after mountain whitefish and rainbow trout, nearby rivers also include Fourth of July and West Fisher. Each can be reached via narrow forest roads or trails. The best hike in the area goes to Geiger Lakes, a pair of subalpine pools sitting near the crest in the Cabinet Mountains Wilderness. The trailhead sits about two miles from the campground up Forest Road 6748, and a steady grade climbs through lodgepole pines to the first lake, which has large boulders on a peninsula that makes a good destination. To reach the second lake in a scenic alpine meadow below Lost Buck Pass, grunt up 600 feet in elevation. Another trailhead requiring a longer drive on the Silver Butte

Road leads to Baree Lake, a six-mile round-trip climb to one of the Cabinet's most southern lakes, known for its wealth of huckleberries in July and August.

The tiny campground tucks into a conifer forest, offering seclusion and utter quiet with only the sound of the creek filtering through the trees. The campground's one small loop spreads out the campsites for privacy.

Campsites, facilities: The campground has four RV and tent campsites. RVs are limited to 32 feet. Facilities include picnic tables, fire grates, and a vault toilet, but no drinking water. Bring your own water, or if you plan to use the creek water, purify or boil it first. Pack out your trash. Leashed pets are permitted.

Reservations, fees: Reservations are not accepted. Campsites are free. Open year-round, but serviced only late May–early September.

Directions: On Highway 2, drive 22 miles southeast from Libby or 66 miles west from Kalispell to the junction with W. Fisher Road (Forest Road 231). Turn onto this dirt road and drive approximately 4.5 miles, swinging left onto Forest Road 2332 at the fork. Drive 0.5 mile to the turnoff to the campground on the left.

GPS Coordinates: N 48° 2.331' W 115° 29.371'

Contact: Kootenai National Forest, Libby Ranger District, Canoe Gulch Ranger Station, 12557 Hwy. 37, Libby, MT 59923-8212, 406/293-7773, www.fs.fed.us/r1/kootenai/.

29 THOMPSON CHAIN OF LAKES PRIMITIVE

Scenic rating: 7

on several lakes in Thompson Chain of Lakes

The Thompson Chain of Lakes consists of 4,655 acres of land containing 18 lakes running in a 20-mile string along Highway 2 between Libby and Kalispell. Some of the lakes are small four-acre ponds; the largest lake tops 1,500 acres. Receding glaciers formed the lakes in a trail of water pockets separated by moraines. Crystal, Horseshoe, and Loon comprise the smaller lakes at the west end. The three Thompson Lakes (Upper, Middle, and Lower) cover the most miles, while McGregor Lake is the largest. The lakes are popular for trout and bass fishing as well as magnets for wildlife. Wake up to the call of loons and watch ospreys dive for fish. Concrete boat ramps for motorboats, canoes, and kayaks are located at Little McGregor, McGregor, Lower Thompson, Upper Thompson, Horseshoe, and Loon Lakes. Some of the lakes have no-wake speed limits.

The campsites are sprinkled along the shorelines singly or in pairs or groups on both sides of the lakes. To locate the Thompson Chain of Lakes primitive campsites, pick up a map at one of the eight pay stations on the road entrances to the lakes. Those campsites adjacent to the highway are the most popular. Most of the campsites are accessed via narrow potholed dirt roads unsuitable for anything larger than a truck camper; however, some of those adjacent to the highway can fit larger rigs.

Campsites, facilities: Thompson Chain of Lakes has 83 primitive campsites and eight group campsites. Sites can have a maximum of two tents, trailers, or RVs, but many can only fit one. Where campsites are concentrated together, a vault toilet is available, but not at the single sites. Facilities include fire rings and some picnic tables. No drinking water is available. Bring your own, or plan to filter or boil the lake water. Leashed pets are permitted.

Reservations, fees: Reservations are not accepted. Campsites cost $7 for those who already have Montana fishing licenses. Otherwise, camping costs $12. Cash or check. Open year-round unless snowbound.

Directions: From Kalispell, drive between 35 and 55 miles westward on Highway 2 to reach Thompson Chain of Lakes.

GPS Coordinates: N 48° 1.451' W 115° 2.446'

Contact: Montana Fish, Wildlife, and Parks, Region 1, 490 N. Meridian Rd., Kalispell, MT 59901, 406/752-5501, http://fwp.mt.gov.

30 LOGAN STATE PARK

Scenic rating: 8

on Middle Thompson Lake in Thompson Chain of Lakes

Sitting midway between Libby and Kalispell on the Highway 2 corridor at 3,300 feet, the Thompson Chain of Lakes strings the Upper, Middle, and Lower Thompson Lakes together with sloughs to make up about 3,000 acres for water recreation. The lakes garner their share of locals, especially on weekends and holidays, and are popular for waterskiing, paddling, and largemouth bass fishing. The bass can range 1–3 pounds in size. Logan Campground sits on the north shore of the middle lake, with a cement boat ramp, dock, trailer parking, and a swimming beach. A half-mile hiking trail leads along the lakeshore to good bird-watching spots. Watch for herons, ospreys, and waterfowl. Loons nest on the lakes, too.

The 17-acre grassy campground circles its two loops under a canopy of western larch, ponderosa pine, and Douglas fir. Without underbrush, the campsites do not have much privacy from each other. Loop B sits closers to the swimming beach and boat launch. Loop A, which leads to the hiking trail, has the playground and showers, and sites 13, 14, 15, and 17 are close to the beach. Squeezed between the lake and the highway, the campground picks up noise from passing vehicles on the highway.

Campsites, facilities: The campground has 37 RV or tent campsites. RVs are limited to 30 feet. Facilities include picnic tables, fire rings with grills, flush toilets, showers, drinking water, a playground, a boat launch, a swimming beach, campground hosts, garbage service, a disposal station, and a horseshoe pit. Firewood is for sale. Leashed pets are permitted. A wheelchair-accessible toilet is available and there's an ADA campsite with an electrical hookup.

Reservations, fees: Reservations are not accepted. For day use, Montana residents have free admission, but all others pay $5 per vehicle. Bikers or hikers cost $3. Campsites cost $15 May–September and $13 October–April. Cash or check. Open year-round.

Directions: From Kalispell drive 45 miles westward on Highway 2, or from Libby drive 40 miles southeast on Highway 2. Turn south at the signed entrance to the campground. GPS Coordinates: N 48° 2.635' W 115° 5.811'

Contact: Montana Fish, Wildlife, and Parks, Region 1, 490 N. Meridian Rd., Kalispell, MT 59901, 406/752-5501, http://fwp.mt.gov.

31 MCGREGOR LAKE

Scenic rating: 8

on McGregor Lake in Kootenai National Forest

At an elevation of 3,998 feet on the easternmost lake in a long chain along Highway 2, McGregor Lake Campground sits on the west end of the long, narrow McGregor Lake. With its short 35-minute drive from Flathead Valley, the 1,522-acre lake is surrounded by summer homes and a small resort. On weekends, the lake packs with water-skiers, boaters, paddlers, and anglers trolling for lake trout or the frequently stocked rainbow trout. The campground allows access to the lake via its boat ramp and a beach for swimming. The lake sits surrounded by a patchwork of Kootenai National Forest and state lands, which offer mountain biking and hiking, but not to exceptionally scenic destinations.

Tucked under large conifers, the campground has two loops with a few of the campsites sitting along the lakeshore. Those rimming the shore are more open and less private than those shaded under trees away from the shore, but they offer views and immediate access to the beach. Truck noise from the highway seeps into the campground.

Campsites, facilities: The campground has 22 RV or tent campsites. RVs are limited to 32 feet. Facilities include picnic tables, fire rings, vault toilets, drinking water, a boat ramp, a campground host, and garbage service, and some firewood is available. Leashed pets are permitted. A wheelchair-accessible toilet is available.

Reservations, fees: Reservations are not accepted. Campsites cost $12. Cash or check. Open mid-May–fall, but serviced only late May–early September.

Directions: From Kalispell, drive 32 miles westward on Highway 2, or from Libby, drive 53 miles southeast on Highway 2. Turn south off the highway at the west end of the lake onto the dirt road leading into the campground. GPS Coordinates: N 48° 1.925' W 114° 54.189'

Contact: Kootenai National Forest, Libby Ranger District, Canoe Gulch Ranger Station, 12557 Hwy. 37, Libby, MT 59923-8212, 406/293-7773, www.fs.fed.us/r1/kootenai/.

32 ASHLEY LAKE NORTH

Scenic rating: 7

west of Kalispell in Flathead National Forest

West of Kalispell in Flathead National Forest, Ashley Lake sits at 3,500 feet. Campers head to Ashley Lake for swimming, canoeing, fishing, and waterskiing, but due to the many homes around the lake—some of them multimillion-dollar summer homes—the area doesn't feel much like wilderness. The lake, which is about five miles long and one mile wide, gets substantial day use from locals. Anglers go after kokanee salmon, westslope cutthroat trout, yellow perch, and large rainbow trout. Some of the rainbow-cutthroat hybrids can get up to five pounds. The boat ramp sits about 0.5 mile west of the campground. Mountain bikers tour the scads of forest roads that crisscross the area, and bird-watchers catch sight of loons and other waterfowl.

The campground is tucked into the north shore of the lake under conifers for shade. The location away from the highway provides quiet once the personal watercraft leave the lake at night. Sites are spread out for privacy, but neighboring campers are visible.

Campsites, facilities: The campground has five RV or tent campsites. RVs are limited to 12 feet. Facilities include picnic tables, fire rings, a vault toilet, swimming area, and boat ramp. Drinking water is not available, so bring your own or plan to purify or boil the lake water. Pack out all garbage. Leashed pets are permitted. A wheelchair-accessible toilet is available.

Reservations, fees: Reservations are not accepted, and camping is free. Open late May–mid-September.

Directions: From Highway 93 in Kalispell, drive west on Highway 2 for 16 miles. Turn north onto the gravel Ashley Lake Road and drive 13 miles following the signs to the campground. (Stay left at the big junction about seven miles up.)

GPS Coordinates: N 48° 12.176' W 114° 37.996'

Contact: Flathead National Forest, Talley Lake Ranger District, 650 Wolfpack Way, Kalispell, MT 59901, 406/758-5204, www.fs.fed.us/r1/flathead/.

33 SYLVIA LAKE

Scenic rating: 7

west of Whitefish in the Salish Mountains in Flathead National Forest

Anglers head to Sylvia Lake for its arctic grayling and westslope cutthroat trout. The 23-acre lake, which sits at 5,189 feet in elevation, is stocked on a frequent cycle by the state. The lake is also popular with canoeists and bird watchers. A trail (#171) across the road climbs 3.5 miles to the summit of Ingalls Mountain, with some views of the Salish Mountains. The area also attracts mountain bikers for its single-track riding on trails and double-track riding on old forest roads. Hunters also use the camp as a base area for hunting in fall. A rough boat ramp aids in launching smaller watercraft onto the lake.

Surrounded by conifers, the campground sits on the lake where you might hear the haunting call of loons in the morning. Due to its distance from pavement, the ultra-quiet campground is usually a place to garner solitude.

Campsites, facilities: The campground has three RV or tent campsites. The maximum length for a trailer is 12 feet. Facilities include picnic tables, rock-ring fire pits, and a pit toilet. Drinking water is not available, so bring your own or plan to purify or boil the lake water. Pack out your trash. Leashed pets are permitted.

Reservations, fees: Reservations are not accepted, and camping is free. Open Memorial Day–Labor Day.

Directions: From Whitefish, drive Highway

93 northwest to Farm to Market Road. Drive 1.8 miles and turn right onto Star Meadows Road (Forest Road 539), which becomes Forest Road 113 when the pavement changes to dirt about 15 miles up. Stay to the left at the next two junctions, following the signs about six miles to Sylvia Lake.

GPS Coordinates: N 48° 20.562' W 114° 49.194'

Contact: Flathead National Forest, Talley Lake Ranger District, 650 Wolfpack Way, Kalispell, MT 59901, 406/758-5204, www.fs.fed.us/r1/flathead/.

34 TALLY LAKE

Scenic rating: 9

west of Whitefish in the Salish Mountains in Flathead National Forest

At 492 feet deep, Tally Lake claims the record as Montana's deepest lake. Located in the heavily forested Salish Mountains at 3,500 feet, the lake attracts weekend campers as well as those out for a day of fishing, waterskiing, paddling, or swimming on the sandy beach. A cement boat ramp, dock, and trailer parking are available. An interpretive site has a spotting scope for watching bald eagles fishing or migratory waterfowl. Several hiking and mountain-biking trails explore the surrounding forest. The 1.25-mile Tally Lake Overlook trail departs from the campground to climb through mature timber. While the walk through the trees provides a close-up view of old-growth forest, the overlook is fast losing its view to crowding trees. Also departing near the campground, a nine-mile loop trail through old-growth forest and in spring fairy slipper orchids also climbs 1,955 vertical feet up Tally Mountain, where it connects with the Boney Gulch Trail to drop back to the road two miles south of the trailhead.

The 23-acre, quiet campground sits on the lake's north shore. The campground loops through mature timber that provides filtered

© BECKY LOMAX

paddling below the cliffs at Tally Lake, the deepest lake in Montana, in Flathead National Forest

shade. Most of the sites are set back from the lakeshore and spread out for privacy, but several on the northwest loop have not only lake frontage, but views of the lake and surrounding mountainside.

Campsites, facilities: The campground has 40 RV or tent campsites. Maximum trailer length for the campground is 40 feet. Facilities include picnic tables, fire rings with grills, vault toilets, drinking water, a disposal station, garbage service, a boat launch, a swimming beach, volleyball, horseshoe pits, and firewood. Leashed pets are permitted. A wheelchair-accessible toilet is available.

Reservations, fees: Reservations are accepted (877/444-6777, www.recreation.gov). Campsites cost $15. Cash or check. Open mid-May–September.

Directions: From Whitefish, drive Highway 93 west 2.5 miles and turn south on Twin Bridges Road for two miles until it reaches Farm to Market Road. Turn left for two more miles and then turn west onto Forest Road

913. Drive nine miles on the dusty dirt road to the campground.

GPS Coordinates: N 48° 24.888' W 114° 35.190'

Contact: Flathead National Forest, Talley Lake Ranger District, 650 Wolfpack Way, Kalispell, MT 59901, 406/758-5204, www.fs.fed.us/r1/flathead/.

35 WHITEFISH LAKE STATE PARK

Scenic rating: 9

in Whitefish on Whitefish Lake

The state park, which sits at 3,000 feet on the south side of Whitefish Lake, with a view of Big Mountain from the beach, is a place to camp more for convenience than quiet. Around 40 trains per day rumble on the tracks adjacent to the campground, which kids and train fanatics love but light sleepers abhor. Local anglers, water-skiers, paddlers, and lake sightseers use the boat launch for the day, and the cordoned-off swimming area attracts families from town to cool off in the summer heat. Downtown Whitefish, with shops, restaurants, groceries, gas, and nightlife, is only two miles away. Whitefish Golf Course with 36 holes is only one mile away. Whitefish Mountain Resort above the lake runs its chairlift in the summer for sightseeing and mountain biking, and the four-mile Danny On Trail connects the summit of Big Mountain with the resort.

With a paved campground road and parking pads, the campsites tuck under a mature forest with substantial undergrowth foliage. None of the campsites sit right on the shoreline, but sites 7, 8, 26, and 25 are closest. Sites 2–13 cluster around a loop separated from the road that day users drive to reach the boat ramp, beach, and parking lot. Sites 14, 15, 22, and 23–25 sit just beneath the slope leading up to the railroad tracks; sites 2–9 are the farthest away from the tracks.

Campsites, facilities: The campground has 25 RV or tent campsites. RVs or trailer combinations are limited to 35 feet. One site is reserved for hikers or bicyclists. Facilities include picnic tables, fire rings with grills, flush toilets, showers, drinking water, a boat ramp with a dock, and a swimming area. Firewood is for sale. Leashed pets are permitted. A wheelchair-accessible toilet is available.

Reservations, fees: No reservations are accepted. Montana residents have free day use, but nonresidents must pay $5 per vehicle. Campsites cost $15. Cash or check. Open May–September.

Directions: From downtown Whitefish, drive Highway 93 west for 1.3 miles. Veer right at the state park sign around the golf course. Take the next right onto State Park Road and follow it about one mile until it crosses the railroad tracks. The entrance sits just past the tracks on the left.

GPS Coordinates: N 48° 25.500' W 114° 22.247'

Contact: Montana Fish, Wildlife, and Parks, Region 1, 490 N. Meridian Rd., Kalispell, MT 59901, 406/752-5501, http://fwp.mt.gov.

36 WHITEFISH KOA

Scenic rating: 7

south of Whitefish

At 3,100 feet, the campground is conveniently near Whitefish as well as only a 35-minute drive from the west entrance to Glacier National Park. Downtown Whitefish, four miles north of the campground, clusters shopping, restaurants, and nightlife within a few blocks. Grocery stores, gas, and other shops line the two miles leading into town. Recreation abounds around town: boating on Whitefish Lake, canoeing the Whitefish River, hiking on Big Mountain, and bicycling the Fish Trails.

A thick forest hides the campground from the highway. Campsites sprinkle across 33 acres of mature forest connected by a gravel road. Open pull-through sites for large RVs allow for satellite reception. Deluxe RV sites include wooden decks. Tent sites sit closer to the bathhouse in grassy or forested locations with options including electricity and water.

Campsites, facilities: There are 25 sites for tents or RVs with a maximum length of 40 feet. RV hookups include sewer, water, and electricity up to 50 amps. Facilities include picnic tables, fire rings, flush toilets, showers, a camp store, a seasonal restaurant, a games center, a playground, and indoor/outdoor pool (mid-April–September only), an adults-only hot tub, wireless Internet, free mini-golf, a disposal station, and firewood. Leashed pets are permitted. A wheelchair-accessible toilet is available.

Reservations, fees: Reservations are accepted. RV hookups run $30–60; tent sites cost $20–36. Cash, check, or credit card. Add on a 7 percent Montana bed tax. Open mid-April–mid-October.

Directions: From Whitefish at the junction of Highways 93 and 40, drive two miles south on Highway 93, or from the junction of Highways 2 and 93 in Kalispell, drive nine miles north on Highway 93. At mile marker 123, turn east into the campground.

GPS Coordinates: N 48° 20.823' W 114° 19.799'

Contact: Whitefish KOA, 5121 Hwy. 93 S., Whitefish, MT 59937, 406/862-4242 or 800/562-8734, www.glacierparkkoa.com.

37 ROCKY MOUNTAIN HI

🚲🛶🏊🎣🐕🎿🚐⛺

Scenic rating: 7

in Kalispell

At 2,950 feet on the east side of Kalispell, Rocky Mountain Hi sits on Spring Creek, almost equidistant from Whitefish, Columbia Falls, and Bigfork. Three golf courses—Northern Pines, Village Greens, and Buffalo Hills—are within six miles. Within five miles of the campground are two fishing access sites on the Flathead River and shopping, box stores, and restaurants in Kalispell. A 25-minute drive connects with the west entrance to Glacier National Park, and 20 minutes on the road leads to Flathead Lake. For kids, the campground has a large playground with a miniature western town and swimming in the creek. A grassy beach lines the creek, and the slow-moving stream works for fishing and canoeing.

The quiet, forested campground sits on the east side of Spring Creek away from the highway noise. Sites 90–98 sit closest to the creek, along with the tent campsites. Many of the pull-through sites sit in a large open area good for clear satellite reception, but with little privacy between sites. Tent sites are separated by wooden privacy fences. The campground has some long-term RVers.

Campsites, facilities: The campground has 98 RV campsites and 10 tent campsites. Pull-through sites can fit the largest RVs. Hookups include sewer, water, electricity up to 50 amps, and cable TV. Facilities include picnic tables, flush toilets, showers, a launderette, swimming area with dock, canoe landing, and camp store. Leashed pets are permitted.

Reservations, fees: Reservations are accepted and recommended for July and August. Hookups run $25–28 for one or two people. Extra people over 12 years old cost $4. Tent sites cost $19. Add on 7 percent Montana bed tax. Cash, check, or credit card. Open year-round.

Directions: From Kalispell, drive Highway 2 north toward Columbia Falls. Turn right on East Reserve Drive and go one mile before turning left onto Helena Flats Road. About 0.8 mile up the road, turn right into the campground.

GPS Coordinates: N 48° 14.969' W 114° 15.279'

Contact: Rocky Mountain Hi RV Park and

Campground, 825 Helena Flats Rd, Kalispell, MT 59901, 406/755-9573 or 800/968-5637, www.glaciercamping.com.

38 COLUMBIA FALLS RV PARK

Scenic rating: 7

in Columbia Falls

Tucked under Columbia Mountain at 3,100 feet, this RV park works for those who want the convenience of driving 20 minutes to the west entrance of Glacier National Park and the quick access to Flathead Valley shopping, restaurants, and recreation. The Columbia Falls post office, outdoor community pool, coffee shop, and restaurants sit within a six-block walk. Big Sky Waterslides, one mile east, opens June–Labor Day. A mountain-biking and hiking trail runs six miles up to the summit of Columbia Mountain for broad views of the valley. At a fishing access and boat launch 0.5 mile to the east, you can float the Flathead River with drift boats, kayaks, rafts, and canoes, and anglers drop lines off the bridge.

Nothing blocks the campground from the highway, so light sleepers should bring ear plugs. Not much privacy exists between sites either; however, the open sites appeal to those requiring satellite reception. Most of the sites are gravel pull-throughs with some extra-large spaces accommodating RVs with double slide-outs. Some seasonal RV residents are here. Most sites garner views of Columbia Mountain or the Whitefish Range. Tent sites sit in a separate large, grassy lawn area. The campground has plans to add 20 new RV super sites for 2010.

Campsites, facilities: The campground has 42 RV campsites and 10 tent campsites. Hookups include sewer, water, electricity up to 50 amps, and cable TV, and some of the sites have phone lines. Facilities include picnic tables, flush toilets, showers, a launderette, wireless Internet, and camp store. Leashed pets are permitted. A wheelchair-accessible toilet is available.

Reservations, fees: Reservations are accepted and highly recommended for July and August. Hookups cost $34; tent sites cost $24–28. Rates cover two people per site; each extra person costs $5. Cash, check, or credit card. Add on 7 percent Montana bed tax. Open mid-April–mid-October.

Directions: From the intersection of Highway 2 and Nucleus Avenue in Columbia Falls, drive 0.25 mile east. The campground sits on the north side of the highway. For those coming from the east, the campground is 0.5 mile west of the bridge over the Flathead River.

GPS Coordinates: N 48° 22.185' W 114° 10.623'

Contact: Columbia Falls RV Park, 103 Hwy. 2 E., Columbia Falls, MT 59912, 406/892-1122 or 888/401-7268, www.columbiafallsrvpark.com.

39 EMERY BAY

Scenic rating: 9

on the east side of Hungry Horse Reservoir in Flathead National Forest

At 3,600 feet on the east side of Hungry Horse Reservoir, Emery Bay Campground is the closest east-side campground to the highway. A cement boat ramp helps launch watercraft for boating, fishing, waterskiing, and paddling. Canoes and kayaks can explore the more sheltered inlets rather than venture out onto the open reservoir where winds can crop up. Mountain-biking and hiking trails are available four miles north in the Coram Experimental Forest. Five miles northeast of the campground, trail #331 also leads to the crest of the Flathead Mountains for stunning views into the Great Bear Wilderness and Glacier National Park.

The quiet campground huddles under a conifer forest that provides partly sunny or shaded sites; however, peek-a-boo views of the reservoir do exist from the bluff that overlooks the main reservoir, Emery Bay, and the Flathead and Swan Mountains. The spacious campsites are spread out, with young trees and tall grass lending privacy between sites. Wildflowers bloom in early summer, too. The parking pads are gravel-and-grass back ins, except for two pull-throughs.

Campsites, facilities: Emery Bay has 26 RV or tent campsites. Trailers are limited to 32 feet. Facilities include picnic tables, fire rings with grills, vault toilets, drinking water, bear boxes, a boat ramp, and campground hosts. Pack out your trash. Leashed pets are permitted. A wheelchair-accessible toilet is available.

Reservations, fees: No reservations are accepted. Campsites cost $13. Cash or check. Open mid-May–September.

Directions: From the town of Hungry Horse, drive 0.6 mile to Martin City and turn east, following signs to the Hungry Horse Reservoir East Road for six miles and veering right at the Y, where the road turns to dusty rough dirt and gravel. Veer right at the campground sign and drop 0.4 mile to the campground.

GPS Coordinates: N 48° 20.062' W 113° 56.957'

Contact: Flathead National Forest, Hungry Horse Ranger District, 10 Hungry Horse Dr., Hungry Horse, MT 59919, 406/387-3800, www.fs.fed.us/r1/flathead/.

40 LOST JOHNNY AND LOST JOHNNY POINT

🚶 🚴 🏊 🛶 ⛵ 🎣 🏕 ♿ 🚐 ⛺

Scenic rating: 9

on the west side of Hungry Horse Reservoir in Flathead National Forest

At an elevation of 3,600 feet on the west side of Hungry Horse reservoir, Lost Johnny and Lost Johnny Point Campgrounds sit less than 0.2 mile apart on Doris Creek inlet's south side. Lost Johnny Point has a cement boat ramp to launch boats for sightseeing, waterskiing, fishing, and paddling, but you can launch hand-carried watercraft from Lost Johnny Campground. North of the inlet, mountain bikers can climb the eight-mile Beta Road, while from its terminus, hikers can ascend three miles to Doris Lake or five miles to Doris Peak for dramatic views of Flathead Valley, the reservoir, and Glacier National Park.

Deep, thick conifers cover both of these quiet campgrounds, providing shade, and underbrush works well as a privacy fence. Lost Johnny Creek runs adjacent to the smaller campground, while Lost Johnny Point Campground, with its paved road and parking pads, tops a bluff on a steep hill with a more open forest and some sites overlooking the reservoir. Due to the paved road access and the proximity to Hungry Horse, the pair fill up faster than other campgrounds on the reservoir. The Forest Service also plans to build a third campground with a three-lane boat ramp and 10 campsites on the inlet's north side at Doris Point.

Campsites, facilities: Lost Johnny Camp has five private RV or tent campsites that can accommodate trailers up to 50 feet, and Lost Johnny Point has 21 RV or tent campsites that can fit trailers up to 40 feet. Facilities include picnic tables, fire rings with grills, drinking water, vault toilets, a boat ramp, and a campground host. Pack out your trash. Leashed pets are permitted. A wheelchair-accessible toilet is available at Lost Johnny Point.

Reservations, fees: No reservations are accepted. The campsites cost $13. Cash or check. Open mid-May–September.

Directions: From the town of Hungry Horse, drive south on the paved West Reservoir Road for nine miles, crossing the dam. Turn left into both campgrounds, located 0.2 mile apart.

Lost Johnny GPS Coordinates: N 48° 18.323' W 113° 58.085'

Lost Johnny Point GPS Coordinates: N 48° 18.601' W 113° 57.813'

Contact: Flathead National Forest, Hungry Horse Ranger District, 10 Hungry Horse Dr., Hungry Horse, MT 59919, 406/387-3800, www.fs.fed.us/r1/flathead/.

41 LID CREEK

Scenic rating: 9

on the west side of Hungry Horse Reservoir in Flathead National Forest

At 3,600 feet on the west side of Hungry Horse Reservoir, Lid Creek sits just at the end of the paved road. A fishing access is at the bottom of the campground, where you can carry small boats, rafts, kayaks, and canoes to the water. A motor or paddle about one mile across the reservoir reaches Fire Island. The nearest large boat launch is at Lost Johnny Point, five miles to the north. The nearest hiking and mountain-biking trail is at the end of Forest Road 895C, about two miles from the campground entrance and 3.5 miles up the Wounded Buck drainage. A three-mile trail climbs to the top of the Swan Crest, meeting up with the Alpine 7 trail, where you can head south to the summit of Strawberry Mountain or Strawberry Lake. The area is favored by huckleberry pickers. Due to the longer drive to reach the campground, it sees fewer people than Lost Johnny.

Known for its quiet and seclusion, the campground sits in thick mixed conifer forest on a large loop on the slope above the reservoir. Tent spaces are tight, small, or lacking in some campsites; you may need to pitch the tent on the parking pad. The campsites are spaced out for privacy. An upper spur offers more primitive campsites. Views from the beach include the rugged Flathead Range across the reservoir.

Campsites, facilities: The campground has 23 RV or tent campsites. Trailers longer than 32 feet are not recommended in the campground. Facilities include picnic tables, fire rings with grills, vault toilets, and campground hosts. No drinking water is available; if you use reservoir water, boil or filter it. Pack out your garbage. Leashed pets are permitted.

Reservations, fees: No reservations are accepted. Campsites cost $11. Cash or check. Open mid-May–September.

Directions: From the town of Hungry Horse, take the Hungry Horse Reservoir's West Reservoir Road south for 15 miles. The paved road crosses the reservoir on the dam and traverses south along the shore. Turn left at the signed entrance onto a gravel road for one mile (go straight through the intersection) into the campground.

GPS Coordinates: N 48° 17.185' W 113° 54.616'

Contact: Flathead National Forest, Hungry Horse Ranger District, 10 Hungry Horse Dr., Hungry Horse, MT 59919, 406/387-3800, www.fs.fed.us/r1/flathead/.

42 FIRE ISLAND

Scenic rating: 8

on Hungry Horse Reservoir in Flathead National Forest

Fire Island is a boat-in campground. While Hungry Horse Reservoir has several islands (all of which permit dispersed camping), only two have established designated campgrounds on them—Elk and Fire. At 3,600 feet, Fire Island sits farther north than Elk and requires no dirt road driving to get to its closest launch ramp at Lid Creek Campground. However, the island's location in the reservoir requires paddling or motoring across open water. The reservoir offers fishing for westslope cutthroat trout. Beach boats completely at night in case winds crop up.

Located on the southwest side of the island, the campsites are primitive, with small spaces for tents tucked into an open forest. The campsites are spread out for privacy in the tall brush and white bear grass blooming in early summer. Unlike Elk Island's gentle beach, Fire Island requires a steep climb up the bank to the campsites. Nonetheless, it still offers quiet and solitude.

Campsites, facilities: The island has four designated tent campsites. Facilities include picnic tables, fire rings with grills, and a pit toilet. Drinking water is not available; bring your own or filter or boil any water dipped from the reservoir. Pack out your trash. Collecting firewood from the beach and downed limbs in the forest is permitted. Leashed pets are permitted.

Reservations, fees: Reservations are not accepted. Campsites are free. Open mid-May–September.

Directions: From the town of Hungry Horse, take the Hungry Horse Reservoir's West Reservoir Road south for 15 miles to Lid Creek Campground. The paved but curvy road crosses the reservoir on the dam and traverses the west shoreline. Turn left at the signed entrance onto a gravel road for one mile to reach the boat launch.

GPS Coordinates: N 48° 17.675' W 113° 53.773'

Contact: Flathead National Forest, Hungry Horse Ranger District, 10 Hungry Horse Dr., Hungry Horse, MT 59919, 406/387-3800, www.fs.fed.us/r1/flathead/.

43 MURRAY BAY

Scenic rating: 9

on the east side of Hungry Horse Reservoir in Flathead National Forest

At 3,600 feet on the east side of Hungry Horse Reservoir, Murray Bay is one of the more coveted campgrounds on the reservoir. The campground's boat ramp aids boaters going for fishing, waterskiing, and sightseeing. Murray Bay is one of the reservoir's better places for paddling, due to the inlets, islands, and more protected water. On Forest Road 1048, the trail to Great Northern Mountain shoots up 4,300 feet in 4.5 miles to the summit for spectacular views of Grant Glacier and Glacier National Park. If snow clings to the upper mountain, the climb can be treacherous and should not be attempted without an ice axe. Mountain bikers ride up to Firefighter Mountain Lookout for panoramic views of the reservoir and knife-like Great Northern Mountain.

The 19-acre ultra-quiet campground sits on a loosely forested, partly sunny larch- and fir-covered square peninsula that sticks out toward Kelly Island. When the reservoir water drops low enough, you can swim or wade across the narrow channel to explore the island. Most of the secluded, roomy campsites have views of the reservoir and the Swan Mountains; however, low underbrush that blooms in July with tall white bear grass permits visibility of other campers. The gravel campground road is narrow and so are the sites; some large RVs may have trouble maneuvering. If the campground is full, more campsites are available at Riverside boat launch one mile north.

Campsites, facilities: The campground has 18 RV or tent campsites. Trailers are limited to 32 feet. Facilities include picnic tables, fire rings with grills, vault toilets, and campground hosts. Pack out your garbage. No drinking water is available; bring your own or filter or boil the lake water. Leashed pets are permitted.

Reservations, fees: No reservations are accepted. Campsites cost $11. Cash or check. Open mid-May–September.

Directions: From the town of Hungry Horse, go east on Highway 2 for 0.6 mile to Martin City and turn eastward, following the signs leading toward the east side of Hungry Horse Reservoir and veering right at the Y, where the road becomes a battle with dust and washboards. Drive 22 miles south on Forest Road 38. Turn right into the campground.

GPS Coordinates: N 48° 15.980' W 113° 48.670'

Contact: Flathead National Forest, Hungry Horse Ranger District, 10 Hungry Horse Dr., Hungry Horse, MT 59919, 406/387-3800, www.fs.fed.us/r1/flathead/.

44 LAKEVIEW

Scenic rating: 8

on the west side of Hungry Horse Reservoir in Flathead National Forest

Lakeview Campground, with an elevation of 3,600 feet, is one of the less crowded destinations on the west side of Hungry Horse Reservoir. Boating and fishing on the reservoir is only available via hand-carried watercraft carried down the bank to the beach. To the west on Forest Road 1633, the 2.5-mile trail #420 climbs to Clayton Lake in Jewel Basin Hiking Area. Locate the road about 3.5 miles north of Lakeview and drive 2.5 miles to the trailhead. The lake is known for its native westslope cutthroat fishery. Due to the campground's late closing in the fall, it is popular with hunters.

The campground sits on a forested slope between the road and the reservoir. The quiet campsites, sitting in a mix of firs and spruce, spread out for privacy and are partly shaded with peek-a-boo views of the lake. Spectacular views greet you at the beach; the knife-like Great Northern and Grant Peak across the lake are snow-covered still in June.

Campsites, facilities: The campground has five RV or tent campsites. Trailers longer than 22 feet are not recommended in the campground. Facilities include picnic tables, fire rings with grills, and a vault toilet. No drinking water is available. Bring your own, or plan to filter or boil water from the creek. Pack out your garbage. Leashed pets are permitted.

Reservations, fees: Reservations are not accepted. Camping is free. Open June–November.

Directions: From the town of Hungry Horse, drive the Hungry Horse Reservoir's West Reservoir Road south for 24 miles. The road crosses the reservoir on the dam and is paved as far as Lid Creek before turning to dirt for about nine miles. Turn left into the campground.

GPS Coordinates: N 48° 13.109' W 113° 48.301'

Contact: Flathead National Forest, Hungry Horse Ranger District, 10 Hungry Horse Dr., Hungry Horse, MT 59919, 406/387-3800, www.fs.fed.us/r1/flathead/.

45 ELK ISLAND

Scenic rating: 10

in Hungry Horse Reservoir in Flathead National Forest

BEST (

Located on the east side of Hungry Horse Reservoir, Elk Island is a boat-in campground at 3,600 feet. Paddling to Elk Island in a sea kayak or canoe yields gorgeous views of Great Northern and Grant Peak, along with the northern Swan Range. (You can also motorboat to the island, launching from any one of the four boat ramps at the north end of the reservoir.) Put in at the Riverside boat launch, which has a cement ramp. Paddle or motor between the Murray Bay Campground and Kelly Island south to Elk Island, beaching on the north side of the island to reach the campsites. If winds come up, stay near the shoreline. If the waters are calm, add tours around Kelly and Elk Islands. On Elk, a 90-minute walk will tour you around the shoreline. Beach boats completely at night in case winds crop up.

The campsites are primitive with small spaces for tents. With lower water levels, some flat sites appear on the beaches. In June, the island blooms with both bear grass and a good crop of mosquitoes. Pull out the camera for the sunset over the Swan Range and the sunrise from the Great Bear Wilderness. The songs of birds, water lapping the shore, and wind are the only sounds on the island.

Campsites, facilities: The island has seven designated tent campsites, plus several more primitive sites. Facilities include picnic tables, fire rings with grills, and pit toilets. Pack out your trash. Drinking water is not available; bring your own or filter or boil any water dipped from the reservoir. Collecting firewood from the beach and downed limbs in the forest is permitted. Leashed pets are permitted.

Reservations, fees: Reservations are not accepted. The campsites are free. Open mid-May–September.

Directions: From the town of Hungry Horse, go east on Highway 2 for 0.6 mile to Martin City and turn eastward, following the signs leading toward the east side of Hungry Horse Reservoir and veering right at the Y onto the gravel road. Drive 21 miles south on the dusty washboard of Forest Road 38. Turn right into Riverside boat launch.

GPS Coordinates: N 48° 14.452' W 113° 47.932'

Contact: Flathead National Forest, Hungry Horse Ranger District, 10 Hungry Horse Dr., Hungry Horse, MT 59919, 406/387-3800, www.fs.fed.us/r1/flathead/.

46 SPRUCE PARK ON THE RIVER

🏊 🛶 🎣 🏠 🐴 🚐 ⛺

Scenic rating: 8

in Kalispell on the Flathead River

At an elevation of 2,900 feet, Spruce Park mixes the convenience of being a few minutes from downtown Kalispell with the ambiance of a riverfront setting backdropped by mountain views. Sitting right on the Flathead River, the campground lures anglers who want to try to hook rainbows or westslope cutthroat trout from the campground's dock. Three golf courses are within seven miles, and the renowned Eagle Bend Golf Club requires only a 20-minute drive. Glacier Park is 30 miles to the northeast. Several fishing accesses on the Flathead River allow for launching boats, rafts, kayaks, and canoes for floating the river.

Most of Spruce Park's campsites sit under large mature firs and cottonwoods with some sites bordering the Flathead River. A paved road loops through the mowed lawn campground, with some large pull-through spaces for big rigs towing boats or cars; sites along the river have views of the northern Swan Mountains. Sites are set close together with little privacy, and highway noise enters the campground.

Campsites, facilities: The campground has 70 RV campsites and 17 tent campsites. Pull-through sites can fit the largest RVs. Hookups include cable TV, sewer, water, and electricity up to 50 amps. Facilities include picnic tables, fire rings, flush toilets, showers, a launderette, wireless Internet, a disposal station, a pet-walking area, a playground, a dock, horseshoes, a game room, a volleyball court, and a camp store. Leashed pets are permitted.

Reservations, fees: Reservations are accepted. Hookups cost $25–28. Tent sites cost $19. Rates are based on one family with their minor children per site or four adults. Add on 7 percent Montana bed tax. Cash, credit card, check, or Canadian currency. Open year-round.

Directions: From Kalispell, drive east on Highway 35 toward Creston. Turn left into the campground about 1.5 miles past the La-Salle/Highway 2 junction.

GPS Coordinates: N 48° 13.440' W 114° 14.825'

Contact: Spruce Park on the River RV Park and Campground, 1985 Hwy. 35, Kalispell, MT 59901, 406/752-6321, www.spruceparkrv.com.

47 EDGEWATER RV RESORT

Scenic rating: 6

on the west side of Flathead Lake

Located on the west side of Flathead Lake in Lakeside, the Edgewater RV Resort sits on one side of the two-lane highway while a marina covers the shoreline. The marina rents power boats, personal watercraft, and paddleboats. Charter fishing and lake cruises are also available. Downtown Lakeside spans only five blocks, so you can walk to the grocery store or restaurants. The town is also home to Tamarack Brewing Company Alehouse and Grill, which serves its microbrews, such as Bear Bottom Blonde and Old 'Stache Whiskey Barrel Porter, along with lunch and dinner.

The campground loops on a paved road through the resort with mowed lawn flanking each paved parking apron. The campground is wide open with no trees for shade, but grabs a clear shot of the sky for satellite reception. Three sites (44–46) sit across the highway closer to the lakeshore. The RV park is adjacent to the resort's motel, and those camping have access to the resort's private swimming beach and dock.

Campsites, facilities: The campground has 38 RV sites. Hookups include water, sewer, and electricity up to 50 amps, and 20 of the sites are pull-throughs at 27 feet wide by 70 feet long—wide enough to accommodate slide-outs. Facilities include picnic tables, pedestal barbecues, flush toilets, showers, a disposal station, modem hookups, a launderette, and access across the highway to the lake, a dock, and swimming. Leashed pets are permitted. A wheelchair-accessible toilet is available.

Reservations, fees: Reservations are accepted. Hookups cost $34. Cash, check, or credit card. Open May–September.

Directions: On Highway 93, find Lakeside 13 miles south of Kalispell and 38 miles north of Polson. The resort sits on the opposite side of the highway from the lake at the north end of town.

GPS Coordinates: N 48° 1.349' W 114° 13.547'

Contact: Edgewater RV Resort, 7140 Hwy. 93 S., Lakeside, MT 59922, 406/844-3644 or 800/424-3798, www.edgewaterrv.com.

48 LAKE MARY RONAN

Scenic rating: 6

on Lake Mary Ronan in the Salish Mountains

Lake Mary Ronan, which sits seven miles west of Flathead Lake at 3,800 feet in the Salish Mountains, doesn't get nearly the traffic that the Flathead Lake parks see, but the lake draws its share of people. At 1,513 acres, the lake is considerably smaller than Flathead Lake, but it still attracts bird-watchers, swimmers, kayakers, canoeists, water-skiers, and mushroom and huckleberry pickers. Anglers go after kokanee, largemouth bass, pumpkinseed, rainbow trout, yellow perch, and westslope cutthroat trout. Trails lead to the beach, which has a concrete boat ramp with an adjacent dock, a small swimming beach, and paved parking for boat trailers.

The quiet, 120-acre park shaded by Douglas firs and western larches tucks its campground back in the shady woods on one gravel loop. The sites around the outside rim of the loop are more private than those inside the circle.

Campsites, facilities: The campground has 31 RV or tent campsites. RVs are limited to 35 feet. Facilities include picnic tables, fire rings with grills, vault toilets, drinking water, a boat launch, and garbage service. Firewood is for sale. Leashed pets are permitted. A wheelchair-accessible toilet is available.

Reservations, fees: No reservations are accepted. Montana residents may use the park free during the day; nonresidents must pay $5 per vehicle or $3 per bike. Camping costs $15, cash or check. The park is open all year but only has services May–September.

Directions: From Kalispell, drive 20 miles south on Highway 93. From Polson, drive 32 miles north on Highway 93. Look for the sign on the west side of the road.

GPS Coordinates: N 47° 55.615' W 114° 22.917'

Contact: Montana Fish, Wildlife, and Parks, Region 1, 490 N. Meridian Rd., Kalispell, MT 59901, 406/752-5501, http://fwp.mt.gov.

49 WEST SHORE STATE PARK

Scenic rating: 9

on the west side of Flathead Lake

Located at 2,900 feet, Flathead Lake has 128 miles of shoreline with waters like clear glass. The glacially fed lake, which draws its waters from Glacier Park, Canada, and the Bob Marshall Wilderness area, grew from ice age glaciers melting 10,000 years ago. Located on the west shore with sunrise views over the Mission and Swan Mountains, the West Shore State Park has the reputation of being the most private state park on the lake. The campground sits on a bluff on Goose Bay with tiny Goose Island about 0.3 mile out in the lake. A concrete boat ramp facilitates launching watercraft for fishing, waterskiing, sailing, kayaking, canoeing, and sightseeing.

The quiet 129-acre park spans a forested hillside with a rocky beach. Filtered sunlight hits the campsites through tall larches and pines. Some of the campsites have peek-a-boo views across the lake to the mountains rising above the opposite shore about eight miles away. The campground road is paved, but parking pads are gravel.

Campsites, facilities: The campground has 31 RV or tent campsites. RVs are limited to 30 feet. Facilities include picnic tables, fire rings with grills, vault toilets, drinking water, garbage service, a playground, and a boat launch. For bicyclists, a bear-resistant food storage locker is available. Firewood is for sale. Leashed pets are permitted. A wheelchair-accessible toilet is available, and an ADA campsite has electrical and water hookups.

Reservations, fees: No reservations are accepted. Montana residents may use the park free during the day; nonresidents must pay $5 per vehicle or $3 per bike. Camping costs $15. Cash or check. Open all year, but serviced only May–September.

Directions: From Kalispell drive 20 miles south on Highway 93, or from Polson drive 32 miles north on Highway 93. Turn east at the signed entrance to drop into the campground.

GPS Coordinates: N 47° 56.958' W 114° 11.027'

Contact: Montana Fish, Wildlife, and Parks, Region 1, 490 N. Meridian Rd., Kalispell, MT 59901, 406/752-5501, http://fwp.mt.gov.

50 BIG ARM STATE PARK

Scenic rating: 10

on the west side of Flathead Lake

BEST (

Flathead Lake covers 188 square miles, but from the vantage of Big Arm State Park, islands cut off some of the wide open water and shrink the size of the lake in appearance. Located on the lake's west side on Big Arm Bay at 2,900 feet, the park faces the morning sunrise coming over the Mission Mountains. Wild Horse Island—a day use state park renowned for its wild horses, bighorn sheep, birds, and wildflowers—sits 5.5 miles across the lake; boat to the island to hike around it. Kayakers and canoeists should watch the weather carefully, as winds can whip the lake into a whitecapped frenzy in minutes. The park also sits on Confederated Salish Kootenai land of the Flathead Reservation; tribal fishing permits are required to fish the lake. The campground includes a cement boat ramp, dock, and trailer parking. With a 2.5-mile nature trail through its prairie grasslands and forest, the park is also good for bird-watching—especially with bald eagles and ospreys fishing in the lake.

Large ponderosa pines and junipers bring filtered shade to the campground. A long swimming beach runs from the boat ramp and dock north to the end of B loop. Campsites are tucked around two narrow, long, paved loops with gravel aprons. Both loops have half of the sites overlooking the lake.

Campsites, facilities: The campground has 40 RV or tent campsites. RVs are limited to 30 feet. Facilities include picnic tables, fire rings with grills, vault toilets, flush toilets, showers, drinking water, garbage service, and a boat launch. The campground also includes a bear-resistant food storage locker for those traveling by bicycle. Firewood is for sale. The campground also rents a yurt. Leashed pets are permitted. A wheelchair-accessible toilet is available.

Reservations, fees: No reservations are accepted. While Montana residents may use the park free during the day, nonresidents must pay $5 per vehicle or $3 per bike. Camping costs $15. Cash or check. Open May–September.

Directions: From Polson, drive 14 miles north on Highway 93, or from Kalispell, drive about 38 miles south on Highway 35. Turn right at the signed entrance. GPS Coordinates: N 47° 48.770' W 114° 18.612'

Contact: Montana Fish, Wildlife, and Parks, Region 1, 490 N. Meridian Rd., Kalispell, MT 59901, 406/752-5501, http://fwp.mt.gov.

51 FINLEY POINT STATE PARK

Scenic rating: 9

on the east side of Flathead Lake

Flathead Lake is the largest natural freshwater lake west of the Mississippi. Finley Point State Park sits at 2,900 feet on the lake's south end on the Flathead Reservation below the Mission Mountains. The point is actually a half-mile-wide spit that sticks out into the lake, forming Skidoo Bay to the northeast and Polson Bay to the southeast—both littered with summer homes along the shores. The proximity to Polson 15 minutes away brings heavy day use to the park. Anglers come here to fish for whitefish, rainbow and bull trout, northern pike, and lake trout that grow up to 20 pounds. A tribal fishing license is required. A boat ramp, marina, boat pump-out, and trailer parking are available. The National Bison Range and Ninepipes National Wildlife Refuge are about 40 minutes south.

The 28-acre campground sits on the shore of Flathead Lake with all of its cramped campsites lined up along the lake facing the sunset. The grassy campground, shaded by mature firs and birches, lacks privacy. From the beach, you'll see summer homes and Polson across the bay. However, the campground's popularity comes from its prime waterfront campsites. Sites 1–4 with tent pads are designated for tents only. Tents are not permitted in the RV sites, which line up in parking-lot fashion in front of their tables and fire rings.

Campsites, facilities: The campground has 12 RV campsites, four tent campsites, and 16 boat campsites. RV hookups include electricity with 30 amps, and the maximum RV length is 40 feet. Facilities include picnic tables, fire rings with grills, flush toilets, drinking water, boat facilities, and a swimming area. Firewood is for sale. Four of the 16 boat slips also have electrical and water hookups. Boats are limited to 25 feet. Leashed pets are permitted. A wheelchair-accessible toilet is available.

Reservations, fees: No reservations are accepted. While Montana residents may use the park for free during the day, nonresidents must pay $5 per vehicle. Campsites and boat camping slips cost $15. Hookups cost $5 additional. Cash or check. Open May–September.

Directions: From Polson, drive seven miles north on Highway 35. Turn left and follow the signs four miles northwest on narrow Finley Point Road. Turn left into the campground. GPS Coordinates: N 47° 45.249' W 114° 5.165'

Contact: Montana Fish, Wildlife, and Parks, Region 1, 490 N. Meridian Rd., Kalispell, MT 59901, 406/752-5501, http://fwp.mt.gov.

52 BLUE BAY

Scenic rating: 10

on the east side of Flathead Lake

Blue Bay commands a spectacular location on Flathead Lake's east side, with views of Wild Horse Island. The campground, which faces southeast down the lake, sets up the majority of its campsites with prime real estate on the waterfront. Owned and operated by the Confederated Salish and Kootenai Tribes, Blue Bay has three parts: a lodge area reserved for groups, the day-use beach and marina, and the campground. The marina includes 32 boat slips, a concrete ramp and boat docks, a fishing pier, boat trailer parking, and a fish-cleaning station. The day-use swim beach has picnic tables, a dock, and a buoyed off area to protect swimmers. Personal watercraft are not permitted.

The campground, on the opposite side of the marina from the day-use area, has another buoyed swim area with a dock at the group shelter and another swim dock with no buoy line located between sites 18 and 19. Large ponderosa pines shade some of the grassy area. Sites 1–6, 41, and 51 are farther apart from their neighbors, while the remainder of the sites line up close to each other. Sites 7–33 line the waterfront. In a row on a bluff behind the waterfront campsites are the sites with hookups. No alcohol is permitted in the campground. Most of the campsites are buffered from the highway by the bluff with the lodges.

Campsites, facilities: The campground has 55 campsites. RV hookups are available at 17 sites with hookups for sewer and water, and some have electricity. Facilities include picnic tables, fire rings, drinking water, garbage service, and flush toilets.

Reservations, fees: Reservations are not accepted. Day use for the area costs $5 per vehicle. Camping costs $15 per vehicle. Hookups cost $30. Cash or check. Open May–September.

Directions: From Polson, drive 13.5 miles north on Highway 35. From Bigfork, drive 14.5 miles south on Highway 35. Turn west at the signed entrance.

GPS Coordinates: N 47° 49.650' W 114° 1.689'

Contact: Confederated Salish and Kootenai Tribes, 51383 Hwy. 93 N., Pablo, MT 59855, 406/675-2700 or 406/253-3813 (campground), www.cskt.org.

53 YELLOW BAY STATE PARK

Scenic rating: 8

on the east side of Flathead Lake

For those looking for a little less hectic experience on Flathead Lake, Yellow Bay may be the answer. It's on the flanks of the Mission Mountains in cherry orchard country. In July, look for stands selling freshly picked cherries along Highway 35; on hot days, you can smell the fruit in the air. Located on the lake's east side, the park sits across from Wild Horse Island—a day use state park with bighorn sheep, eagles, and wild horses. With 10 miles of water in between, power boaters go from this eastern side, but kayakers and canoeists tend to stick to the east shoreline, visiting the island only from the west side of the lake. The park also sits on the Flathead Reservation; tribal fishing permits are required to fish the lake. Located in sheltered Yellow Bay, the 15-acre park sidles up to the Flathead Lake shoreline with a wide, sandy southeast-facing beach for swimming and Yellow Bay Creek running through the park. A concrete ramp with a dock aids boat launchers for fishing, waterskiing, and sightseeing.

Although the access off the highway is paved, the road is steep and narrow. Picking up traffic noise, the tent sites sit back from the beach, tucked under a thick canopy of trees between the campground and the highway.

Campsites, facilities: The campground has only four walk-in tenting sites. Facilities include picnic tables, pedestal grills, flush toilets, drinking water, and garbage service. Wood fires are not permitted; bring your own charcoal. Bear-resistant food storage lockers are also available, a boon for bicyclists. Leashed pets are permitted.

Reservations, fees: No reservations are accepted. While Montana residents may use the park free during the day, nonresidents must pay $5 per vehicle or $3 per bike. Camping costs $15. Cash or check. Open May–September.

Directions: From Polson, drive 15 miles north on Highway 35, or from Bigfork, drive 13 miles south on Highway 35. Turn west at the signed entrance to the park.

GPS Coordinates: N 47° 52.532' W 114° 1.728'

Contact: Montana Fish, Wildlife, and Parks, Region 1, 490 N. Meridian Rd., Kalispell, MT 59901, 406/752-5501, http://fwp.mt.gov.

54 WAYFARERS STATE PARK

Scenic rating: 9

on the east side of Flathead Lake

Sitting at 2,900 feet on the largest natural freshwater lake in the West, Wayfarers State Park hops in high season with fishing, sailing, waterskiing, paddling, and sightseeing. For boaters, a concrete launch ramp, boat trailer parking, dock, and pump-out service are available. A 1.5-mile hiking trail climbs through the 67-acre forested park with scenic overlooks

of the lake. The park is also adjacent to Bigfork, with its summer theater, restaurants, and shopping. Wayfarers is the closest designated campground to Jewel Basin, a 15,349-acre hiking area in mountain goat terrain with 50 miles of trails that loop between 27 alpine lakes. The Wild Mile of the Swan River yields advanced white-water kayaking right outside Bigfork.

The paved entrance road passes an osprey nest as it drops to the lake, where the boat launch and picnic area sit on the beach, with the campground a five-minute walk away. Most of the campground loops through a shady canopy of mature firs and ponderosa pines. Sites 10–15 have more privacy than sites 19–25, which sit on a big meadow. Sites 1–4 also sit on the meadow, right at the campground entrance with more traffic. A couple of tight sites are pull-throughs reserved for RVs only; maximum trailer combination is 50 feet. A few sites are for tents only.

Campsites, facilities: The campground has 26 RV or tent campsites. RVs are limited to 50 feet. Facilities include picnic tables, fire rings with grills, vault and flush toilets, showers, drinking water, garbage service, a disposal station, a playground, and a bear-resistant food storage locker for bikers. Firewood is for sale. Leashed pets are permitted. A wheelchair-accessible toilet is available, and there's a 30-amp electrical hookup at site 24, an ADA site.

Reservations, fees: No reservations are accepted. Montana residents may use the park free during the day; nonresidents must pay $5 per vehicle or $3 per bike. Camping costs $15. Cash or check. Open all year, but serviced only May–September.

Directions: From Bigfork, drive 0.5 mile south on Highway 35. Turn west at the signed entrance into the park.

GPS Coordinates: N 48° 4.120' W 114° 4.849'

Contact: Montana Fish, Wildlife, and Parks, Region 1, 490 N. Meridian Rd., Kalispell, MT 59901, 406/752-5501, http://fwp.mt.gov.

55 HANDKERCHIEF LAKE

Scenic rating: 7

west of Hungry Horse Reservoir in Flathead National Forest

At 3,850 feet on the west side of Hungry Horse Reservoir above Graves Bay, the 30-acre Handkerchief Lake sits only two miles from Graves Bay. The lake makes for nice canoeing; no boat launch is available, but trails lead to the shore. Fishing is available for native trout, too. Continue up the road another two miles to reach the Graves Creek Trailhead. The trail climbs in five miles to Black Lake—a native westslope cutthroat fishery—in Jewel Basin Hiking Area, with views of Mount Aeneas and the Great Bear Wilderness across the reservoir. The campground is used by hunters in the fall.

The campground has a unique layout. You park on a pull-off on the road, but sites are spread out all along the shore below the road. The campsites sit in a deep forest of thick spruce and firs with privacy between campsites created from abundant underbrush. Only natural sounds fill the campground, making it prized for its quiet.

Campsites, facilities: The campground has nine RV or tent campsites. Trailers are limited to 22 feet. Facilities include picnic tables, fire rings with grills, and vault toilets. No drinking water is available; bring your own, or plan to filter or boil water from the creek. Pack out your trash. Leashed pets are permitted.

Reservations, fees: Reservations are not accepted. Camping is free. Open June–November.

Directions: From the town of Hungry Horse, take the Hungry Horse Reservoir West Road south for 35 miles. The road crosses the reservoir on the dam and is paved as far as Lid Creek (halfway) before turning to dusty washboards and potholes. At 35 miles, turn right onto Forest Road 897 and drive two miles to the campground.

GPS Coordinates: N 48° 8.631' W 113° 49.574'

Contact: Flathead National Forest, Hungry Horse Ranger District, 10 Hungry Horse Dr., Hungry Horse, MT 59919, 406/387-3800, www.fs.fed.us/r1/flathead/.

56 GRAVES BAY

Scenic rating: 8

on the west side of Hungry Horse Reservoir in Flathead National Forest

On the west side of the reservoir, Graves Bay Campground (sometimes called Graves Creek) sits on the largest bay—stretching almost three miles long. The elevation is 3,600 feet. A primitive boat launch is available—best for hand-carried small boats, canoes, and kayaks. The narrow bay's water offers a protected place to paddle. Waters tumble from Jewel Basin down to the bay, which increases beach size as the reservoir drops during the summer. The Graves Creek Trail, which departs from above Handkerchief Lake, climbs to Black Lake into Jewel Basin Hiking Area for views of Mount Aeneas and the Great Bear Wilderness across the reservoir.

The quiet, forested campground sits at the head of Graves Bay. The campsites sit along the creek on a spur road opposite the bay. The Forest Service has plans to remove the campsites on the reservoir side of the road and develop the sites on the west side of the road with a vault toilet and an ADA camping site. If this campground is full, try Handkerchief Lake three miles away.

Campsites, facilities: The campground has 10 RV or tent campsites. Trailers longer than 22 feet are not recommended in the campground. Facilities include picnic tables, fire rings with grills, and vault toilets. No drinking water is available. Bring your own, or plan to filter or boil water from the creek. Pack out your garbage. Leashed pets are permitted.

Reservations, fees: Reservations are not accepted. Camping is free. Open June–September.

Directions: From the town of Hungry Horse, take the Hungry Horse Reservoir West Road south for 35 miles. The road crosses the reservoir on the dam and is paved as far as Lid Creek, about halfway. After that, the curvy dirt road becomes interminable dust and washboards. Turn west into the campground. GPS Coordinates: N 48° 7.625' W 113° 48.643'

Contact: Flathead National Forest, Hungry Horse Ranger District, 10 Hungry Horse Dr., Hungry Horse, MT 59919, 406/387-3800, www.fs.fed.us/r1/flathead/.

57 DEVIL'S CORKSCREW

Scenic rating: 7

on the east side of Hungry Horse Reservoir in Flathead National Forest

The long dirt road on the east side of the reservoir into Devil's Corkscrew deters many people. Before departing from the town of Hungry Horse, gas up and check the spare tire in preparation for the dust, washboards, and lack of services. Located at 3,600 feet, the campground has a primitive boat launch for small boats, kayaks, and canoes. Larger boats must launch from ramps located 10 miles in either direction. The 35-mile-long Hungry Horse Reservoir is known for its native fishery. Within short drives north and east on the forest road, you can find trailheads. The six-mile Logan Creek Trail (#62) climbs into the Great Bear Wilderness, and a four-mile rougher trail leads to the site of Baptiste Lookout for views of the reservoir.

The Forest Service thinned the campground area several years ago, opening up the thick forest for partial sun. The quiet small campground sits back in the trees from the shore

with campsites spread out for privacy. This is one prized for its quiet and solitude.

Campsites, facilities: The campground has four RV or tent campsites. Trailers are limited to 32 feet. Facilities include picnic tables, fire rings with grills, and a vault toilet. Drinking water is not available; bring your own. Pack out your trash. Leashed pets are permitted.

Reservations, fees: Reservations are not accepted. The campsites are free. Open mid-May–September.

Directions: From the town of Hungry Horse, go east on Highway 2 for 0.6 mile to Martin City and turn eastward, following the signs leading toward the east side of Hungry Horse Reservoir and veering right at the Y onto the gravel road. Drive 32 miles south on Forest Road 38. Turn right into the campground. GPS Coordinates: N 48° 6.610' W 113° 41.801'

Contact: Flathead National Forest, Spotted Bear Ranger District, 10 Hungry Horse Dr., Hungry Horse, MT 59919, 406/387-3800, www.fs.fed.us/r1/flathead/.

58 PETER'S CREEK

Scenic rating: 8

on the east side of Hungry Horse Reservoir in Flathead National Forest

The long, dusty road on the east side of the reservoir into Peter's Creek deters many people. Gas up, and check the spare tire before you depart. At an elevation of 3,600 feet on the east shore of the 35-mile-long reservoir, the campground is prized for its sheer remoteness. You can launch hand-carried watercraft from the campground, but larger boats need to launch from the Crossover boat launch about 4.5 miles farther south of Peter's Creek. It offers a cement low-water boat ramp for water-skiers, sightseers, and anglers going for the native species in the reservoir. Mountain biking is available on a tangle of forest roads on the flanks of the Flathead Mountains.

A thick forest of larch and Douglas fir covers the small two-acre campground, but with enough openings through the trees for views of the Swan Range across the reservoir. The quiet, secluded campsites are spaced out along the reservoir, with loads of undergrowth for privacy, but they are small and cramped, with very small tent spaces. Short trails lead down to the reservoir, where the beach grows larger throughout the summer as the dam draws the water down.

Campsites, facilities: The campground has seven RV or tent campsites. Trailers are limited to 22 feet. Facilities include picnic tables, fire rings with grills, and a vault toilet. Drinking water is not available; filter or boil any water dipped from the creeks. Pack out your trash. Leashed pets are permitted. A wheelchair-accessible toilet is available.

Reservations, fees: Reservations are not accepted. Camping is free. Open mid-May–September.

Directions: From the town of Hungry Horse, go east on Highway 2 for 0.6 mile to Martin City. Turn eastward, following the signs leading toward the east side of Hungry Horse Reservoir and veering right at the Y onto the gravel road. Drive 37 miles south on Forest Road 38. Turn right to drop into the campground.

GPS Coordinates: N 48° 3.408' W 113° 38.678'

Contact: Flathead National Forest, Spotted Bear Ranger District, 10 Hungry Horse Dr., Hungry Horse, MT 59919, 406/387-3800, www.fs.fed.us/r1/flathead/.

59 SWAN LAKE

Scenic rating: 9

in Swan Valley in Flathead National Forest

BEST (

At 3,100 feet, Swan Lake—a long, skinny cold-water lake located just southeast of Bigfork in the Swan Valley—gets packed with recreational boaters and water-skiers. The lake, with a swimming beach, dock, and boat ramp, is surrounded by the high Swan Mountains. The south end of the lake attracts paddlers for bird-watching along the Swan River National Wildlife Refuge, and anglers go for the rainbow and westslope cutthroat trout. Local hikes lead to lookouts and lakes. A four-mile climb tops Sixmile Mountain, the site of an old lookout at the north end of the southern Swan Crest Trail (Alpine 7), and a seven-mile trail ascends to Bond and Trinkus Lakes, which cuddle in basins just below the crest.

Shaded by big cedars, the picnic area sits right on the beach of Swan Lake, while the campground tucks its two loops back into trees on the opposite side of the highway. Underbrush lends a sense of privacy between many of the campsites; those on the outsides of the loops have more privacy than those on the inside. The Forest Service holds campfire programs in the evenings. Catering to cyclists, the campground has bike lanes and one bicycle-only campsite.

Campsites, facilities: The campground has 36 RV or tent campsites. The campground can accommodate trailers up to 50 feet. Facilities include picnic tables, fire rings with grills, vault toilets, drinking water, campground hosts, and garbage service. Leashed pets are permitted. A wheelchair-accessible toilet is available.

Reservations, fees: Reservations are accepted (877/444-6777, www.recreation.gov). Campsites cost $15. Cash or check. Open mid-May–September.

Directions: From two miles north of Bigfork, drive east on Highway 83 and 19.7 miles south to Swan Lake. From Seeley Lake, drive 56.5 miles north on Highway 83. Turn east into the campground.

GPS Coordinates: N 47° 56.187' W 113° 51.033'

Contact: Flathead National Forest, Swan Lake Ranger District, 200 Ranger Station Rd.,

Bigfork, MT 59911, 406/837-7500, www.
fs.fed.us/r1/flathead/.

60 SPOTTED BEAR

Scenic rating: 9

south of Hungry Horse Reservoir in Flathead
National Forest

BEST (

Gas up the vehicle to drive to Spotted Bear,
and take along emergency tire repair equipment, for no services exist on the long dusty
access road, and cell phones won't work.
Located at 3,700 feet at the confluence of
the Spotted Bear River and South Fork of
the Flathead River, the campground features
fishing in both rivers. A Wild and Scenic
River, the South Fork also provides Class II
rafting, canoeing, or kayaking. Nearby trails
for hiking, mountain biking, and horseback
riding depart to Spotted Bear Lake (2 miles),
Spotted Bear Lookout (a long 7-mile climb),
and Meadow Creek Gorge (10 miles). The
Spotted Bear Ranger Station, which is staffed
seven days per week, sits across Spotted Bear
River, and the Diamond R Guest Ranch is
across the road. Find the footbridge across
the South Fork River behind ranger station
to reach the river for fishing and swimming
holes.

Located on a bench above the confluence
of the rivers, the campground sits partly
shaded under a loose forest of Douglas firs
and western larch, with underbrush adding to
privacy. Due to its distance from pavement,
the campground offers the rare commodities
of silence and solitude. The campsites, with
gravel parking pads, are spread out on both
sides of the campground loop, with half of the
sites high above Spotted Bear River.

Campsites, facilities: The campground has 13
campsites for RVs or tents. Trailers are limited
to 32 feet. Facilities include picnic tables, fire
rings with grills, a vault toilet, drinking water,
garbage service, bear boxes, and campground
hosts. Leashed pets are permitted. A wheelchair-accessible toilet is available.

Reservations, fees: No reservations are accepted. Campsites cost $10. Cash or check.
Open mid-May–September.

Directions: From the town of Hungry Horse,
go east on Highway 2 for 0.6 mile to Martin
City and turn eastward, following the signs
leading toward the east side of Hungry Horse
Reservoir and veering right at the Y just outside Martin City, where the road becomes an
interminable battle with dust and washboards.
Drive 54 miles south on Forest Road 38. Turn
right into the campground.
GPS Coordinates: N 47° 55.531' W 113°
31.700'

Contact: Flathead National Forest, Spotted
Bear Ranger District, 10 Hungry Horse Dr.,
Hungry Horse, MT 59919, 406/387-3800,
www.fs.fed.us/r1/flathead/.

61 BEAVER CREEK

Scenic rating: 8

south of Hungry Horse Reservoir in Flathead
National Forest

At 4,150 feet on Spotted Bear River over 60
miles from pavement, Beaver Creek is the
last campground before jumping off into
the Bob Marshall Wilderness. Don't go here
on a whim: The distance will take you several hours, and no services are available en
route. Be sure your spare tire is pumped up
and ready for use. Within five miles of the
campground are five trailheads—Silvertip,
Upper Big Bill, Lower Big Bill, South Creek,
and Meadow Creek—with trails winding up
long drainages into the heart of the wilderness. The 34-mile-long Spotted Bear River
south of the campground supports mountain
whitefish, native westslope cutthroat, and the
threatened bull trout for fly-fishing. Due to
flooding, the riverbed is broad, with braided
streams weaving through rocks and sand in

late summer. Hunters use the campground in fall.

Due to its remote location, the tiny campground offers utter quiet, except for the sound of the river. The secluded forested campground spreads out its sites for privacy, and undergrowth adds to it. Should the campground be full, the Forest Service permits dispersed camping in this area. Choose a site that shows previous use rather than starting a new site, and follow Leave No Trace principles.

Campsites, facilities: The campground has four RV or tent campsites. Trailers are limited to 32 feet. Facilities include picnic tables, fire rings with grills, and a vault toilet. Drinking water is not available; filter or boil any water dipped from the river. Pack out your trash. Leashed pets are permitted.

Reservations, fees: Reservations are not accepted. The campsites are free. Open June–November.

Directions: From the town of Hungry Horse, go east on Highway 2 for 0.6 mile to the Martin City turnoff and head eastward, veering right at the Y onto the dusty gravel road that traverses the east side of Hungry Horse Reservoir. Drive 54 miles south on Forest Road 38 and then 8.5 miles east on Forest Road 568. Turn right into the campground. GPS Coordinates: N 47° 55.458' W 113° 22.442'

Contact: Flathead National Forest, Spotted Bear Ranger District, 10 Hungry Horse Dr., Hungry Horse, MT 59919, 406/387-3800, www.fs.fed.us/r1/flathead/.

62 THOMPSON FALLS STATE PARK

🧍🚴🛶🎣🛥️🎿🐴♿🚐⛺

Scenic rating: 8

west of Thompson Falls on the Clark Fork River

Located less than five minutes from downtown Thompson Falls or Rivers Bend Golf Course, the 36-acre state park sits under firs and tall ponderosa pines right on the Clark Fork River. The campground overlooks the river, flowing with a few riffles to slow downriver in Noxon Reservoir. The campground's boat ramp, located between the B and C loops, is suitable for small boats. For a full-sized boat launch, head 0.5 mile north on Blue Slide Road across the bridge. The river is popular for boating, waterskiing, paddling, and fishing. Seven miles east of the campground, you can see bighorn sheep at the KooKooSint viewing area November–mid-April. In the campground, a trail tours the riverbank and loops around a small pond that houses turtles, frogs, and fish. The park also provides good bird-watching: ospreys, hawks, Canadian geese, and songbirds.

Recent thinning at the campground increased the filtered sunlight reaching the grassy campsites, which sit in two loops. C loop's sites 16 and 17 are the most private and closest to the river. Bring earplugs for sleeping, as the trains pass on the railroad tracks across the river all night long.

Campsites, facilities: The campground has 17 RV or tent campsites. Fourteen sites can accommodate RVs up to 30 feet. Facilities include picnic tables, fire rings with grills, vault toilets, drinking water, a boat launch, nature trail, campground hosts, and a group site with covered tables. Firewood is available for purchase. Leashed pets are permitted. A wheelchair-accessible toilet is available.

Reservations, fees: Reservations are not accepted. Camping costs $15. For day use, state parks charge $5 per vehicle for nonresidents; Montana residents have free day use. Cyclists only need to pay $3 for day use. Cash or check only. Open May–September.

Directions: From Thompson Falls, drive Highway 200 one mile northwest. At milepost 49.5, turn right onto Blue Slide Road. Drive 1.5 miles to the entrance on the west side of the road. Coming from the west on Highway 200, turn left onto Birdland Bay Road at mile marker 47.5 and drive 0.5 mile to the entrance on the right.

GPS Coordinates: N 47° 35.564' W 115° 20.256'

Contact: Montana Fish, Wildlife, and Parks, Region 1, 490 N. Meridian Rd., Kalispell, MT 59901, 406/752-5501, http://fwp.mt.gov.

63 COPPER KING

Scenic rating: 7

on the Thompson River in Lolo National Forest

Drive up the Thompson River Road, and you'll find your neck craning upward. Huge rock outcroppings and cliffs frame the steep-walled valley. Sitting at 2,700 feet, Copper King is the only campground accessible via pavement. Anglers visit Copper King to fish the river for brook, brown, or rainbow trout. Floaters also paddle the river. During high water, some Class II and Class III rapids add froth to the river just below the campground.

Tucked under large cedar trees, the tiny campground encompasses two acres. The campground's tight corners and short parking pads relegate this campground to truck campers, mini-bus campers, and tents. The first campsite is the only one set back in the trees away from the river; the others all border the river. Sites 2 and 5 are more private, but sites 3 and 4 have mountain views. Site 5 is the largest, with a double-sized table. (If this campground is full, you can drive one more mile to the Clark Memorial Campground.) Only one thing encroaches on the singing robins and sound of the river—the rumble from logging trucks hidden in the woods across the river. However, they do not drive at night.

Campsites, facilities: The campground has five RV or tent campsites. RVs are limited to small vehicles. Trailers are not recommended on the Thompson River Road. Facilities include picnic tables, fire rings with grills, and a vault toilet, but no drinking water. Bring your own water, or if you plan to use the river water, boil or purify it before drinking. Pack out your trash. Leashed pets are permitted. A wheelchair-accessible toilet is available.

Reservations, fees: Reservations are not accepted. Campsites cost $5. Cash or check. Open late May–late September.

Directions: From Thompson Falls, drive five miles northeast on Highway 200. On the west side of the Thompson River, turn north onto the paved Thompson River Road and drive four miles. Turn right into the campground. (Stay off the east side road. It sees logging trucks kicking up dust and turns into a private road.)

GPS Coordinates: N 47° 37.165' W 115° 11.344'

Contact: Lolo National Forest, Plains/Thompson Falls Ranger District, P.O. Box 429, Plains, MT 598859, 406/826-3821, www.fs.fed.us/r1/lolo/.

64 CLARK MEMORIAL

Scenic rating: 7

on the Thompson River in Lolo National Forest

Located at 2,400 feet in elevation one mile north of Copper King, Clark Memorial Campground sits on the Thompson River near a memorial grove of huge western red cedars, which grow only in areas that receive abundant moisture. The Thompson River cuts through the steep-walled canyon, home to bighorn sheep. You can launch rafts and kayaks from the campground to paddle Class II–III rapids down to Copper King or all the way to the Clark Fork River. The river, which usually runs clear even during high water, produces only small 8- to 12-inch trout.

Contrary to the heavily forested Copper King, this campground sits more in the open, with views of the rugged mountains that pinch the river. Unfortunately, the open area also allows for watching loud logging trucks on the road across the river. Luckily, they don't drive at night. The grassy campground lines the river, with the site at the south end claiming the most privacy.

Campsites, facilities: The campground has five RV or tent campsites. Trailers are not recommended on the Thompson River Road due to its skinny width and sharp corners, and the campground is suitable only for small RVs. Facilities include picnic tables, fire rings with grills, a vault toilet, but no drinking water. Bring your own water, or if you plan to use the river water, boil or purify it before drinking. Leashed pets are permitted. A wheelchair-accessible toilet is available.

Reservations, fees: Reservations are not accepted. Campsites cost $5. Cash or check only. Open late May–late September.

Directions: From Thompson Falls, drive six miles northeast on Highway 200. On the west side of the Thompson River, turn north onto the paved Thompson River Road and drive five miles. The road turns to dirt and narrows just past Copper King. A few pullouts sit along the road to deal with oncoming vehicles. (Stay off the east side road. It sees logging trucks kicking up dust and turns into a private road.)

GPS Coordinates: N 47° 37.937' W 115° 10.417'

Contact: Lolo National Forest, Plains/Thompson Falls Ranger District, P.O. Box 429, Plains, MT 598859, 406/826-3821, www.fs.fed.us/r1/lolo/.

65 CASCADE

Scenic rating: 7

on the Clark Fork River in Lolo National Forest

BEST (

Across the road from the Clark Fork River, sitting at 2,900 feet, Cascade is the only designated campground on Highway 135, so it frequently fills up—especially with its close proximity to a hot spring resort. Four miles east of the campground, Quinn's Hot Springs

welcomes drop-ins for about $9 per person. Sink into the two hot tubs and four soaking pools before hopping in the 65-degree cold pool. The resort, which is open daily and refills the pools nightly rather than using chemicals, also has a swimming pool, a restaurant, and tavern. Five miles west of the campground, a fishing access allows for launching drift boats, rafts, canoes, and kayaks onto the Clark Fork River. The Cascade National Recreation Trail begins at the campground, and a one-mile nature walk leads to Cascade Falls overlook and views of the Clark Fork River.

Adjacent to the paved highway, the four-acre campground is tucked under a shady canopy of ponderosa pines and larch. The narrow canyon walls shade the campground until filtered sun arrives late in the morning. Both truck and train noise enters the campground. Low brush lends some privacy, but you'll see a few neighboring campers. If the campground fills up, locate free dispersed, primitive campsites between the campground and the fishing access. As long as no sign is posted banning camping, it is legal to camp at large in the national forest.

Campsites, facilities: The campground has nine RV or tent campsites. Facilities include picnic tables, fire grates, vault toilets, and drinking water. Pack out your trash. Leashed pets are permitted. A wheelchair-accessible toilet is available.

Reservations, fees: Reservations are not accepted. Campsites cost $10. Cash or check. Open late May–late September.

Directions: From St. Regis drive 17 miles northeast on Highway 135, or from Paradise drive south on Highway 200 across the Clark Fork River and turn west onto Highway 135 for 6.2 miles. Turn south into the campground.

GPS Coordinates: N 47° 18.385' W 114° 49.504'

Contact: Lolo National Forest, Plains/Thompson Falls Ranger District, P.O. Box 429, Plains, MT 598859, 406/826-3821, www.fs.fed.us/r1/lolo/.

66 HOLLAND LAKE

Scenic rating: 10

in Swan Valley in Flathead National Forest

BEST (

At an elevation of 4,150 feet near the southern end of the Swan Valley, Holland Lake provides a leap-off point into the Bob Marshall Wilderness. Both backpackers and horse-packing trips depart from here. Surrounded by the rugged Swan Mountains, the lake itself is very popular for boating, waterskiing, fishing, and paddling, but weekdays and off-season offer quieter exploration. Hiking trails depart right from the campground. A 1.5-mile easy hike hugs the lake to Holland Falls, roaring and spewing mist. A steep 3.5-mile trail climbs to Holland Lookout for dramatic views into the wilderness area, and a 12-mile loop ties together Upper Holland Lake and the smaller Sapphire Lake in an alpine bowl of wildflowers and huckleberry bushes. The historic lodge—which has a restaurant and bar—also rents canoes and kayaks and leads horseback trail rides. Owl Creek Packer Camp, with two stock ramps, vault toilets, and drinking water, sits 0.5 mile away.

The quiet campground snuggles under a fir forest canopy on the lake and adjacent to the rustic Holland Lake Lodge, with trails that run between the campsites and the lake. Lakefront sites include 1, 2, 3, 5, 6, 18, 20, 21, 23, 30, 32, 34, and 36. Some of the sites are very private due to thick foliage; others are more open with minimal understory.

Campsites, facilities: The campground has 40 RV or tent campsites. RVs are limited to 50 feet. Facilities include picnic tables, fire rings with grills, flush and vault toilets, drinking water, campground hosts, a boat ramp, a disposal station, and garbage service. Leashed pets are permitted. A wheelchair-accessible toilet is available.

Reservations, fees: Reservations are accepted (877/444-6777, www.recreation.gov). Campsites cost $15. Cash or check. Open mid-May–September.

Directions: From the start of Highway 83 two miles north of Bigfork, drive 35.2 miles south past Condon to Holland Lake Road. From Seeley Lake, drive 19.3 miles north on Highway 83 to Holland Lake Road. Turn east and drive 2.5 miles to the Y, and turn left. Follow the signs to the campground.

GPS Coordinates: N 47° 27.099' W 113° 36.526'

Contact: Flathead National Forest, Swan Lake Ranger District, 200 Ranger Station Rd., Bigfork, MT 59911, 406/837-7500, www.fs.fed.us/r1/flathead/.

67 LINDBERGH LAKE

Scenic rating: 7

in Swan Valley in Flathead National Forest

Southwest of Holland Lake, at an elevation of 4,400 feet, Lindbergh Lake draws fewer campers. It still sees its share of water-skiers, anglers, and paddlers, but the four-mile-long lake is nearly twice as big as Holland Lake, allowing more room to spread out. A boat ramp allows launching onto the lake. Streams from the Mission Mountain Wilderness feed the 815-acre lake, which sits at 4,494 feet in elevation and fosters several trout species plus mountain whitefish, kokanee salmon, northern pike minnow, longnose suckers, and yellow perch. Recent years have seen stocking of kokanee and westslope cutthroat trout. The campground lends itself well for mountain biking with a maze of old logging roads in the area. Most of the hiking trails require dirt road drives to get to the trailheads, but they lead to high clear lakes in the Mission Mountain Wilderness.

The campground tucks under a thick forest of spindly conifers, with plenty of shrubs and small trees lending privacy to most of the campsites. The sites are small but spread out. Due to the distance from the highway, the campground is quiet.

Campsites, facilities: The campground has 22 RV or tent campsites. The maximum length for RVs is 20 feet. Facilities include picnic tables, fire rings with grills, and vault toilets. No drinking water is available. Bring your own, or haul it from the lake. Be sure to purify or boil the lake water before use. Pack out your trash. Leashed pets are permitted. A wheelchair-accessible toilet is available.

Reservations, fees: Reservations not accepted. The campground has been free, but the Forest Service plans to start charging a fee for camping. Open May–September.

Directions: From the start of Highway 83 two miles north of Bigfork, drive 36.5 miles south past Condon to Forest Road 79. From Seeley Lake, drive 18 miles north on Highway 83 to Forest Road 79. Turn west and drive four miles to the campground road (79C).

GPS Coordinates: N 47° 24.241' W 113° 43.588'

Contact: Flathead National Forest, Swan Lake Ranger District, 200 Ranger Station Rd., Bigfork, MT 59911, 406/837-7500, www.fs.fed.us/r1/flathead/.

68 RAINY LAKE

Scenic rating: 8

north of Seeley Lake in Lolo National Forest

Accessed via a short, dirt forest road, Rainy Lake is a favorite of those who like small, primitive off-beat campgrounds. The campground sits at 4,100 feet on the divide at the southern end of the Swan Valley. Although the campground itself holds debris from recent thinning in the form of stumps and small slash piles, and some of the campsites show excessive wear, the small lake attracts float tube anglers and visitors who want to lounge on the grassy shore with the snow-covered Swan Range reflecting in the water. The lake is also close enough to the parking lot to carry lightweight canoes and kayaks down to the shore.

Three of the walk-in sites sit back in the mixed forest, two with peek-a-boo views of the lake. But the one walk-in site on the peninsula commands a view not only of most of the lake, but also the Swan Mountains. The one small, open drive-up site has no views. Except for the drive-up site, the campsites are spread out, but all are within sight of each other, which makes for little privacy but a very quiet location.

Campsites, facilities: The campground has one RV or tent campsite suitable only for a small RV and four walk-in tent campsites. Facilities include picnic tables, fire rings with grills, a vault toilet, and bear pole. The walk-in sites provide large flat areas for tents. No drinking water is available; if you plan to use lake water, boil or purify it before drinking. Leashed pets are permitted. Pack out your trash.

Reservations, fees: Reservations are not accepted. Camping is free. Open May–November.

Directions: Turn west off Highway 83 at milepost 27 onto Forest Road 4357. Drive 0.5 mile on the dirt road to where the road loops in a dead end.

GPS Coordinates: N 47° 20.205' W 113° 35.603'

Contact: Lolo National Forest, Seeley Lake Ranger District, HC-31, Box 3200, Seeley Lake, MT 59868, 406/677-2233, www.fs.fed.us/r1/lolo/.

69 LAKE ALVA

Scenic rating: 7

north of Seeley Lake in Lolo National Forest

Located north of Seeley Lake, Alva is one of the string of lakes tied along the upper Clearwater River. Sitting at 4,198 feet in elevation, the 298-acre lake is fed by cold water from the Mission Mountains and the Swan Mountains. With a small grassy swimming beach, a boat launch, and boat trailer parking, the lake yields four species of trout plus an array of lake fish—redside shiners, suckers, and yellow perch—and has been stocked with westslope cutthroat trout and kokanee. The lake also harbors nesting loons—both at the head and on the tiny island. To see the knife-like Swan Range, paddle or boat to the opposite shore of the lake. (Wish the campground had those views!) For hiking, drive five miles up the Clearwater Loop Road 4370, following the signs, to hike the Clearwater Lake Loop trail. The loop road also works for mountain biking.

Sitting between the highway and the lake, Alva picks up road noise through the trees. Large spruces, larches, and subalpine firs tower over the campground, which sprinkles its campsites around three paved loops with paved parking pads set above the lake. The loop nearest the lake holds two group campsites. Due to the thick foliage, none of the campsites has a view of the lake, but the sites are private and loaded with clumps of bear grass. The campground offers interpretive programs; check the bulletin board for the schedule.

Campsites, facilities: The campground has 41 RV or tent campsites. RVs are limited to 22 feet long. Facilities include picnic tables, fire rings with grills, vault toilets, drinking water, garbage service, and campground hosts. Leashed pets are permitted. A wheelchair-accessible toilet is available.

Reservations, fees: Reservations are not accepted, except for the two group campsites (877/444-6777, www.recreation.gov). Campsites cost $10. Each extra vehicle costs $5. Cash or check. Open Memorial Day weekend–September.

Directions: At milepost 26.1 on Highway 83 north of Seeley Lake, turn west on Forest Road 1098 for 0.4 mile to enter the campground. GPS Coordinates: N 47° 19.470' W 113° 35.078'

Contact: Lolo National Forest, Seeley Lake Ranger District, HC-31, Box 3200, Seeley Lake, MT 59868, 406/677-2233, www.fs.fed.us/r1/lolo/.

70 LAKESIDE

Scenic rating: 7

north of Seeley Lake in Lolo National Forest

As the name implies, the Lakeside campground sits at 4,100 feet right on the side of a lake—Lake Alva. The campground may be listed on older maps as Old Alva Campground. Lakeside also squeezes in the Clearwater River Valley between the Alva and Inez campgrounds. With shoreline campsites, launching hand-carried watercraft is easy. Those who want to launch larger boats must do so at Alva Campground. Fishing is available. The lake also harbors nesting loons—both at the head and on the tiny island. To see the knife-like Swan Range, paddle or boat to the opposite shore of the lake. For hiking, drive five miles up Clearwater Loop Road 4370, following the signs, to hike the Clearwater Lake Loop trail. The loop road also works for mountain biking.

While you can camp overlooking the lake, only a short steep slope separates the sites from the highway, which is within earshot and sight. The long, skinny campground is in two parts, connected by a 0.3-mile single-lane, narrow, curvy dirt road with a few pullouts in case vehicles meet. Trailers will have trouble backing up on this stretch. The campground road dead-ends in a small loop. Each section has three campsites and a vault toilet. The large sites are separated from each other under fir trees. Site 2 is a walk-in site on a shaded bluff overlooking the lake. Handicapped-accessible site 3 is very large, with extra tables and parking spots. Sites 4, 5, and 6 require driving the narrow road to the end of the campground.

Campsites, facilities: The campground has five RV or tent campsites and one walk-in tent campsite. Only small RVs are suitable; trailers are not recommended. Facilities include picnic tables, fire rings with grills, vault toilets, and garbage service. Bring your own water; or if you use lake water, boil or purify it first.

Leashed pets are permitted. A wheelchair-accessible toilet is available.

Reservations, fees: Reservations are not accepted. Campsites cost $10. Each extra vehicle costs $5. Cash or check. Open Memorial Day weekend–September.

Directions: From Highway 83 north of Seeley Lake, turn west into the entrance of the campground at milepost 25.6.

GPS Coordinates: N 47° 18.903' W 113° 34.705'

Contact: Lolo National Forest, Seeley Lake Ranger District, HC-31, Box 3200, Seeley Lake, MT 59868, 406/677-2233, www.fs.fed.us/r1/lolo/.

71 LAKE INEZ

Scenic rating: 7

north of Seeley Lake in Lolo National Forest

Tucked between the Swan and Mission Mountains two miles south of Lake Alva sits another one of the Clearwater River's chain of lakes. At 4,100 feet, the 288-acre Lake Inez is popular for swimming, fishing, boating, and waterskiing. Get out on the lake for the views of the southern Swan Mountains. Due to its location, it has the same fishing, mountain-biking, and hiking options as Lake Alva. For those with canoes to paddle its willow-laden north shore, bird-watching is prime. Look for red-necked grebes, bald eagles, rufous hummingbirds, American redstarts, flycatchers, and sparrows. The lakes along this chain make good habitat for loons, too, with suitable nesting areas protected from human disturbance and a substantial supply of fish. Listen in the morning or evening for the haunting call of the loon. About 60 pairs of loons nest in this chain of lakes, but only about 30 offspring survive.

The campground sits at the north end of Lake Inez on a dirt road. Find the primitive boat ramp with small grassy parking for boat trailers at the campground's north end as well

as the three main campsites with the vault toilet. Undeveloped sites 4 and 5 sit farther south on the road, with lake views. Site 5 only has parking for a small vehicle.

Campsites, facilities: The campground has three RV or tent campsites, plus two primitive campsites. Facilities include fire rings with grills at all campsites, but picnic tables and a vault toilet for the first three campsites. Drinking water is not available. Bring your own, or if you plan to use lake water, purify it by filtering or boiling. Pack out your trash. Leashed pets are permitted.

Reservations, fees: Reservations are not accepted. Camping is free. Open May–November.

Directions: From Highway 83 north of Seeley Lake, the campground has two entrances, neither marked by obvious signs on the road. Turn west into the north entrance at milepost 24.1 or into the south entrance at milepost 22.9.

GPS Coordinates: N 47° 17.701' W 113° 34.111'

Contact: Lolo National Forest, Seeley Lake Ranger District, HC-31, Box 3200, Seeley Lake, MT 59868, 406/677-2233, www.fs.fed.us/r1/lolo/.

72 SEELEY LAKE

Scenic rating: 9

on Seeley Lake in Lolo National Forest

At 4,000 feet between the Swan and Mission Mountains, Seeley Lake is the largest of the upper Clearwater River's lakes. The 1,031-acre lake cranks with the noise of water-skiers, Jet Skiers, and power boaters. The big picnic area spans a long grassy beach that includes a cordoned-off swimming area, cement boat launch, and boat trailer parking. The campground also attracts quiet paddlers because of the Clearwater Canoe Trail, which feeds into the lake from the Clearwater River. The

© BECKY LOMAX

paddling the Clearwater Canoe Trail to Seeley Lake in Lolo National Forest

Campsites, facilities: The campground has 29 RV or tent campsites. The maximum recommended trailer length is 32 feet. Facilities include picnic tables, fire rings, flush toilets, drinking water, garbage service, a swimming beach, and a boat launch. Leashed pets are permitted. A wheelchair-accessible toilet is available.

Reservations, fees: Reservations are not accepted. Campsites cost $10. Each extra vehicle costs $5. Cash or check. Open Memorial Day weekend–Labor Day.

Directions: From milepost 14 on Highway 83 in the town of Seeley Lake, turn west onto Boy Scout Road and drive 3.2 miles. Turn right into the campground.

GPS Coordinates: N 47° 11.560' W 113° 31.214'

Contact: Lolo National Forest, Seeley Lake Ranger District, HC-31, Box 3200, Seeley Lake, MT 59868, 406/677-2233, www.fs.fed.us/r1/lolo/.

3.5-mile trail paddles through a dense willow marsh full of the music of songbirds such as ruby crowned kinglets. Located on the west side of the lake just opposite the River Point campground, Seeley Lake campground grabs a bigger view of the south Swan Mountains from the beach than other campgrounds in the area. The popular campground fills up on weekends and holidays.

A paved road leads up the west side of the lake to the 11-acre campground. The campground's road is narrow and curvy; large trees pinch the corners as it winds through the two loops. While the road is paved, the parking aprons are mostly dirt. Large spruces, monster larches, and subalpine firs shade most of the campground. The sites have little privacy, but they are very roomy. None of the campsites sit right on the lake, but sites 28 and 29 are right across from the beach. Sites 5, 7, and 8 are more private because they're on a side inlet from the lake.

73 BIG LARCH

Scenic rating: 8

on Seeley Lake in Lolo National Forest

Big Larch is a busy campground, thanks to its location one mile from the town of Seeley Lake and right on the east side adjacent to the highway. At 4,000 feet, it sits on the largest of the upper Clearwater River's lakes and offers fishing, boating, waterskiing, paddling, and swimming. Two sandy swimming beaches sprawl along the shoreline. The campground also has a 0.5-mile nature trail. Loaded with bird-watching, the Clearwater Canoe Trail is easy to access from this side of the lake as the put-in and take-out sit 5–10 minutes up the highway. The campground also sits closest to the most popular trail in the area—the Morrell Falls National Recreation Trail. Located seven miles up Morrell Creek Drive, the easy-walking 2.5-mile trail (open to mountain bikers and hikers) wanders past a series of small lakes and ponds before finishing at the 90-foot-tall falls. The trail sees a steady stream of hikers on weekends. Forest roads attract mountain bikers.

A paved road wanders through the campground with a mix of dirt, gravel, and paved parking aprons in the three overlapping loops. As the name suggests, huge larch trees along with some equally large Ponderosa pines shade much of the campground. In this type of forest, however, little underbrush survives, so most of the campsites are open beneath the trees, affording very little privacy. Sites 1–30 in the first two loops have shorter but wider campsites. Sites 34–49 are longer but narrower. Check the bulletin board at the check-in station for evening interpretive programs.

Campsites, facilities: The campground has 50 RV or tent campsites. Trailers are limited to 32 feet. Facilities include picnic tables, fire rings with grills, vault toilets, drinking water, garbage service, a large swimming beach, and a concrete boat launch. Leashed pets are permitted. A wheelchair-accessible toilet is available.

Reservations, fees: Reservations are not accepted. Campsites cost $10. Each extra vehicle costs $5. Cash or check. Open Memorial Day weekend–September.

Directions: From Seeley Lake, drive one mile north on Highway 83. Turn west at the signed entrance into the campground.

GPS Coordinates: N 47° 11.533' W 113° 29.638'

Contact: Lolo National Forest, Seeley Lake Ranger District, HC-31, Box 3200, Seeley Lake, MT 59868, 406/677-2233, www.fs.fed.us/r1/lolo/.

74 RIVER POINT

Scenic rating: 9

on Seeley Lake in Lolo National Forest

Of the three campgrounds on Seeley Lake in between the Mission and Swan Mountains,

the eight-acre River Point is the smallest. It sits at 4,000 feet at the foot of the lake where the broad, slow-moving Clearwater River exits the lake. With the proximity to the town of Seeley Lake, the campground is convenient for running to town for groceries, gas, gift shops, and restaurants. This campground is also the closest to Seeley Lake's golf course south of town. The Morrell Falls National Recreation Trail is within an 11-mile drive. The day-use area of the campground sits on both Seeley Lake and the Clearwater River. Views from the beach include the south Swan Peaks. The campground, however, only borders the river. Despite the lake frontage, no boat launch ramp is available. Use the one at Seeley Lake Campground 1.2 miles north. However, you can launch rafts, canoes, and kayaks from the river campsites, plus the beach in the day-use area.

A paved road leads to and through the one-loop campground, which has paved parking aprons. Large spruces, larches, and subalpine firs shade most of the roomy campsites, but with little understory and only short brush, the campsites have little privacy. Sites 11, 12, 14, 17, 19, and 20 sit on the river.

Campsites, facilities: The campground has 26 RV or tent campsites. Trailers are limited to 22 feet. Facilities include picnic tables, fire rings with grills, vault toilets, drinking water, garbage service, and a swimming beach. Leashed pets are permitted. A wheelchair-accessible toilet is available.

Reservations, fees: Reservations are not accepted. Campsites cost $10. Each extra vehicle costs $5. Cash or check. Open Memorial Day weekend–Labor Day.

Directions: In the town of Seeley Lake at milepost 14 on Highway 83, turn west onto Boys Scout Road on the north side of Pyramid Lumber Company. Drive two miles to the campground, which sits on the north side of the road.

GPS Coordinates: N 47° 11.252' W 113° 30.889'

Contact: Lolo National Forest, Seeley Lake

Ranger District, HC-31, Box 3200, Seeley Lake, MT 59868, 406/677-2233, www.fs.fed.us/r1/lolo/.

75 PLACID LAKE STATE PARK

🚶 🏊 🛶 🚤 🎣 🐴 ♿ 🚐 ⛺

Scenic rating: 8

south of Seeley Lake in Lolo National Forest

At 4,100 feet, Placid Lake State Park sits on one of the smaller pools in the upper Clearwater River's chain of lakes. The 31-acre lake is tiny in comparison to its northern sisters, but still attracts boaters for waterskiing, fishing, sightseeing, paddling, and wildlife-watching. Look for ospreys fishing, but keep your distance from nesting loons. Because private homes surround much of the shoreline, the water hops with Jet Skiers and boat noise (not exactly placid!) on weekends and hot August days. A short foot trail departs from site 18 to tour the shoreline. The boat docks include slips for 13 boats.

The 32-acre campground sits on the shore of Placid Lake, with the campsites tucked on three loops in the trees. A wide, potholed dirt road leads to the campground, but the campground road and parking pads are paved. Sites 1, 2, 3, 5, 6, 7, 12, 16, and 17 sit adjacent to the beach. Large ponderosas and firs partly shade campsites, but the lack of undergrowth yields little privacy.

Campsites, facilities: The campground has 40 RV or tent campsites. RVs are limited to 25 feet. Up to eight people and two camping units (vehicles or tents) are allowed per site. Facilities include picnic tables, fire grates, flush toilets, pay showers, drinking water, a disposal station, a swimming beach, boat docks, boat trailer parking, and a concrete boat ramp. Firewood is for sale. Leashed pets are permitted. A wheelchair-accessible toilet is available, and sites 16 and 17 are reserved for disabled campers.

Reservations, fees: No reservations are accepted. Day use costs $5 per vehicle for nonresidents while Montana residents get in for free. Campsites cost $15. Seniors and campers with disabilities pay $7.50. Hookups cost an addition $5. Cash or check. Open May–November.

Directions: From the Clearwater Junction (look for the big cow at the junction of Highways 83 and 200), drive 10 miles north on Highway 83. From Seeley Lake, drive Highway 83 south for three miles. Turn west onto the Placid Lake Road at milepost 10.2, and drive 2.7 miles. At the campground sign, turn left, then make an immediate right to reach the entrance in 0.3 mile.

GPS Coordinates: N 47° 7.102' W 113° 30.147'

Contact: Montana Fish, Wildlife, and Parks, Region 1, 490 N. Meridian Rd., Kalispell, MT 59901, 406/752-5501, http://fwp.mt.gov.

76 SALMON LAKE STATE PARK

🚶 🏊 🛶 🚤 🎣 🐴 ♿ 🚐 ⛺

Scenic rating: 8

south of Seeley Lake in Lolo National Forest

At 3,900 feet, the 631-acre Salmon Lake is the last lake in the chain of the Clearwater lakes. Small steep-walled mountains constrict the valley into a narrow channel that holds the lake, forming a natural impoundment for the Clearwater River. A few islands—some with private homes—also sit in the lake, which is popular for fishing, boating, paddling, and waterskiing. The 42-acre long, narrow park has separate entrances for the campground and day use area, which holds the cement boat ramp, boat trailer parking, 60-foot boat dock, and cordoned-off swimming beach. A foot trail with lupines, arrowleaf balsamroot, and shooting stars in spring connects the campground loop with the day-use area.

North of the day-use area, the campground

squeezes between the lake and highway, with most of the campsites in one loop under firs and larch. Sites 1, 2, and 21 sit closest to the lake. Sites 22 and 23 sit in the old boat ramp area on the beach. Sites 1, 2, 4, 5, and 7 have lake views. Sites 10–15 sit adjacent to the highway, but given how narrow the campground is, no one is far from the lake nor the highway noise. The amphitheater hosts evening interpretive programs.

Campsites, facilities: The campground has 20 RV or tent campsites. RVs are limited to 25 feet. Facilities include picnic tables, fire rings with grills, flush toilets, pay showers, drinking water, a disposal station, campground hosts, a swimming beach, and a boat launch. Firewood is for sale. Leashed pets are permitted. A wheelchair-accessible toilet is available, and the ADA site has electrical hookups.

Reservations, fees: No reservations are accepted. Day use costs $5 per vehicle for nonresidents but is free for Montana residents. Campsites cost $15. Seniors and campers with disabilities are charged $7.50. Hookups cost $5 more. Cash or check. Open May–November.

Directions: From the Clearwater Junction (look for the big cow at the junction of Highways 83 and 200), drive seven miles north on Highway 83. From Seeley Lake, drive Highway 83 south for six miles. At milepost 7, turn west into the campground. The day-use entrance is at milepost 6.5.

GPS Coordinates: N 47° 5.542' W 113° 23.831'

Contact: Montana Fish, Wildlife, and Parks, Region 1, 490 N. Meridian Rd., Kalispell, MT 59901, 406/752-5501, http://fwp.mt.gov.

ROCKY MOUNTAIN FRONT

© BECKY LOMAX

BEST CAMPGROUNDS

In eastern Montana, the sage-scented prairie

churns forever. With very few trees, it rolls westward, broken only by a pot-hole pond here or a river there. But in one abrupt sweep, the Rocky Mountain Front pops up like a wall, looming as monstrous snow-clad purple peaks. For campers, the Front yields a wondrous combination of campgrounds where the flat prairie collides with the rugged peaks of the Continental Divide.

The open prairie dotted with cow towns offers wind-blown places to camp along reservoirs, while long river valleys snake into the mountains with shaded, more-protected campgrounds. The Front attracts campers for fishing, boating, hiking, horseback riding, hunting, and mountain biking. It also acts as a gateway into the Bob Marshall Wilderness Area, where 9,000-foot-high summits flank a towering 22-mile-long, 1,000-foot-high limestone escarpment called the Chinese Wall.

Prepare for weather extremes while camping and recreating on the Front. High winds contort ridgeline trees into avant garde sculptures, blow trains off their tracks in winter, and cause white-knuckled driving in RVs. The Front also fluctuates wildly in temperatures, having set records for swinging up to 100 degrees in 24 hours, and Rogers Pass claims fame as one of the top 10 coldest spots in the world.

How ironic that such a harsh environment produces quirks that sustain abundant wildlife. The Front's winds turn it into one of the largest golden eagle migratory flyways in North America. The national forests, game preserves, and wildlife refuges burgeon with elk, bighorn sheep, deer, grizzly bears, mountain lions, coyotes, pronghorn antelope, and birds.

From the Blackfeet Reservation in the north to the Canyon Ferry Reservoir in the south, large tracts of unpopulated public land with campgrounds flank towns. Helena, Montana's capital, houses only 28,000 people — a population comparable to 3 percent of the downtown San Francisco population. Great Falls, which holds double the population of Helena, is the largest city in the area, but most of the Front's population is centered in tiny towns like Choteau (pronounced "SHOW-toe"), which has a mere 1,800 residents.

Campers exploring the Rocky Mountain Front find themselves confined to minimal roads. Only one freeway (I-15) runs north to south through the prairie, linking up Great Falls with Helena. A narrow, more-scenic two-lane highway (Highway 89) that requires several hours to drive parallels the freeway farther west, connecting the tiny towns closer to the Front mountain ranges. Routes over the Continental Divide dwindle to two: Highway 200 squeezes over Rogers Pass north of Helena, and Highway 12 scoots even higher over MacDonald Pass west of Helena. Beyond that, the more-common paved, skinny two-laners and the more-pervasive washboard gravel or potholed dirt routes comprise the web of the Front's roadways to reach campgrounds.

On the Front, waterways draw the most campers. Upper Missouri River dams create reams of reservoirs, each holding shoreline campgrounds that fill on hot summer days with water-skiers, sailors, canoeists, Jet Skiers, and swimmers. Holter Lake butts up against the Beartooth Wildlife Management Area, providing opportunities for watching elk and raptors. Hauser Lake forms the entrance to Gates of the Mountains Wilderness, the route of Lewis and Clark. Canyon Ferry Lake, the largest, sees the most use of any lake in the state. Anglers go after its rainbow trout, walleye, perch, and ling, as do the bald eagles that nest here.

Those looking for more remote places to camp wrestle the bumpy dirt roads that creep into the Lewis and Clark or Helena National Forest. The forests form several doorways to the immense Bob Marshall Wilderness Complex — a roadless area the size of Rhode Island. The wilderness is crisscrossed with hiking and horse-packing trails that snake past bighorn sheep herds and climb through wildflower fields to precipice-clinging lookouts. Streams teem with native trout, and big game attracts hunters. Front country campers find Forest Service campgrounds the norm, rather than manicured RV parks.

The Rocky Mountain Front is unique. From its glimmering peaks to its golden prairie echoing with the lone cry of red-tailed hawk, it yields a rare beauty that hasn't been marred by the creep of million-dollar homes.

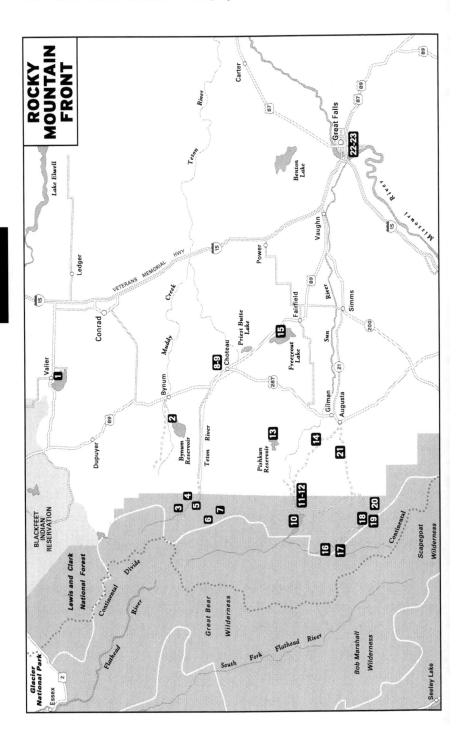

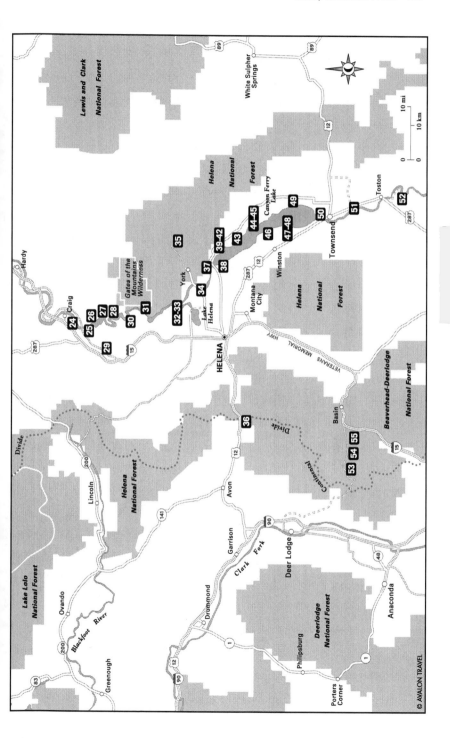

© AVALON TRAVEL

◼ LAKE FRANCES

🚶♿🚴🏊🎣🚣⛴️❄️🏠🐕🚗⛺

Scenic rating: 7

in Valier on the Blackfeet Indian Reservation

At an elevation of 3,800 feet on the prairie on the Blackfeet Indian Reservation, Lake Frances attracts campers for water recreation. In summer, swimming, fishing, boating, waterskiing, sailing, windsurfing, and Jet Skiing are favored. In winter, ice fishing and snowmobiling are popular. The lake has three boat ramps and docks—on the east end, in Valier, and on the west end—but as water levels drop in late summer, sometimes launching can be difficult. Anglers go after walleye, northern pike, and yellow perch. From the hiking and biking trail along the lakeshore, you get a view of the Rocky Mountains in the distance.

The campground is composed of three interconnected loops, all with back-in parking pads. Eleven sites sit right on the shoreline, but several others also have lake views. Perimeter trees provide spots of shade in the sunny campground. Sites are close together, offering little privacy, but with its location across the little-used air strip from town and away from the highway, the campground is quiet. An additional overflow primitive campground with only a pit toilet is at the southeast end of the lake.

Campsites, facilities: The campground has 50 RV campsites that can accommodate large RVs and 10 primitive tent campsites. Facilities include picnic tables, fire rings with grills, flush toilets, a disposal station, garbage service, a boat ramp, a fish-cleaning station, and a playground. Leashed pets are permitted.

Reservations, fees: Reservations are not accepted. Campsites cost $15 for electrical hookups; tent sites cost $7. Cash or check. Open year-round.

Directions: From Highway 44 on the west end of Valier, turn south onto Teton Avenue, which becomes Lake Frances Road. Drive 0.9 mile to the campground entrance on the right. To find the primitive overflow campground on the lake's southeast end, drive 2.2 miles east of Valier on Highway 44 and turn south onto Division Street for 2.1 miles. The campground is on the right just before the dam.

GPS Coordinates: N 48° 18.046' W 112° 15.591'

Contact: Valier Area Development Corporation, P.O. Box 568, Valier, MT 59486, 406/279-3600.

◼ BYNUM RESERVOIR

🏊🎣⛴️🚣🐾🏠♿⛺

Scenic rating: 7

west of Bynum northwest of Choteau

The 3,205-acre Bynum Reservoir is one of the myriad of small lakes dotting the prairie of the Rocky Mountain Front. Sitting at 4,198 feet in elevation west of the small village of Bynum, the lake draws anglers for its rainbow trout and yellow perch. It also contains walleye, but a fish consumption advisory is in effect for that species here due to mercury buildup. A concrete boat ramp is available, but it is unusable during drought conditions. Contact the Region 4 office for the reservoir's current water levels. Find a small general store, post office, and the Two Medicine Dinosaur Center in Bynum. The center displays bones from the world's longest dinosaur, a model skeleton of a seismosaurus, and the first baby dinosaur remains found in North America. The Blackleaf Wildlife Management Area—home to mountain goats, elk, and golden eagles—is about 25 minutes to the west.

The campground is primitive and part of the fishing access site run by the state. The sites line up along the shore of the reservoir in a hot, sunny, treeless, grassy area along the dirt campground road. The campground and lake yield expansive views of the Front range peaks in the distance, but when winds crop up, no trees are available as windbreaks. The campground is far enough away from the highway that the only sounds you'll hear are the wind, the waterfowl, and sometimes the western chorus frog. When water levels drop low in August, the rim becomes dusty.

Campsites, facilities: The campground has four RV and tent campsites that can accommodate only smaller RVs. Facilities include picnic tables, fire rings with grills, vault toilets, and boat ramp. Pack out your trash. Leashed pets are permitted. A wheelchair-accessible toilet is available.

Reservations, fees: Reservations are not accepted. Campsites cost $7 with a Montana fishing license and $12 without a Montana fishing license. Cash or check. Open year-round.

Directions: From Bynum at the signed turnoff, drive west on the dirt county road for 4.2 miles. Veer left at the signed fork for 0.6 mile, and turn left for 1.2 miles to reach the reservoir. Follow the road 0.6 mile eastward to reach the fishing access site and campground.

GPS Coordinates: N 47° 57.593' W 112° 24.382'

Contact: Montana Fish, Wildlife, and Parks, Region 4, 4600 Giant Springs Rd., Great Falls, MT 59405, 406/454-5840, http://fwp.mt.gov.

3 WEST FORK

Scenic rating: 7

on the West Fork of the Teton River in Lewis and Clark National Forest

At 5,700 feet in elevation, the West Fork campground sits at the confluence of the West Fork with the Teton River in a narrow, forested valley dwarfed by high peaks. Hiking trails with trailheads located within 0.25 mile depart to several destinations. Mount Wright requires a steep four-mile climb to reach the summit and its panoramic wilderness views, bighorn sheep, and mountain goats. Three other trails depart for drainages in the Bob Marshall Wilderness Area—the shortest is the West Fork Trail (#114), which climbs over Teton Pass at the Continental Divide in about seven miles. The wilderness boundary is only one mile from the campground. Brown and rainbow trout as well as mountain whitefish inhabit both the West Fork and the Teton River. The campground is a favorite for hunters in the fall.

The access to reach the forested campground requires long miles of dirt road driving, but the reward is solitude, along with the sound of the West Fork of the Teton River. The Forest Service discourages RVs and trailers from the campground; however, smaller RVs and truck campers will fit on the dirt parking pads and narrow road. Campsites are a mix of shade and partial sun.

Campsites, facilities: The campground has six tent sites that also work for small RVs. Facilities include picnic tables, fire rings with grills, pit toilets, and a hand pump for drinking water. Pack out your trash. Leashed pets are permitted.

Reservations, fees: No reservations are accepted. Camping is free. Open late May–November.

Directions: From four miles north of Choteau, turn off Highway 89 at milepost 46.5, heading west on Teton River Road (also Forest Road 144) toward Teton Pass Ski Area. Drive 33 miles to the campground, climbing up to the ski area and dropping again to the river. (The pavement turns to gravel and dirt, loaded with washboards and potholes, around milepost 18.)

GPS Coordinates: N 47° 57.741' W 112° 48.474'

Contact: Lewis and Clark National Forest, Rocky Mountain Ranger District, 1102 N. Main Ave., P.O. Box 340, Choteau, MT 59422, 406/466-5341, fax 406/466-2237, www.fs.fed.us/r1/lewisclark.

4 ELKO

Scenic rating: 7

on the West Fork of the Teton River in Lewis and Clark National Forest

At 5,300 feet in elevation, Elko Campground sits in the Lewis and Clark National Forest about five air miles east of the boundary of the Bob Marshall Wilderness. The campground isn't necessarily a destination in itself, but works as a good overflow site should Cave Mountain fill up. Across the road from the campground, the exceptionally clear waters of the West Fork of the Teton River contain rainbow, brown, and brook trout. The North Fork Teton River Trail (#107) departs nearby and heads four miles through Box Canyon. It's a cool trail for hot days since it requires fording the river several times. The campground is popular with hunters in fall.

The campground sits very close to the dusty road, although road traffic abates into silence after dark. Two of the sites are well-used, with broad spaces for tents. The third, less-used site is overgrown with thimbleberry and thistle. Tall firs partially shade the campsites, which sit very close together. The site on the right as you drive in sits near a seasonal stream.

Campsites, facilities: The campground has three RV or tent campsites. Due to the uneven, rocky, short parking pads and little turnaround room, only small RVs can squeeze in here. Facilities include picnic tables, fire rings with grills, and a pit toilet. No water is available; bring your own, or if you use river water, boil or purify it first. Pack out your trash. Leashed pets are permitted.

Reservations, fees: No reservations are accepted. Camping is free. Open late May–November.

Directions: From Choteau, drive about four miles north on Highway 89 to milepost 46.5. Turn west onto Teton River Road (Forest Road 144) and drive 27 miles. The pavement will turn to gravel and dirt with copious washboards around milepost 18. The campground is unsigned on the east side of the road.

GPS Coordinates: N 47° 55.476' W 112° 45.792'

Contact: Lewis and Clark National Forest, Rocky Mountain Ranger District, 1102 N. Main Ave., P.O. Box 340, Choteau, MT 59422, 406/466-5341, fax 406/466-2237, www.fs.fed.us/r1/lewisclark.

5 CAVE MOUNTAIN

Scenic rating: 8

on the West Fork of the Teton River in Lewis and Clark National Forest

BEST (

At 5,200 feet in elevation, Cave Mountain Campground sits in the Lewis and Clark National Forest at the confluence of the Middle Fork with the West Fork of Teton River—both trout fisheries in exceptionally clear waters after spring runoff. The Bob Marshall Wilderness is accessed via the Route Creek Trail (#108) over a high pass six miles up the Middle Fork. The trailhead, which is equipped for stock (hitch rails, feeding trough, loading ramp) is a five-minute drive up the road. The same trail also connects with the Lonesome Ridge Trail (#154), which crosses into the South Fork of the Teton River drainage. The campground is popular with hunters in fall.

The quiet campground is surrounded by a rail fence to keep out cattle grazing under permit in the area. Aspens, pines, and firs shade many of the campsites, with low vegetation between them. However, sites are spread out to offer privacy, especially site 14 at the end of the loop. Seven sites overlook the river; the others back up to the hillside. Sites 8, 10, and 12 offer views of the area's dramatic cliffs and better river views. Sites 3 and 4 have spaces for large or multiple tents.

Campsites, facilities: The campground has 14 RV or tent campsites. The gravel back-in

The Teton River flows from the Bob Marshall Wilderness past Cave Mountain Campground on the Rocky Mountain Front.

parking pads can fit RVs up to 50 feet. Facilities include picnic tables, fire rings with grills, vault toilets, and drinking water. Pack out your trash. Leashed pets are permitted. One vault toilet is wheelchair accessible.

Reservations, fees: No reservations are accepted. Campsites cost $6. Cash or check. Open late May–November.

Directions: From Choteau, drive four miles north on Highway 89 to milepost 46.5. Turn west onto Teton River Road (Forest Road 144) and drive 22.6 miles. The pavement will turn to gravel and dirt with copious washboards around milepost 18. At the sign for the campground, turn left and drive for 0.4 mile. The entrance road crosses a one-lane bridge, swings right, crosses a second short bridge, and continues straight past the next junction to the campground entrance on the right. GPS Coordinates: N 47° 53.399' W 112° 43.595'

Contact: Lewis and Clark National Forest, Rocky Mountain Ranger District, 1102 N. Main Ave., P.O. Box 340, Choteau, MT 59422, 406/466-5341, fax 406/466-2237, www.fs.fed.us/r1/lewisclark.

6 MILL FALLS

Scenic rating: 8

on the South Fork of the Teton River in Lewis and Clark National Forest

BEST (

Mill Falls Campground sits in the Lewis and Clark National Forest near the South Fork of the Teton River, a trout fishery. From the campground, you can hike 0.1 mile to its namesake waterfall. A popular trailhead departs 1.5 miles farther up the road for the small scenic alpine Our Lake (2.5 miles) and Headquarters Pass (3 miles), which marks the entrance to the Bob Marshall Wilderness. The Headquarters Pass Trail is also used to scramble up the Class 4 slopes to the summit of Rocky Mountain, one of the highest peaks in the region. The area also is popular for fall hunting.

The tiny, shaded, quiet campground is tucked back off the road. Its entrance looks like a jeep trail, and its narrow, rocky, potholed, rutted road with overhanging branches can only accommodate smaller RVs. Trailers will not have room to turn around. Sites 3 and

4 pair up close together on the right as you drive in. Also close together, sites 1 and 2 sit at the back of the campground, with large tent spaces adjacent to a small creek.

Campsites, facilities: The campground has four RV or tent campsites. The small uneven, rocky parking pads, however, can only fit smaller camper-truck RVs. Facilities include picnic tables, fire rings with grills, and a pit toilet. No drinking water is provided; bring your own. Pack out your trash. Leashed pets are permitted.

Reservations, fees: No reservations are accepted. Camping is free. Open late May–November.

Directions: From Choteau, drive four miles north on Highway 89 to milepost 46.5. Turn west onto Teton River Road (Forest Road 144) and drive 16.9 miles to the Ear Mountain Outstanding Area sign. Turn left onto the gravel road and cross the single-lane bridge. Immediately after the bridge, turn right onto South Fork Road. Drive 3.1 miles, veering right at the Nature Conservancy Pine Butte Guest Ranch sign. Follow the bumpy, washboard Forest Road 109 for 5.4 miles to the signed campground entrance on the right.

GPS Coordinates: N 47° 51.519' W 112° 46.389'

Contact: Lewis and Clark National Forest, Rocky Mountain Ranger District, 1102 N. Main Ave., P.O. Box 340, Choteau, MT 59422, 406/466-5341, fax 406/466-2237, www.fs.fed.us/r1/lewisclark.

⁊ GREEN GULCH

Scenic rating: 7

on the South Fork of the Teton River in Lewis and Clark National Forest

Tiny Green Gulch primitive campground sits at 5,560 feet in elevation in the Lewis and Clark National Forest near the South Fork

of the Teton River. The river is a trout fishery with rainbows, brook, and brown trout. The 12-mile-long Green Gulch Trail (#127) tours a deeply wooded valley after fording the river and reaches a pass at 7,232 feet, where it drops into Sheep Gulch. The area is popular for fall hunting. It also has quick access within a 10-minute drive to the trailhead for Our Lake (2.5 miles) and Headquarters Pass (3 miles)—both much more scenic trails than the Green Gulch trail.

The shaded, quiet, primitive campground is tucked on the Green Gulch side road closer to the South Fork of the Teton River than Mill Falls. Both sites offer ample room for tents, and with only two sites, you get privacy.

Campsites, facilities: The campground has two RV or tent campsites. The small parking pads, however, can only fit smaller RVs and trailers. Facilities include picnic tables, fire rings with grills, and a pit toilet. No drinking water is provided; bring your own. Pack out your trash. Leashed pets are permitted.

Reservations, fees: No reservations are accepted. Camping is free. Open late May–November.

Directions: From Choteau, drive four miles north on Highway 89 to milepost 46.5. Turn west onto Teton River Road (Forest Road 144) and drive 16.9 miles to the Ear Mountain Outstanding Area sign. Turn left onto the gravel road and cross the single-lane bridge. Immediately after the bridge, turn right onto South Fork Road. Drive 3.1 miles, veering right at the Nature Conservancy Pine Butte Guest Ranch sign. Follow the bumpy, washboard Forest Road 109 for 4.4 miles to Green Gulch Road and veer left onto it for 0.2 mile to the campground.

GPS Coordinates: N 47° 51.839' W 112° 45.466'

Contact: Lewis and Clark National Forest, Rocky Mountain Ranger District, 1102 N. Main Ave., P.O. Box 340, Choteau, MT 59422, 406/466-5341, fax 406/466-2237, www.fs.fed.us/r1/lewisclark.

8 CHOTEAU

Scenic rating: 4

in Choteau west of Great Falls

Located in Choteau, the campground is convenient for exploring the town. The community swimming pool is within one mile, and the nine-hole golf course is less than 0.5 mile away, north of the campground across a field. Open daily in summer, the Old Trail Museum on the north end of town includes fossils, Native American artifacts, pioneer history, and wildlife exhibits. Choteau's Rodeo Grounds host rodeo events and music concerts. Eureka Reservoir, eight miles northwest on Teton Canyon Road, provides fishing and boating. Four miles south of town, Freezeout Lake annually draws bird-watchers in March, when the lake crowds with 300,000 snow geese and 10,000 tundra swans on their migration north, but birding is also good in the fall.

The campground sits on the outskirts of town, but right on the highway. However, the route isn't a major trucking thoroughfare, so road noise dwindles at night. A handful of small trees dot the campground, but most of the grassy campsites are open, sunny, and close to each other. Because it lacks trees for windbreaks, the campground can see hefty winds. From the campground, views span pastures and neighboring houses.

Campsites, facilities: The campground has 55 RV and 20 tent campsites. Facilities include picnic tables, fire rings, drinking water, flush toilets, showers, a launderette, a store, a disposal station, a playground, a game room, horseshoe pits, and hookups for sewer, water, and electricity. Leashed pets are permitted.

Reservations, fees: Reservations are accepted. Hookups cost $28–32. Tent sites cost $18. Montana bed tax will be added. Cash, check, or credit card. Open mid-April–mid-November.

Directions: From Choteau at the junction of Highways 89 and 221, drive 0.75 mile east on Highway 221 to the campground. The campground sits on the north side of the road.

GPS Coordinates: N 47° 48.956' W 112° 9.985'

Contact: Choteau Campground, 85 Hwy. 221, Choteau, MT 59422, 406/466-2615 or 800/562-4156.

9 CHOTEAU CITY PARK

Scenic rating: 4

in Choteau west of Great Falls

The city park campground is one block off the downtown main strip in Choteau, an easy option for those bicycling the Rocky Mountain Front. A two-block walk leads to restaurants downtown and the community swimming pool. The nine-hole golf course is less than one mile away. Open daily in summer, the Old Trail Museum on the north end of town includes fossils, Native American artifacts, pioneer history, and wildlife exhibits. Choteau's Rodeo Grounds host rodeo events and music concerts. Eureka Reservoir, eight miles northwest on Teton Canyon Road, provides fishing and boating. Four miles south of town, Freezeout Lake draws bird-watchers in March, when the lake crowds with 300,000 snow geese and 10,000 tundra swans on their migration north, but also offers birding in the fall.

The campground is part of Choteau's city park. Nine of the campsites sit on the hot west side, with views of a warehouse and grain silos and only a few perimeter willow and cottonwood trees for shade. The other five campsites are more secluded, tucked on the east side under bigger, thicker trees next to a tiny creek. Due to the shade, these sites usually have green grass while the others are brown dry grass. A gravel walking path runs through the park. You may want to bring earplugs—the park is only a half block away from the railroad tracks. The campground road is a combination of gravel and pavement, with level sites for tents or RVs.

Campsites, facilities: There are 14 RV and tent campsites. The west-side campsites can accommodate any length of RV. Facilities include picnic tables, a few fire pits or rock fire rings at some of the sites, drinking water, flush toilets, a dump station, and garbage service. Leashed pets are permitted.

Reservations, fees: No reservations are accepted. Campsites cost $8 per night. Open May–September.

Directions: In downtown Choteau, turn east off Highway 89 at the campground sign onto 1st Street NE and drive one block. Turn right at the park sign, drive 0.1 mile, and turn left into the campground. You can also get to the campground entrance via 1st Street SE.

GPS Coordinates: N 47° 48.695' W 112° 10.719'

Contact: Choteau Park and Campground, City of Choteau, P.O. Box 619, Choteau, MT 59422, 406/466-2510.

Trail (#201), which heads along the reservoir's shore. You can mountain bike the trail up to the wilderness boundary (7 miles) and continue on to climb Sun Butte (9.5 miles) for a panoramic view of the area. The Mortimer Gulch National Recreation Trail (7 miles) offers views of Sawtooth Ridge and the reservoir.

The quiet campground's two loops feature partially shaded, partially private campsites. Some are tucked under aspens, others under large Douglas firs. Those in the upper loop tend to have more shade than those in the lower loop. One of the campsites has a pull-through parking pad, but the remainder are paved back-ins.

Campsites, facilities: The campground has 28 RV or tent campsites that can accommodate vehicles up to 48 feet. Facilities include picnic tables, fire rings with grills, vault toilets, and drinking water. Pack out your trash. Leashed

10 MORTIMER GULCH

Scenic rating: 9

on Gibson Reservoir in Lewis and Clark National Forest

Located near 5,000 feet in the Lewis and Clark National Forest, Mortimer Gulch is the only designated campground on the 1,289-acre Gibson Reservoir. The reservoir is surrounded by dramatically steep upthrust ridges that mark the edge of the Front. A steep cement ramp, a dock, and trailer parking aid in launching boats for fishing, sightseeing, and waterskiing. The reservoir also houses rainbow, brook, and westslope cutthroat trout, and arctic grayling. The campground is popular in early summer when the reservoir's water levels are higher; in fall, hunters flock to the campground because it's a seven-mile hike away from the Sun River Game Preserve. A hiking trail drops from the campground to the boat launch area and connects with the North Fork of the Sun River

© BECKY LOMAX

Bighorn sheep are just one of the game species on the Sun River Game Preserve, near Gibson Reservoir.

pets are permitted. A wheelchair-accessible toilet is available.

Reservations, fees: No reservations are accepted. Campsites cost $8. Cash or check. Open late May–November; however, water is turned off after Labor Day.

Directions: Drive out of town on Manix Street in Augusta, which becomes the Sun River Road (Forest Road 108). Drive 3.7 miles to a signed intersection. Turn right and drive 15 miles on dirt, where the road turns to pavement again. Continue driving 6.8 miles on the pavement, which climbs up above the dam. Turn left into the campground at the sign. GPS Coordinates: N 47° 36.748' W 112° 46.133'

Contact: Lewis and Clark National Forest, Rocky Mountain Ranger District, 1102 N. Main Ave., P.O. Box 340, Choteau, MT 59422, 406/466-5341, fax 406/466-2237, www.fs.fed.us/r1/lewisclark.

11 SUN CANYON LODGE
🏃‍♂️🚵‍♀️🚣‍♂️🎣🏊‍♂️🛶🐎🏕️⛷️♿🚐⛺

Scenic rating: 7

east of Gibson Reservoir in Lewis and Clark National Forest

At 4,600 feet in Lewis and Clark Forest, the rustic Sun Canyon Lodge is a bucolic Montana outfitter with trophy antlers on the wall of the octagon 1920s log lodge. The lodge nestles below the towering cliffs one mile south of the North Fork of the Sun River below the Gibson Reservoir dam. The river contains rainbow, brook, and cutthroat trout that can be caught by wade fishing. Within a 10-minute drive to the west, Gibson Reservoir offers lake fishing, hiking and mountain-biking trails, boating, and swimming. Departing from Sun Canyon Lodge, the Home Gulch–Lime Trail (#267, 15 miles) offers spring wildlife-watching opportunities, but more scenic trails depart from the reservoir area.

The campground is part of the Sun Canyon Lodge complex of restaurant, cabins, and corrals, with campsites lined up along the perimeter of a grassy meadow against aspen trees. Its location off the Sun Canyon Road yields quiet, but the campsites are visible from the restaurant and the parking area.

Campsites, facilities: The campground has 10 RV or tent campsites that can accommodate large RVs. Facilities include picnic tables, drinking water, flush toilets, showers, a disposal station, garbage service, a coin-operated launderette, a restaurant, a bar, trail rides, a playground, boat tours, horse corrals, and outfitting services for fishing and hunting. Leashed pets are permitted. A wheelchair-accessible toilet is available.

Reservations, fees: Reservations are accepted. RV camping costs $10 without electrical hookups and $15 with electrical hookups. Tent camping costs $5. Using the disposal station costs $10, and showers cost $3 per person. Cash, check, or credit card. Open May–November.

Directions: From Augusta, follow the signs to Gibson Reservoir. Drive out of town on Manix Street, which becomes Sun River Road (Forest Road 108). Drive 3.7 miles to a signed intersection. Turn right and drive 15 miles on dirt to where the road turns to pavement again. Continue three more miles to the Sun Canyon Lodge sign and turn left, traveling for one more mile. GPS Coordinates: N 47° 36.303' W 112° 43.296'

Contact: Sun Canyon Lodge, P.O. Box 327, Sun River Rd., Augusta, MT 59410, 406/562-3654 or 888/749-3654, www.suncanyonlodge.com.

12 HOME GULCH
🏃‍♂️🚵‍♀️🚣‍♂️🎣🛶🚤🐎🏕️♿🚐⛺

Scenic rating: 7

on Sun River east of Gibson Reservoir in Lewis and Clark National Forest

Located at 4,580 feet in Lewis and Clark National Forest, Home Gulch nestles below the towering cliffs along the North Fork of the Sun River below the Gibson Reservoir dam. Within a five-minute drive, funky Sun Canyon Lodge offers a coin-operated launderette, showers, trail rides, a disposal station, and a cafe displaying the stuffed trophies from local hunts. The campground is popular with hunters in the fall, and the North Fork of the Sun River contains rainbow, brook, and cutthroat trout that can be caught by wade fishing. Gibson Reservoir, with fishing, hiking and mountain-biking trails, boating, and swimming is a 10-minute drive to the west. Departing from Sun Canyon Lodge, the Home Gulch–Lime Trail (#267, 15 miles) offers spring wildlife-watching opportunities, but more scenic trails depart from the reservoir area.

The campground squeezes between the Sun Canyon Road and the North Fork of the Sun River. Aspen and alder trees lend partial shade to the campsites. The campground is quiet but does get a fair amount of weekend traffic during the day on the adjacent road, but not at night when the sound of the river is pervasive. A narrow dirt road winds through the campground, which has gravel parking pads; one is a pull-through and the rest are back-ins. Most of the campsites overlook the river.

Campsites, facilities: The campground has 15 RV or tent campsites that can accommodate vehicles up to 45 feet long. Facilities include picnic tables, fire rings with grills, vault toilets, and hand pumps for drinking water. Pack out your trash. Leashed pets are permitted. A wheelchair-accessible toilet is available.

Reservations, fees: No reservations are accepted. Campsites cost $6. Cash or check. Open late May–November, but the water is shut off after Labor Day.

Directions: From Augusta, follow the signs to Gibson Reservoir. Drive out of town on Manix Street, which becomes Sun River Road (Forest Road 108). Drive 3.7 miles to a signed intersection. Turn right and drive 15 miles on dirt to where the road turns to pavement again. Continue 1.8 miles farther on the pavement and turn right at the sign into the campground.

GPS Coordinates: N 47° 36.981' W 112° 43.698'

Contact: Lewis and Clark National Forest, Rocky Mountain Ranger District, 1102 N. Main Ave., P.O. Box 340, Choteau, MT 59422, 406/466-5341, fax 406/466-2237, www.fs.fed.us/r1/lewisclark.

13 PISHKUN RESERVOIR

Scenic rating: 8

north of Augusta and southwest of Choteau

The 1,518-acre Pishkun Reservoir is a prairie lake below the Rocky Mountain Front. Long, rough, gravel and dirt access roads lead to it from Choteau or Augusta. Sitting at 4,370 feet in elevation, the lake draws anglers for its northern pike, rainbow trout, and yellow perch. Used also in winter for ice fishing, it is stocked regularly with rainbow trout and sometimes kokanee. The concrete boat ramp is unusable during drought conditions. Contact the Region 4 office for current water levels. Also a wildlife management area, the reservoir is a good place for watching waterfowl, loons, and peregrine falcons.

The primitive campground is part of the fishing access site run by the state. Its campsites line up along the shore in a hot, sunny, windy, treeless, grassy area along the dirt campground road facing the dramatic, expansive views of the Front range peaks. The campground is so distant from any highway that wind is the only sound. The state discourages trailers and RVs from using the campground due to the rough condition of the access road, but smaller RVs and truck-campers often visit the campground anyway. Despite how spread out the campsites are, you'll still see your neighboring campers.

Campsites, facilities: The campground has five RV and tent campsites that can accommodate only smaller RVs. Facilities include picnic tables with shelters, fire rings with grills, vault toilets, and a boat ramp. Pack out your trash. Leashed pets are permitted.

Reservations, fees: Reservations are not accepted. Campsites cost $7 with a Montana fishing license and $12 without a Montana fishing license. Cash or check. Open year-round.

Directions: From Choteau, drive 0.5 mile south on Highway 287 and turn southwest for 19 miles on the Pishkun Road. Turn left at the signed entrance to the fishing access site to reach the campground. From Augusta, drive 11.3 miles north on Highway 287 and turn left onto West Spring Valley Road for 7.3 miles as it jogs north and west again. Turn right onto the Pishkun Access Road for 4.8 miles and then turn left onto Pishkun Road for 0.8 mile to the campground entrance on the left.

GPS Coordinates: N 47° 41.666' W 112° 28.650'

Contact: Montana Fish, Wildlife, and Parks, Region 4, 4600 Giant Springs Rd., Great Falls, MT 59405, 406/454-5840, http://fwp.mt.gov.

14 WILLOW CREEK RESERVOIR

Scenic rating: 8

north of Augusta

The 1,314-acre Willow Creek Reservoir is a prairie lake below the Rocky Mountain Front accessible via a rough gravel road. At 4,150 feet in elevation, the lake draws anglers for its rainbow and brook trout. Used also in winter for ice fishing, it is stocked regularly with rainbow trout. The concrete boat ramp is unusable during drought conditions and late in the summer; contact the Region 4 office for current water levels. Also a wildlife management area, the reservoir is a good place for watching waterfowl and loons, and it attracts hunters in fall.

The primitive campground is part of the fishing access site run by the state. Its spread-out campsites line up along the shore in a hot, sunny, windy, treeless, grassy area along the dirt campground road. Some of the campsites face east toward the lake's island, but the Front peaks are also in view to the west. Other campsites can nab reflections of the Front peaks in the water on calm days. The campground is so distant from any highway that wind is the only sound. The state discourages trailers and RVs from using the campground because of the rough condition of the access road, but smaller RVs and truck-campers often visit the campground anyway.

Campsites, facilities: The campground has six RV and tent campsites that can accommodate only smaller RVs. Facilities include picnic tables, fire rings with grills, vault toilets, and a boat ramp. Pack out your trash. Leashed pets are permitted.

Reservations, fees: Reservations are not accepted. Campsites cost $7 with a Montana fishing license and $12 without a Montana fishing license. Cash or check. Open year-round.

Directions: From Augusta, drive out of town on Manix Street, which becomes the Sun River Road (Forest Road 108). Drive 3.7 miles to a signed intersection. Turn right for 1.6 miles and turn right again at the fishing access site sign onto Willow Creek Road for 1.2 miles. Turn left for 0.1 mile to reach the campground.

GPS Coordinates: N 47° 32.842' W 112° 26.358'

Contact: Montana Fish, Wildlife, and Parks, Region 4, 4600 Giant Springs Rd., Great Falls, MT 59405, 406/454-5840, http://fwp.mt.gov.

15 FREEZEOUT LAKE

Scenic rating: 8

south of Choteau

BEST (

Freezeout Lake sits on a 11,466-acre wildlife state management area at 3,770 feet in elevation south of Choteau. The lake—actually one lake and six ponds—provides outstanding wildlife-watching. In late March and early April, as many as 300,000 snow geese and 10,000 tundra swans congregate on the lake amid a cacophony of squawks on their migration northward. For the best experience, watch in early morning as thousands of birds lift off the lake to go feed in nearby grain fields to prepare for their flight to Saskatchewan and then the arctic. Over 200 species of birds use the Freezeout area—either for migration or nesting. Winter brings upland game birds and raptors, spring and fall have waterfowl migrations, and summer includes ducks, herons, shorebirds, sandhill cranes, swans, and raptors. You can call 406/467-2646 for an automated waterfowl update. Perimeter roads are open

year-round. Interior roads are closed during hunting season (October–mid-January) for upland game birds and waterfowl. Dike roads are closed to motorized vehicles but open for hiking. A paved walking path leads to a waterfowl blind. Only nonmotorized boats are permitted on the lake.

The primitive campground squeezes between the highway and Pond 5 in an open field divided by hedgerows of brush into back-in grassy campsites. The campground is sunny and windy, and receives noise from a handful of trucks at night. But that doesn't compare with the deafening noise of thousands of snow geese at once.

Campsites, facilities: The campground has 12 RV and tent campsites that can accommodate small RVs. Facilities include picnic tables, vault toilets, and primitive boat ramps. Pack out your trash. Leashed pets are permitted. A wheelchair-accessible toilet and campsite are available, along with a paved trail to a viewing blind.

Reservations, fees: Reservations are not accepted. Camping is free. Open year-round; however, motorized vehicles are restricted

Freezeout Lake, a popular birding campground, sees thousands of snow geese in March.

October–mid-January when internal roads are closed.

Directions: From Choteau, drive Highway 89 southeast for 12.3 miles. Turn west at the headquarters office. Drive 0.3 mile to a four-way junction. Turn right, continuing for 0.3 mile. Turn right and go 0.1 mile to the campground entrance.

GPS Coordinates: N 47° 40.180' W 112° 0.947'

Contact: Montana Fish, Wildlife, and Parks, Region 4, 4600 Giant Springs Rd., Great Falls, MT 59405, 406/454-5840, http://fwp. mt.gov.

16 SOUTH FORK SUN RIVER

Scenic rating: 7

on the South Fork of the Sun River in Lewis and Clark National Forest

At 5,300 feet, the South Fork of the Sun River Campground is in Lewis and Clark National Forest at one of the most popular trailheads to access the wilderness for backpacking, horse packing, fishing, hunting, and mountain climbing. The 22-mile-long Chinese Wall can be reached via trail in about 18 miles. The Sun River attracts anglers for brown trout, mountain whitefish, and rainbow trout. The South Fork of the Sun Trail (#202), which is part of the Continental Divide Trail, parallels the South Fork of the Sun River to access the Scapegoat Wilderness to the south and the Bob Marshall Wilderness to the north.

This campground is busy and dusty, due to the trailhead. The campground loop is adjacent to parking for hikers and for stock trailers, which can be packed with up to 20 trucks and trailers that are visible from every campsite. Even though the campground sits on the river, none of the campsites have private river frontage, although you can walk the 100 feet to it. Lodgepole pines lend partial shade to the campground, with campsites surrounded by tall grass. While Benchmark offers much more privacy and camping ambiance, some hikers prefer camping here for the convenience to the trailhead.

Campsites, facilities: The campground has seven RV or tent campsites that can accommodate smaller RVs. Facilities include picnic tables, fire rings, hand pumps for drinking water, and vault toilets. Pack out your trash. Leashed pets are permitted. A wheelchair-accessible toilet and campsite are available, although the campsite has become overgrown.

Reservations, fees: No reservations are accepted. Camping costs $8. Cash or check. Open late May–November.

Directions: From Augusta, follow County Road 435 for 0.3 mile to the Nilan Reservoir sign. Turn right onto Eberl Street. Follow the road as it swings south and then west again, where the road turns to gravel, becoming Forest Road 235. Drive 14.2 miles to an intersection and continue straight for 16.2 miles until the road dead-ends in the campground.

GPS Coordinates: N 47° 30.108' W112°53.283'

Contact: Lewis and Clark National Forest, Rocky Mountain Ranger District, 1102 N. Main Ave., P.O. Box 340, Choteau, MT 59422, 406/466-5341, fax 406/466-2237, www.fs.fed.us/r1/lewisclark.

17 BENCHMARK

Scenic rating: 7

on Straight Creek in Lewis and Clark National Forest

Located at 5,300 feet in the Lewis and Clark National Forest, Benchmark is a remote Forest Service station with an airstrip and a popular access for those entering the wilderness for hiking, backpacking, horse packing, fishing, and hunting. The 22-mile-long Chinese Wall can be reached via trail in about

18 miles. The campground sits between Straight and Wood Creeks, both tributaries to the South Fork of the Sun River that harbor mottled sculpin and rainbow trout. The 15.2-mile Straight Creek Trail (#212) departs 0.2 mile from the campground, and one mile north the South Fork of the Sun Trail (#202), which is part of the Continental Divide Trail, parallels the river to access the Scapegoat Wilderness to the south and the Bob Marshall Wilderness to the north.

A mixed aspen and conifer forest shades the campground, which is suited for those with stock. The two loops on the right have feeding troughs for horses, plus hitching rails and loading ramps are available. To accommodate stock trailers, the parking pads are large, triple-wide back-ins. The loop to the left is not set up for horses. Low grass covers the forest floor, while lodgepole pines lend partial shade. The spaced out sites are private due to shorter pine trees growing between sites. Sites 18, 19, 20, 24, and 25 have views but also look across the airstrip. Site 16 has a bear pole for hanging food. Most of the campsites have large, flat tent spaces.

Campsites, facilities: The campground has 25 RV or tent campsites that can accommodate RVs up to 30 feet. Facilities include picnic tables, fire rings, hand pumps for drinking water, stock equipment, and pit and vault toilets. Pack out your trash. Leashed pets are permitted. A wheelchair-accessible toilet is available.

Reservations, fees: No reservations are accepted. Campsites cost $6. Cash or check. Open late May–November.

Directions: From Augusta, follow County Road 435 for 0.3 mile to the Nilan Reservoir sign. Turn right onto Eberl Street. Follow the road as it swings south and then west again, where the road turns to gravel, becoming Forest Road 235. Drive 14.2 miles to an intersection and turn left for another 15.2 miles on the Benchmark Road. At the campground sign, turn left, driving across the single-lane bridge, and swing left for another 0.2 mile.

GPS Coordinates: N 47° 29.207' W 112° 52.942'

Contact: Lewis and Clark National Forest, Rocky Mountain Ranger District, 1102 N. Main Ave., P.O. Box 340, Choteau, MT 59422, 406/466-5341, fax 406/466-2237, www.fs.fed.us/r1/lewisclark.

18 WOOD LAKE

Scenic rating: 9

at Wood Lake in Lewis and Clark National Forest

At 5,799 feet in elevation, Wood Lake is a small, shallow lake on Benchmark Road in the Lewis and Clark National Forest just east of the Scapegoat Wilderness Area. The lake is popular with anglers for its westslope cutthroat trout; you can often see six or more people fly-fishing along its shore. A primitive boat ramp is available, but motors are not permitted.

Sitting across the road from the lake, the aspen, lodgepole, and fir campground is enclosed with a rail fence to keep cattle grazing under permit in the area from entering. It sits very close to Benchmark Road, where every vehicle kicks up dust, which filters into the campsites adjacent to the road. Sites 2, 3, and 5 are more open, with views of the forested slopes. In July, cow parsnips, black-eyed susans, and cinquefoil bloom around the campsites, which are close together and lacking foliage. Site 7 is a small, private site with a view of a small rocky gorge; a rough trail cuts through the fence and tours it. Sites 11 and 12 sit in a second area to the left when you drive in. These sites are open, with views of Wood Lake across the road, and with extra parking pads for trailers or additional vehicles.

Campsites, facilities: The campground has 12 RV or tent campsites that can accommodate a maximum RV length of 22 feet. Facilities include picnic tables, fire rings with grills, vault toilets, and hand pumps for drinking water. Leashed pets are permitted. A wheelchair-accessible toilet is available.

Reservations, fees: No reservations are accepted. Camping costs $6. Cash or check. Open late May–November.

Directions: From Augusta, follow County Road 435 for 0.3 mile to the Nilan Reservoir sign. Turn right onto Eberl Street. Follow the road as it swings south and then west again, where the road turns to gravel, becoming Forest Road 235. Drive 14.2 miles to an intersection and turn left onto Benchmark Road. Drive nine miles to Wood Lake. The campground entrance is on the right just before the lake.

GPS Coordinates: N 47° 25.706' W 112° 47.697'

Contact: Augusta Information Station, 405 Manix St., P.O. Box 365, Augusta, MT 59410, 406/562-3247.

19 FORD AND WOOD CREEKS PRIMITIVE

🏃 🛶 🐾 🚙 ⛺

Scenic rating: 7

on the Benchmark Road in Lewis and Clark National Forest

At an elevation of 5,600 feet in Lewis and Clark National Forest, the Benchmark Road parallels Ford and Wood Creeks, two Rocky Mountain Front trout streams. Dispersed primitive campsites flank both sides of the road, some on the creeks and others in pine forest settings on the opposite side of the road. A few are open and visible from the road. Locate the campsites on dirt spur roads. Some are marked with numbered tent icon signs; others are unmarked. Scout the roads first before driving in blind—especially if you are pulling a small trailer or driving an RV. Not all of the sites have turnaround room.

The primitive campsites along the road are attractive for their solitude and privacy broken only by the sounds of nature. Some are forested while others sit in partly sunny aspen groves. Follow Leave No Trace principles when camping at these dispersed sites, using only pre-existing fire rings and driving only on jeep trails.

Campsites, facilities: The Benchmark Road has 13 dispersed campsites for small RVs or tents. Facilities include rock fire rings. No drinking water is available. If you choose to use the creek water, boil or purify it first. Pack out your trash. Leashed pets are permitted.

Reservations, fees: No reservations are accepted. Camping is free. Open May–November.

Directions: From Augusta, follow County Road 435 for 0.3 mile to the Nilan Reservoir sign. Turn right onto Eberl Street. Follow the road as it swings south and then west again, where the road turns to gravel becoming Forest Road 235. Drive 14.2 miles to an intersection and turn left onto the Benchmark Road. Find dispersed campsites on both sides of the road between MP 4.5 and the Benchmark airstrip.

Contact: Lewis and Clark National Forest, Augusta Ranger Station, 1102 N. Main Ave., P.O. Box 340, Choteau, MT 59422, 406/466-5341, fax 406/466-2237, www.fs.fed.us/r1/lewisclark.

20 DOUBLE FALLS

🏃 🛶 🐾 🚙 ⛺

Scenic rating: 7

on Wood Creek in Lewis and Clark National Forest

At 5,500 feet on Ford Creek in Lewis and Clark National Forest, Double Falls sits on the road to Benchmark, one of the most popular entrances to the Scapegoat and Bob Marshall Wildernesses. It is named for the falls just east of the campground. A 0.1-mile trail follows the north side of the creek to the falls. The campground is also the trailhead for Petty Ford Creek Trail (#244). With views of Crown and Steamboat Mountains, the 3.5-mile trail climbs out of Ford Creek and drops to Petty Creek. Ford Creek harbors brook trout.

This small, primitive campground is reached via a steep, narrow, rocky dirt road. The road can be muddy in wet weather. While high clearance vehicles are not mandatory, they will manage the rocks better. Both campsites sit right on the river, hence the campground's appeal despite its primitive status. One campsite is open with a views across the meadow (full of pink sticky geraniums in July) and of the mountainsides. The other campsite on the east end of the campground is tucked behind tall firs for more privacy. Both have large, flat spaces for tents and rough dirt parking pads.

Campsites, facilities: The campground has two RV or tent campsites that can accommodate only smaller RVs and trailers. Facilities include picnic tables, fire rings with grills, and a vault toilet. No drinking water is available. Pack out your trash. If you choose to use the creek water, boil or purify it first. Leashed pets are permitted.

Reservations, fees: No reservations are accepted. Camping is free. Open May–November.

Directions: From Augusta, follow County Road 435 for 0.3 mile to the Fishing Access for Nilan Reservoir sign. Turn right onto Eberl Street. Follow the road as it swings south and then west again, where the road turns to gravel, becoming Forest Road 235. Drive 14.2 miles to an intersection and turn left onto the Benchmark Road. Continue on 4.5 miles to the campground entrance, which sits on the left.

GPS Coordinates: N 47° 24.443' W 112° 43.329'

Contact: Augusta Information Station, 405 Manix St., P.O. Box 365, Augusta, MT 59410, 406/562-3247.

21 NILAN RESERVOIR

Scenic rating: 9

west of Augusta

At an elevation of 4,440 feet, west of Augusta on the road to Benchmark, Nilan Reservoir is one of the most scenic of the Rocky Mountain Front reservoirs due to its surrounding prairie and the looming peaks. The 520-acre reservoir offers boating for motorized craft as well as canoes and kayaks. For anglers, the reservoir houses rainbow and brown trout. It is also a popular ice-fishing location in winter. Bird-watchers can see a variety of birds, from raptors to American pelicans.

The campground sprawls along the south shore of Nilan Reservoir, with open gravel, rock, and dry grass campsites in pairs. The lack of trees makes them sunny and affords outstanding views of the front range, but winds whip right through them. Mornings tend to be calm, with the water often reflecting the peaks, but breezes pick up in the afternoon. Sites 1–6, which are large gravel pull-throughs, have the best views but, due to the road, get dusted by passing vehicles; sites 7 and 8 sit adjacent to the dusty road away from the water on the boat ramp spur. Sites 3 and 4 each have their own small jetty; site 2 has a small windbreak from cottonwood trees. Due to the rough road access, the state does not recommend the campground for trailers or RVs, but plenty of people drive in with both.

Campsites, facilities: The campground has eight RV or tent campsites that can accommodate midsized RVs. Facilities include picnic tables, fire rings with grills, vault toilets, and a boat ramp. No drinking water is available. If you choose to use the reservoir water, boil or purify it first. Pack out your trash. Leashed pets are permitted.

Reservations, fees: No reservations are accepted. Camping costs $7 if you have a Montana fishing license or $12 without. Cash or check. Open year-round.

Directions: From Augusta, follow County Road 435 for 0.3 mile to Fishing Access for Nilan Reservoir sign. Turn right onto Eberl Street. Follow the road as it swings south and then west again, where the road turns to gravel, becoming Forest Road 235. Drive seven miles to the campground. Sites will be on the right side of the road over the next 0.3 mile.

GPS Coordinates: N 47° 28.387' W 112° 31.074'

Contact: Montana Fish, Wildlife, and Parks, Region 4 Office, 4600 Giant Springs Rd., Great Falls, MT 59405, 406/454-5840, http://fwp.mt.gov.

22 DICK'S RV PARK

Scenic rating: 5

In Great Falls

At an elevation of 3,505 feet, Dick's RV Park is convenient for exploring the C.M. Russell Museum, which celebrates the work of the famous western artist, and the Lewis and Clark Interpretive Center, with displays about the Corps of Discovery, as well as hiking trails and bicycling paths. Although the campground sits along the Sun River, the confluence of the Sun River with the Missouri River is less than a five-minute drive away. The campground is also a five-minute drive from two golf courses and fishing, boating, and floating on the Missouri River, along with hiking and biking trails at Giant Springs Heritage State Park.

The older campground squeezes between the Sun River and a four-lane freeway with trucking traffic, and it picks up noise from the nearby railroad. Both pull-through and back-in sites are available, with small plots of grass between sites. The cramped sites are very close together with no privacy. The sunny campground has only a few trees. Some long-term residents live here.

Campsites, facilities: The campground has 141 RV sites that can fit large RVs, 20 tent campsites, and 30 unserviced overflow sites. Hookups include water, sewer, electricity, and cable TV. Facilities include picnic tables, flush toilets, showers, a coin-operated launderette, coin-operated car wash, drinking water, store with movie rentals, wireless Internet, cable TV, a dog walk, propane for sale, and a recreation hall. Leashed pets are permitted.

Reservations, fees: Reservations are accepted. Hookups cost $26–36. Tent sites cost $19. Cash, check, or credit card. Open year-round.

Directions: From I-15 at Great Falls, take Exit 278 (10th Avenue S.) onto Highway 87/89/200 heading east. Take Exit 0, turning north onto 14th Street. Turn right at 13th Avenue SW and drive two blocks, going under the railroad bridge. The campground entrance is on the right.

GPS Coordinates: N 47° 29.456' W 111° 19.998'

Contact: Dick's RV Park, 1403 11th St. SW, Great Falls, MT 59404, 406/452-0333, www.dicksrvpark.com.

23 GREAT FALLS KOA

Scenic rating: 5

In Great Falls

At an elevation of 3,505 feet, the Great Falls KOA is convenient for exploring three of the town's main attractions: the C.M. Russell Museum Complex, Giant Springs Heritage State Park, and the Lewis and Clark Interpretive Center. Great Falls also has three golf courses and fishing, boating, and floating on the Missouri River, along with hiking and biking trails.

This manicured grassy campground provides partial shade from the cottonwood trees, and some of the sites have privacy from bushes. Sites include full hookups, partial hookups, dry camping, and tent villages with partial shade and fenced grass. The quiet location on the edge of town still picks up a little noise from large trucks on the highway. Shower facilities include family rooms, and a covered outdoor kitchen is available. Mornings start with an all-you-can-eat pancake breakfast with chokecherry syrup. On summer evenings, entertainment includes bluegrass music and cowpoke poetry performed by the River Town Rounders.

Campsites, facilities: The campground has 120 RV and tent campsites that can accommodate rigs of any length. Hookups include water, sewer, and electricity (50 amps available), and the tent village area includes hookups for water and electricity. Facilities include picnic tables, pedestal grills, flush toilets, showers, a coin-operated launderette, drinking water, a playground, a swimming pool, water slides and park, a hot tub, a game room, movie nights, fresh veggies in the garden, basketball and volleyball courts, a dog walk, wireless Internet, modem dataports, cable TV, café, a camp store, firewood for free, propane for sale, and a dump station. Leashed pets are permitted.

Reservations, fees: Reservations are accepted. Hookups cost $49–56. Tent sites cost $38–45. Rates cover two people. For over two people, add on $10 per adult and $8 per child. Children five years old and under stay free. Six people maximum are permitted per campsite. Kamping cabins cost $65–87. Cash, check, or credit card. Open year-round.

Directions: From I-15 in Great Falls, take Exit 278 and drive five miles east on Highways 87/89/200 (also called 10th Avenue S.) to the east edge of the city. Turn south onto 51st Street S. and drive 0.3 mile to the campground entrance on the corner where the road turns west.

GPS Coordinates: N 47° 29.269' W 111° 13.304'

Contact: Great Falls KOA, 1500 51st St. S, Great Falls, MT 59405, 406/727-3191 or 800/562-6584, www.greatfallskoa.com.

24 WOLF BRIDGE

Scenic rating: 4

on the Missouri River north of Helena

On the Missouri River north of Holter Dam, Wolf Bridge, at 3,500 feet, is a popular fishing

and boating access, but not a prime camping location. You can launch upriver at Holter Dam Campground and float two miles back to the camp, or you can float from Wolf Bridge eight miles north to Craig. Anglers go after a variety of game fish, which include black crappie, brown trout, burbot, channel catfish, mountain whitefish, northern pike, paddlefish, rainbow trout, sauger, shovelnose sturgeon, smallmouth bass, walleye, and yellow perch.

Squeezed up against the road and bridge, the campground is really a strip of dry grass along the edge of a large gravel parking lot and boat launch—a fishing access site run by the state. It's a place to camp for convenience rather than ambiance. Two of the sites have flat spaces for tents. The campground has no trees for shade or to block wind. The area does have a bench along the river for watching the passing boats. Campsite 1 is the closest to the river. Individual parking pads do not exist; just pull up next to a picnic table.

Campsites, facilities: The campground has five RV or tent campsites that can accommodate larger RVs. Facilities include picnic tables, fire rings with grills, vault toilets, and a boat ramp. No drinking water is available. If you choose to use the river water, boil or purify it first. Pack out your trash. Leashed pets are permitted. A wheelchair-accessible toilet is available.

Reservations, fees: No reservations are accepted. Camping costs $7 if you have a Montana fishing license or $12 without. Cash or check. Open year-round.

Directions: From I-15 north of Helena, take Exit 226 at Wolf Creek. From Wolf Creek on the south side of the freeway, drive Recreation Road for 3.3 miles and turn left after crossing the bridge over the Missouri River.

GPS Coordinates: N 47° 1.198' W 112° 0.612'

Contact: Montana Fish, Wildlife, and Parks, Region 4 Office, 4600 Giant Springs Rd., Great Falls, MT 59405, 406/454-5840, http://fwp.mt.gov.

25 HOLTER DAM

Scenic rating: 6

on Holter Lake north of Helena

Below Holter Dam on the west bank of the Missouri River, at 3,550 feet, Holter Dam Campground drones with the constant noise of the dam, and views are of the dam as well as the surrounding arid mountain slopes. Yet it attracts many anglers, who fish from shore or hop on rafts or drift boats to float the Missouri River for its game fish. During high water, the dam may need to release water; a siren and lights alert those in the river channel to move up into the campground.

The campground is in two parts, adjacent to the boat launch area. The first part (sites 1–11) centers around a large gravel parking lot with picnic tables with shade covers. Sites 1 and 11 sit on the water, but the remainder line up on the grass on the opposite side of the parking lot from the river. Only a couple of large willow trees provide shade. Sites 13–17 line up with double-wide back-in gravel parking pads and no covers on the tables. Neither of the sections affords privacy due to the lack of trees and close quarters.

Campsites, facilities: There are 33 RV or tent campsites that can accommodate midsized RVs. Facilities include picnic tables, fire rings with grills, vault toilets, drinking water, a gravel boat launch, boat trailer parking, dock, garbage service, firewood for sale, and a campground manager on site. Leashed pets are permitted. Site 7 and toilets are wheelchair-accessible.

Reservations, fees: No reservations are accepted. Campsites cost $10. Day use of the park costs $2. Cash or check. Open early May–October.

Directions: From I-15 north of Helena, take Exit 226 at Wolf Creek. From Wolf Creek on the south side of the freeway, drive Recreation Road for 3.3 miles and turn right just before the bridge over the Missouri River. Drive two miles. The road has large washboards and potholes that make driving the two miles a challenge.

GPS Coordinates: N 46° 59.705' W 112° 00.682'

Contact: Bureau of Land Management, 106 N. Parkmont, P.O. Box 3388, Butte, MT 59702, 406/533-7600, www.blm.gov/mt/st/en.html.

26 HOLTER LAKE

Scenic rating: 8

on the Missouri River north of Helena

Located at 3,600 feet on the east shore of Holter Lake north of Helena, this campground sits on the Missouri River in a lake created by Holter Dam. From the campground, you can boat south into Gates of the Mountains Wilderness for sightseeing along the route that Lewis and Clark traveled. The lake is popular for waterskiing and fishing for black crappie, brown trout, burbot, channel catfish, mountain whitefish, northern pike, paddlefish, rainbow trout, sauger, shovelnose sturgeon, smallmouth bass, walleye, and yellow perch. A marina with boat rentals and gas sits 0.5 mile south on Beartooth Road.

Sitting on a bluff above the lake, the campground appears as a green, mowed-lawn oasis amid the surrounding dry grassland and pine hills. Two interconnected paved loops waltz through the cramped, crowded open campground, which has no privacy between sites. Only a few short cottonwoods offer shade for hot days, causing most campers to cower in the cool shadow of their trailer or RV. Paved walkways connect the campground to the beach, boat launch, and fishing jetty. Sites 3, 5, 6, 7, 8, 10, 12, 13, 15, and 18 overlook the lake. A separate walk-in tent area is available.

Campsites, facilities: There are 33 RV or tent campsites, plus an additional open walk-in tenting area without assigned sites. The gravel parking pads can accommodate midsized RVs.

© BECKY LOMAX

Holter Lake, home to several campgrounds, is formed on the Missouri River by a downstream dam.

Facilities include picnic tables, fire rings with grills, vault toilets, drinking water, a paved multi-lane boat launch, boat trailer parking, docks, boat slips, a fish-cleaning station, garbage service, swimming area, and campground manager on-site. Leashed pets are permitted. Toilets are wheelchair-accessible. Camping is limited to seven days.

Reservations, fees: No reservations are accepted. Campsites cost $10. Day use of the park costs $2. Cash or check. Open early May–October.

Directions: From I-15 north of Helena, take Exit 226 at Wolf Creek. From Wolf Creek on the south side of the freeway, drive Recreation Road for 3.3 miles until you cross the Missouri River on a bridge; turn right onto paved Beartooth Road for 2.3 miles. The campground is on the right.

GPS Coordinates: N 46° 59.640' W 111° 59.436'

Contact: Bureau of Land Management, 106 N. Parkmont, P.O. Box 3388, Butte, MT 59702, 406/533-7600, www.blm.gov/mt/st/en.html.

27 LOG GULCH

Scenic rating: 9

on the Missouri River north of Helena

Log Gulch, at 3,600 feet on the east shore of Holter Lake, a reservoir on the Missouri River, provides access for fishing and a sandy swimming beach. It is the closest launch for boating up the Oxbow to Gates of the Mountains Wilderness. Once at the Gates, you can hike one hour into Mann Gulch, a National Historic Landmark that marks the site of a tragic wildfire in 1949 that killed 13 firefighters. Crosses up the steep hillside mark where each firefighter died.

The campground flanks a hillside with three different options for camping—none with privacy. The main campground circles in several paved loops upslope in the gulch. A few of these lawn campsites have pull-through gravel parking pads, a cottonwood or pine tree for partial shade, and views of the lake (from the sites at the top of the loop). A second area—Little Log—climbs a steep hill with staggered terraced campsites, some with peek-a-boo views of the lake. A third area— a large, flat, treeless, gravel parking lot for RVs to back into—offers prime views of spiny Sleeping Giant Mountain and the lake. Watch for rattlesnakes around the campground.

Campsites, facilities: There are 70 RV or tent campsites; some can accommodate the largest RVs. Facilities include picnic tables, fire rings with grills, vault toilets, drinking water, a paved multi-lane boat launch, boat trailer parking, docks, boat slips, a fish-cleaning station, garbage service, swimming area, and campground manager on-site. Leashed pets are permitted. Toilets are wheelchair-accessible.

Reservations, fees: No reservations are accepted. Campsites cost $10. Day use of the park costs $2. Cash or check. Open early May–October.

Directions: From I-15 north of Helena, take Exit 226 at Wolf Creek. From Wolf Creek on the south side of the freeway, drive Recreation Road for 3.3 miles until you cross the bridge over the Missouri River; turn right onto Beartooth Road for 6.5 miles. After passing Holter Lake campground, the paved road turns to bumpy oiled dirt and narrows with sharp, blind corners, but pavement resumes just before the campground.

GPS Coordinates: N 46° 57.683' W 111° 56.601'

Contact: Bureau of Land Management, 106 N. Parkmont, P.O. Box 3388, Butte, MT 59702, 406/533-7600, www.blm.gov/mt/st/en.html.

28 DEPARTURE POINT

Scenic rating: 8

on the Missouri River north of Helena

BEST (

At 3,600 feet on Holter Lake's east shore, Departure Point is a tiny campground one bay south of Log Gulch. A narrow paved road connects it with the larger campground, but be prepared for its sharp, blind corners. The campground is as far as you can drive along the shoreline of Holter Lake's east side, and it sits at the northern entrance to the Beartooth Wildlife Management Area, where you can see elk, deer, bighorn sheep, and a variety of raptors and birds. Go for wildlife drives either in early morning or evening when sightings are usually best.

The tiny campground has only four sites on a paved parking lot set above the day use area and beach. The double-wide parking strips cram together, but the sunset views across the lake are stunning. A paved trail connects the parking lot with the day-use area and swimming beach. The distance is short enough that you can launch canoes and sea kayaks from here to tour the Oxbow. Larger boats can be launched at Log Gulch and beached here. Rattlesnakes are in the area; caution is advised.

Campsites, facilities: Four RV campsites can accommodate midsized RVs. Facilities include picnic tables, fire rings with grills, vault toilets, drinking water, garbage service, and a buoyed swimming area. Leashed pets are permitted. Toilets are wheelchair-accessible.

Reservations, fees: No reservations are accepted. Campsites cost $10. Day use of the park costs $2. Cash or check. Open early May–October.

Directions: From I-15 north of Helena, take Exit 226 at Wolf Creek. From Wolf Creek on the south side of the freeway, drive Recreation Road for 3.3 miles until you cross the bridge over the Missouri River; turn right onto paved Beartooth Road for seven miles. The paved surface will change to a rough, oiled dirt road about a lane and a half wide for a couple of miles. Drive slowly—it is narrow with blind corners.

GPS Coordinates: N 46°57.391' W 111° 56.418'

Contact: Bureau of Land Management, 106 N. Parkmont, P.O. Box 3388, Butte, MT 59702, 406/533-7600, www.blm.gov/mt/st/en.html.

29 PRICKLY PEAR RIVER

Scenic rating: 6

on the Prickly Pear River north of Helena

On the Prickly Pear River, a tributary of the Missouri River, three state-run fishing access campsites dot this stream, which attracts anglers with its brown and rainbow trout. At 3,760 feet in elevation, the camps snuggle into Prickly Pear Canyon—a dramatic geological slice through layered pink rock. The campsites are divided into two locations—the Lichen Cliff on the north and Prickly Pear to the south.

Despite the side road locations, both campgrounds fill with noise from the paralleling I-15 and railroad tracks. The Prickly Pear campsite sits 20 feet from the tracks. The two Lichen Cliff campsites are pull-overs off the road, better suited to midsized RVs, even though the state does not recommend trailers or RVs. The Prickly Pear campsite, tucked down a short spur road, offers a better tent area secluded from the road. Lichen Cliff campsites sit right on the stream, but at Prickly Pear, you must walk across the railroad tracks to several two-minute trails to reach the creek.

Campsites, facilities: The campgrounds have three RV or tent campsites. Lichen Cliff can accommodate larger RVs, but the Prickly Pear spot is suitable only for smaller RVs. Small trailers can fit, but the campsite has minimal turnaround space. Facilities include picnic tables, fire rings with grills, and vault toilets. No drinking water is available. If you choose to use the stream water, boil or purify it first. Pack out your trash. Leashed pets are permitted.

Reservations, fees: No reservations are accepted. Camping costs $7 if you have a Montana fishing license or $12 without. Cash or check. Open year-round.

Directions: From I-15 north of Helena, take Exit 226 at Wolf Creek and drive south on Recreation Road, or take Exit 219 and drive north on Spring Creek Road. The milepost numbering starts at the south and begins renumbering again at Lyons Creek Road around milepost 3. Find Prickly Pear at milepost 0.8 between Exit 219 and Lyons Creek Road. Find Lichen Cliff at milepost 1.6 between Lyons Creek Road and Wolf Creek.

GPS coordinates for Lichen Cliff: N 46° 56.316' W 112° 7.300'

GPS coordinates for Prickly Pear: N 46° 55.004' W 112° 7.371'

Contact: Montana Fish, Wildlife, and Parks, Region 4 Office, 4600 Giant Springs Rd., Great Falls, MT 59405, 406/454-5840, http://fwp.mt.gov.

30 BEARTOOTH LANDING

Scenic rating: 8

on the Missouri River north of Helena

On west shore of the Missouri River on Holter Lake, at 3,600 feet, Beartooth Landing is a small boat-in only campground below the Sleeping Giant. It sits just downstream from the 2,225-mile mark on the Missouri, across from Ming Bar, which has shallow water over a sandy swimming basin. Boating from the north requires navigating 10.2 river miles through the convoluted Oxbow from Log Gulch, roughly double the air miles. You can also boat in 6.8 miles from the south through the steep-walled canyon of Gate of the Mountains. The campground sits 1.8 miles upstream from Mann Gulch National Historic Site and the north entrance to Gates of the Mountains and across the river from the Beartooth Wildlife Management Area, with pronghorns, deer, elk, bighorn sheep, raptors, and songbirds.

The tiny, north-facing, partially shaded campsites sit along the shore, with views of Beartooth Mountain. No dock is available, so boats must be beached. During the day, the area bustles with motorboats—water-skiers, sightseers, and anglers—but in the evening, quiet pervades the river. Rattlesnakes are in the area; caution is advised.

Campsites, facilities: The campground has four tent sites. Facilities include picnic tables, fire rings with grills, and a vault toilet. No drinking water is available. Pack out your trash. Leashed pets are permitted.

Reservations, fees: No reservations are accepted. Camping is free. Open early May–October.

Directions: To launch from the north on Holter Lake, drive I-15 north of Helena to Exit 226 at Wolf Creek. From Wolf Creek on the south side of the freeway, drive Recreation Road for 3.3 miles until you cross the bridge over the Missouri River; turn right onto Beartooth Road for 6.5 miles. The paved road turns to bumpy oiled dirt and narrows with sharp, blind corners, but pavement resumes just before the Log Gulch Campground, where you can launch a boat. Kayaks and canoes can also launch 0.6 mile farther south at Departure Point Recreation Area. To launch from the south, drive 20 miles north of Helena on I-15 to Exit 209 and then east on Gates of the Mountains Road for 2.7 miles to Gates of the Mountains Marina.

GPS Coordinates: N 46° 53.131' W 111° 56.458'

Contact: Bureau of Land Management, 106 N. Parkmont, P.O. Box 3388, Butte, MT 59702, 406/533-7600, www.blm.gov/mt/st/en.html.

31 COULTER

Scenic rating: 10

in Gates of the Mountains in Helena National Forest

BEST (

Located on the Missouri River at 3,610 feet in elevation, Coulter is a boat-in only campground in the Gates of the Mountains, a steep-walled narrow gorge named by Lewis

and Clark. The campground sits about midway through the canyon on the east shore. You can launch from Gates of the Mountains Marina ($5 for boats from trailers and $3 for kayaks and canoes) and travel 3.3 miles downstream, or launch from the north at Log Gulch or Departure Point to travel 11.7 miles upstream. Both routes can be windy. The campground sits about 1.5 miles south of the entrance to Mann Gulch, a National Historic Landmark honoring 13 firefighters who lost their lives in 1949 (their crosses still stand on the hillside), and 0.8 mile south of the Meriwether picnic area, which has trails, interpretive displays, and a boat dock. A fire burned some of the surrounding wilderness in 2007. Trails also go upstream from the campground to several overlooks. Watch for ospreys and bald eagles fishing.

The campground sits on a grassy hillside with campsites in the open sun or tucked back in more secluded pines and junipers that offer

© BECKY LOMAX

Coulter campground is located on the Missouri River in the Gates of the Mountains canyon.

partial shade. After the day boaters and the tour boat disappear, a quiet descends on the canyon.

Campsites, facilities: The campground has seven tent sites. Facilities include picnic tables, fire rings, a vault toilet, and boat docks. Pack out your trash. Leashed pets are permitted.

Reservations, fees: No reservations are accepted. Camping is free. Open late May–September.

Directions: To launch boats from the south, drive 20 miles north of Helena on I-15 to Exit 209 and then east on Gates of the Mountains Road for 2.7 miles to Gates of the Mountains Marina. To launch boats from the north, drive I-15 north of Helena to Exit 226 at Wolf Creek. From Wolf Creek on the south side of the freeway, drive Recreation Road for 3.3 miles and turn right onto the half paved/half bumpy oiled dirt Beartooth Road for 6.5 miles to Log Gulch Campground, where you can launch a boat. Kayaks and canoes can also launch 0.6 mile farther south at Departure Point Recreation Area.

GPS Coordinates: N 46° 51.570' W 111° 54.439'

Contact: Helena National Forest, Helena Ranger District, 2001 Poplar, Helena, MT 59601, 406/449-5490, www.fs.fed.usfr1/helena.

32 BLACK SANDY

🚶 🏊 🚣 🎣 🛶 🐎 🔥 ♿ 🚐 ⛺

Scenic rating: 8

on Hauser Lake north of Helena

On the west side of Hauser Lake, south of Hauser Dam at 3,835 feet in elevation, the 43-acre campground, which sits just north of White Sandy Campground, has the benefit of both a lake and canyon scenery as the walls rise straight from the water. The lake is a reservoir on the Missouri River, and the campground sits on the Lewis and Clark Trail; interpretive information is available. A hiking trail leads one mile along the lake. Hauser Lake is popular for waterskiing, swimming, boating, and fishing for kokanee salmon, trout, and other game fish.

Most of the campsites cram along the river frontage with no privacy and nearly on top of each other. Grass surrounds cement pads under the picnic tables. The campground bakes on hot days; only one-third of the sites have willows to offer some shade. The sun drops behind the canyon walls early to begin cooling off the campground for evening. Level, back-in gravel parking pads access most campsites. Two of the walk-in tent sites have river frontage; the other two sit up on a flat bench with views. The tent sites are dry, dusty, and lack trees.

Campsites, facilities: The campground has 29 RV or tent campsites, plus four walk-in tent sites. Parking pads can accommodate trailers up to 35 feet. Facilities include picnic tables, fire rings with grills, vault and flush toilets, a boat ramp, dock, boat slips, drinking water, garbage service, a dump station, campfire programs, and a campground host. Leashed pets are permitted. Toilets are wheelchair-accessible.

Reservations, fees: No reservations are accepted. Camping costs $15. For day use, Montana residents get in free; nonresidents pay $5 per vehicle. Cash or check. Open year-round.

Directions: From I-15 north of Helena, take Exit 200 and drive west on Lincoln Road for 5.1 miles. Turn left at the signed junction onto Hauser Dam Road for three miles, which turns to a wide gravel boulevard in 0.2 mile. At the fork where the pavement resumes, swing left, following the sign to Black Sandy State Park. The campground entrance will be on the right after the dump station and sign.

GPS Coordinates: N 46° 44.848' W 111° 53.185'

Contact: Montana Fish, Wildlife, and Parks, Region 4 Office, 4600 Giant Springs Rd., Great Falls, MT 59405, 406/454-5840, http://fwp.mt.gov.

33 WHITE SANDY

Scenic rating: 8

on Hauser Lake north of Helena

Located on the west side of Hauser Lake south of Hauser Dam, the campground sits at 3,835 feet in elevation just south of Black Sandy Campground. The lake is on the Missouri River where it begins to narrow into a canyon with steep cliff walls. The campground sits on the Lewis and Clark Trail. Hauser Lake is popular for fishing, swimming, boating, and waterskiing. The lake houses kokanee salmon, walleye, yellow perch, mountain whitefish, and several species of trout.

White Sandy is a new campground. As such, its trees are very small, affording no shade or windbreaks yet. The sites, however, are bigger and more spacious than in the adjacent state park, so they gain more privacy by distance, even though you can see the neighbors. The grassy campground has two separate areas for campsites. The upper spur has five sites that back in against a hill with a turnaround loop at the end; these have views of the lower bluff and lake. The lower bluff area is more popular for its 14 lakefront sites. Most of the gravel back-in parking pads are double-wide.

Campsites, facilities: The campground has 34 RV or tent campsites that can accommodate larger RVs. Facilities include picnic tables, fire rings with grills, vault toilets, a boat ramp, a dock, a fish-cleaning station, drinking water, garbage service, firewood for sale, and a campground host. Leashed pets are permitted. Site 14 and toilets are wheelchair-accessible.

Reservations, fees: No reservations are accepted. Camping costs $10. Cash or check. Open May–October.

Directions: From I-15 north of Helena, take Exit 200 and drive west on Lincoln Road for 5.1 miles. Turn left at the signed junction onto Hauser Dam Road for three miles, which turns to a wide gravel boulevard in 0.2 mile. At the fork where the pavement resumes, swing right, following the sign to Black Sandy State Park. The road climbs over a bluff and drops into the campground in 0.2 mile.

GPS Coordinates: N 46° 44.503' W 111° 53.251'

Contact: Bureau of Land Management, 106 N. Parkmont, P.O. Box 3388, Butte, MT 59702, 406/533-7600, www.blm.gov/mt/st/en.html.

34 DEVIL'S ELBOW

Scenic rating: 9

on the Missouri River north of Helena

BEST (

At an elevation of 3,700 feet on the west side of Hauser Lake on the Missouri River, the Devil's Elbow campground sits where the river makes a sharp oxbow around a peninsula before entering a steep-walled slot canyon. The campground sits on that peninsula about one mile north of the York Bridge, the access to the Gates of the Mountains Wilderness and Helena National Forest. The scenic drive through the narrow rocky canyon across the bridge is worth the time. The campground sits below the Two Camps Vista, which affords a dramatic view of the area as well as interpretive information on the Lewis and Clark expedition. Hiking trails connect to Clark's Bay picnic area and the vista. Hauser Lake is popular for swimming, boating, waterskiing, and fishing for kokanee salmon, trout, and other game fish.

The spacious, sunny campground has three grassy loops on a sagebrush bluff above the lake. Young trees scatter throughout the open camp's double-wide gravel parking pads. Some areas are fenced above steep cliffs. Sites are spread out to feel private, but you can see the neighbors. In loop A, sites 1, 3, 5, 6, and 7 overlook the water. In loop B, sites 18, 20,

21, 22, and 24 have water views. Loop C sits farther back from the edge of the bluffs, but with expansive views across the water to distant mountains.

Campsites, facilities: The campground has 41 RV or tent campsites that can accommodate larger RVs on their double-wide parking pads. Facilities include picnic tables, fire rings with grills, vault toilets, a boat ramp, docks, boat slips, boat trailer parking, a fish-cleaning station, drinking water, garbage service, firewood for sale, and a campground host. Leashed pets are permitted. Toilets are wheelchair-accessible.

Reservations, fees: No reservations are accepted. Camping costs $10. Day-use only costs $2. Cash or check. Open May–October.

Directions: From I-15 in Helena, take Exit 193 to the east side of the freeway and go north on Washington Street for 0.8 mile. Turn east onto Canyon Ferry Road for 0.7 mile. Turn north onto York Road and drive 11.6 miles to the signed campground entrance on the right. Drop 0.5 mile down into the campground. GPS Coordinates: N 46° 42.021' W 111° 48.272'

Contact: Bureau of Land Management, 106 N. Parkmont, P.O. Box 3388, Butte, MT 59702, 406/533-7600, www.blm.gov/mt/st/en.html.

35 VIGILANTE

Scenic rating: 8

in the Big Belt Mountains of Helena National Forest

Tucked at an elevation of 4,400 feet at the west end of the deep Trout Creek Canyon in the Big Belt Mountains, Vigilante Campground is the only designated campground for exploring this area of Helena National Forest. The Vigilante Trail (#247)—a National Recreation Trail—begins at the campground and climbs six miles into a hanging valley with an overlook into Trout Creek Canyon. The last 300-foot section requires climbing through steep crevasses in the rocks. The Trout Creek Canyon Trail (#270), which begins with a one-mile wheelchair-accessible paved section, traverses up the canyon for three miles, with clear views of its limestone walls. Shaded areas of the canyon stay cool in the heat of summer, and an interpretive brochure identifies features along the trail, including the original road, which was washed out in a 1981 flood. The canyon is also good for bird- and wildlife-watching.

The quiet, secluded campground snuggles at the bottom of a canyon, where you have a choice of shady or sunny campsites. Some campsites have a forest duff floor; others are grassy. The campground is small, so you will see the neighbors, but enough undergrowth is present in places to make you feel private. Prepare for an onslaught of mosquitoes in early summer.

Campsites, facilities: The campground has 18 RV or tent campsites that can accommodate only smaller RVs. Facilities include picnic tables, fire rings, drinking water, and vault toilets. Pack out your trash. Leashed pets are permitted. A wheelchair-accessible toilet is available.

Reservations, fees: No reservations are accepted. Campsites cost $5. Cash or check. Open late May–September.

Directions: From I-15 in Helena, take Exit 193 to the east side of the freeway and go north on Washington Street for 0.8 mile. Turn east onto Canyon Ferry Road for 0.7 mile. Turn north onto York Road and drive 12.6 miles to the York Bridge. After crossing the bridge, drive 10 miles on the York-Trout Creek Road to the campground. The entrance is on the right. GPS Coordinates: N 46° 46.020' W 111° 39.024'

Contact: Helena National Forest, Helena Ranger District, 2001 Poplar, Helena, MT 59601, 406/449-5490, www.fs.fed.usfr1/helena.

36 CROMWELL DIXON

Scenic rating: 6

on MacDonald Pass in Helena National Forest

At 6,260 feet in elevation at the top of Mac-Donald Pass west of Helena, Cromwell Dixon Campground sits on the Continental Divide. Bicyclists use the campground while doing long-distance rides. The campground is more one for convenience when traveling west from Helena rather than a destination in itself.

With the campground's proximity to Highway 12—a trucking route—noise pervades the area even at night. The paved campground road loops around a hillside of mature Douglas fir and lodgepole pines. A few of the pines are turning rust-colored due to attacking beetles. Fireweed and cow parsnip meadows also flank the campground, offering a mix of choices for campsites. Open to the wind, grassy sites 6 and 8 have sunny expansive views across meadows; other sites tuck protected and shaded under big trees with a forest duff floor. Some sites include large, shapely granitic boulders that kids find fun for climbing. Most of the gravel parking pads are back-ins. Because of the hillside, only some of the sites have level tent spaces. The sites at the end of the loop are closer together than those that are further spaced out at the beginning of the loop.

Campsites, facilities: The campground has 15 RV or tent campsites. Some of the sites can fit midsized RVs, and site 9 offers a big pull-through. Facilities include picnic tables, fire rings, vault toilets, and drinking water. Pack out your trash. Leashed pets are permitted. A wheelchair-accessible toilet is available.

Reservations, fees: No reservations are accepted. Campsites cost $8. Cash or check. Open late May–September.

Directions: From Helena, go 15 miles west on Highway 12. At milepost 27.8, turn south off the highway at the campground sign and immediately turn right over the cattle grate for 0.2 mile to the campground entrance.

GPS Coordinates: N 46° 33.427' W 112° 18.892'

Contact: Helena National Forest, Helena Ranger District, 2100 Poplar, Helena, MT 59601, 406/449-5490, www.fs.fed.us/r1/helena.

37 RIVERSIDE

Scenic rating: 7

on the Missouri River north of Canyon Ferry Dam

Most people who visit Riverside Campground, which sits at 3,700 feet, head onto the Missouri River. You can launch from here to float, motor, or paddle downstream as far as Hauser Dam, which is 15 river miles north. Campers stay here rather than up on Canyon Ferry Reservoir because they prefer the feel of the slow-moving river to the lake. A primitive, dirt boat ramp and dock aid in launching small motorboats, rafts, drift boats, kayaks, and canoes. Boat trailer parking is available. One wheelchair-accessible fishing platform is also available.

Surrounded by dry sagebrush and juniper hillsides, the wide-open, breezy, and sunny campground sits just below the Canyon Ferry Dam, which is visible and emits a constant audible drone. Four interconnected loops make up most of the campground, and the bulk of the campsites circle two of them. Sites 1–4, 6–9, and 20 have river frontage, with their picnic tables a few feet from the shoreline. The lack of trees equals no privacy, shade, or windbreaks, but the flat grassy sites afford plenty of room for setting up large tents. Site 21 sits off by itself overlooking the boat launch.

Campsites, facilities: The campground has 38 RV or tent campsites. Facilities include picnic tables (three are covered), fire rings with grills, vault toilets, garbage service, drinking water, a boat ramp, horseshoe pits, and campground hosts. Leashed pets are permitted. A wheelchair-accessible toilet and campsite (site 1) on the river are available.

Reservations, fees: No reservations are accepted. Campsites cost $8. Cash or check. Open May–September.

Directions: From I-15 in Helena, take Exit 193 to the east side of the freeway and go north on Washington Street for 0.8 mile. Turn east onto Canyon Ferry Road for 14.3 miles to the Canyon Ferry Dam. Cross the dam, driving 1.2 miles. Turn north onto Jimtown Road for one mile, veering left at both junctions, until you reach the campground entrance on the right.

GPS Coordinates: N 46° 39.376' W 111° 44.194'

Contact: Bureau of Reclamation, Montana Area Office, Canyon Ferry Field Office, 7661 Canyon Ferry Rd., Helena, MT 59602, 406/475-3921, www.usbr.gov/gp/mtao/canyonferry/.

38 FISHHAWK

Scenic rating: 8

on the northwest shore of Canyon Ferry Reservoir

On bluffs at 3,850 feet above Canyon Ferry Reservoir, Fishhawk Campground is a treat for tent campers. While it does not have lake access for boating, it does provide views of the intricate web of islands, peninsulas, and coves at the north end of the lake, and you can climb down to the rocky lakeshore. The campsites face the sunrise, with views of the Big Belt Mountains flanking the lake's east side.

The unnumbered walk-in campsites are divided by rocky outcrops and tall ponderosa pines that offer a bit of shade and privacy, but most of the campsites are quite sunny—especially the one adjacent to the toilet. Many campers bring tarps for shade as well as rain protection. Sagebrush and junipers also grow on the hillside, casting a scent into the air after

rains. Each of the sites has flat spaces for tents, and some can fit more than one tent. Even from the vantage point of the bluffs, you can hear motorboats on the lake during the day, but the noise disappears at night. Bring binoculars for watching bald eagles and ospreys fishing. The gravel entry road is narrow and curves sharply around the loop that contains the parking areas. Bear in mind that you must hike uphill to the toilet here from most of the campsites.

Campsites, facilities: The campground has five walk-in tent campsites. Facilities include picnic tables and fire rings with grills at some of the campsites and a vault toilet. Bring your own water. Pack out your trash. Leashed pets are permitted. A wheelchair-accessible toilet and one site are available.

Reservations, fees: No reservations are accepted. Campsites cost $8. Cash or check. Open year-round; however, services are available only May–September.

Directions: From I-15 in Helena, take Exit 193 to the east side of the freeway and go north on Washington Street for 0.8 mile. Turn east onto Canyon Ferry Road for 13.4 miles to West Shore Drive. Turn south and drive 0.5 mile on the narrow, paved, hilly single-lane road. The campground entrance is on the left.

GPS Coordinates: N 46° 37.935' W 111° 43.063'

Contact: Bureau of Reclamation, Montana Area Office, Canyon Ferry Field Office, 7661 Canyon Ferry Rd., Helena, MT 59602, 406/475-3921, www.usbr.gov/gp/mtao/canyonferry/.

39 COURT SHERIFF

Scenic rating: 7

on the northeast shore of Canyon Ferry Reservoir

On the rugged north end of Canyon Ferry Reservoir at 3,800 feet, Court Sheriff is the closest campground to the Canyon Ferry Visitor Center, 0.7 mile to the west. While it doesn't have a boat ramp, it has plenty of easy-access shoreline for launching hand-carried watercraft. (You can launch larger boats at Chinamen's Gulch, 0.3 mile south, or at Kim's Marina about 0.5 mile south.) A few islands sit offshore, and lagoons divide parts of the campground, giving the landscape a playful look. The islands also grant destinations for exploration. Much of the shoreline is muddy and willowy, but open areas are available for beaching boats. Anglers go after walleye, rainbow trout, brown trout, ling, and perch in the lake and ice fish in winter.

Almost half of the campsites have waterfront—on either the lake or one of the lagoons. The grassy, open, sunny campground affords little privacy or shade, but a few sites have large pines for partial shade. Large flat tent spaces are available, and several campsites have paved, double-wide, back-in parking to accommodate trailers. A few pull-through sites are also available. This is a busy end of the lake, humming with the noise of personal watercraft and motorboats until the sun goes down. The campground faces the sunset.

Campsites, facilities: The campground has 49 RV or tent campsites that can accommodate midsized RVs. Facilities include picnic tables, fire rings with grills, vault toilets, drinking water, garbage service, boat trailer parking, and campground hosts. Leashed pets are permitted. Wheelchair-accessible toilets are available.

Reservations, fees: No reservations are accepted. Campsites cost $10. Cash or check. Open year-round; however, services are available only May–September.

Directions: From I-15 in Helena, take Exit 193 to the east side of the freeway and go north on Washington Street for 0.8 mile. Turn east onto Canyon Ferry Road for 14.3 miles to the Canyon Ferry Dam. Continue 1.7 miles past the dam to milepost 10.8 and turn right. GPS Coordinates: N 46° 39.488' W 111° 42.608'

Contact: Bureau of Reclamation, Montana Area Office, Canyon Ferry Field Office, 7661 Canyon Ferry Rd., Helena, MT 59602, 406/475-3921, www.usbr.gov/gp/mtao/canyonferry/.

40 CHINAMEN'S GULCH

Scenic rating: 7

on the east shore of Canyon Ferry Reservoir

Located on the west shore of the north end of Canyon Ferry Reservoir at 3,800 feet, Chinamen's Gulch sits in a small, narrow canyon that descends to the lakeshore. Contrary to other campgrounds that spread out along the shore, this campground has a tiny beach area. But it includes a shallow area for swimming, a primitive gravel boat launch, and a small dock. The beach flanks a small bay off the main lake, which offers game fishing in summer and ice fishing in winter.

Chinamen's Gulch Campground is a slice of a hot, dry, dusty narrow canyon that faces the sunset. Large ponderosa pines cover some of the upper sites, offering shade, but some of these are dying due to attacking pine beetles. The lower 12 campsites are small and terraced with views of the water and each other. Most sit west-facing in full sun. The upper campsites are more spread out, with large boulders and big trees dividing some of the sites for a little privacy. You'll still be able to see a few neighbors, though. Most of the sites have dirt floors with little surrounding ground cover. Even though the campground is on the busy north end of the lake, it quiets at night.

Campsites, facilities: The campground has 45 RV or tent campsites that can accommodate smaller RVs and trailers. Facilities include picnic tables, fire rings with grills, vault toilets, drinking water, garbage service, a boat ramp, dock, and campground hosts. Leashed pets are permitted. Wheelchair-accessible toilets are available.

Reservations, fees: No reservations are accepted. Campsites cost $8. Cash or check. Open year-round; however, services are available only May–September.

Directions: From I-15 in Helena, take Exit 193 to the east side of the freeway and go north on Washington Street for 0.8 mile. Turn east onto Canyon Ferry Road for 14.3 miles to the Canyon Ferry Dam. Continue two miles past the dam to milepost 11.1 and turn right, descending on a dirt washboard road down into the campground.
GPS Coordinates: N 46° 39.046' W 111° 42.540'

Contact: Bureau of Reclamation, Montana Area Office, Canyon Ferry Field Office, 7661 Canyon Ferry Rd., Helena, MT 59602, 406/475-3921, www.usbr.gov/gp/mtao/canyonferry/.

41 KIM'S MARINA AND RV RESORT

Scenic rating: 6

on the east shore of Canyon Ferry Lake

Kim's Marina is one of three marinas on the 33,500-acre Canyon Ferry Lake. Located at 3,800 feet in elevation, the marina and RV resort sit on the northeast corner of the lake in a sheltered bay. The resort services boaters, water-skiers, and anglers going after the walleye, rainbow trout, brown trout, ling, and perch that inhabit the reservoir.

The campground is cramped wall-to-wall with RVs. Premium sites on the water for dry camping and electrical-only hookups cost more than those off the waterfront. Full hookup sites are set back in the campground, some on a large, dry, gravel hillside. A paved road loops through the grassy campground, but the parking pads—all back-ins—are gravel. A few big willows dot the shoreline along the waterfront sites for partial shade, but most of the sites are sunny. The campground has several

permanent trailer homes, plus rents long-term RV sites, and the bay is busy with motorboats during the day as the marina houses around 165 boats.

Campsites, facilities: The campground maintains 105 RV sites. Facilities include picnic tables, pedestal grills, flush toilets, showers, drinking water, a token-operated launderette, a store with fishing tackle, a disposal station, horseshoe pits, tennis courts, boat rentals, docks, boat trailer parking, boat slips, buoyed swimming beach, and hookups for sewer, water, and electricity. Leashed pets are permitted.

Reservations, fees: Reservations are accepted. Hookups cost $24–27. Dry camping costs $15–16. Fees are based on four people per site; each additional person costs $3. A 7 percent Montana bed tax will be added to camping fees. Showers cost $2. Use of the RV and boat disposal station costs $5. Launching a boat costs $10. Open year-round; however, services are available only May–September.

Directions: From I-15 in Helena, take Exit 193 to the east side of the freeway and go north on Washington Street for 0.8 mile. Turn east onto Canyon Ferry Road for 14.3 miles to the Canyon Ferry Dam. Cross the dam, driving another 2.5 miles around the head of the lake. The marina is on the right at milepost 11.5.
GPS Coordinates: N 46° 39.144' W 111° 42.070'

Contact: Kim's Marina and RV Resort, 8015 Canyon Ferry Rd., Helena, MT 59602, 406/475-3723, www.kimsmarina.com.

42 JO BONNER

Scenic rating: 6

on the east shore of Canyon Ferry Reservoir

Located on the east shore of Canyon Ferry Reservoir at 3,800 feet, Jo Bonner Campground sits at the head of a long bay that is flanked with summer homes. It is the farthest south of the busy north-end campgrounds, which attract water-skiers, sailors, Jet Skiers, windsurfers, and anglers. Game fish opportunities include brook trout, brown trout, burbot, rainbow trout, walleye, and yellow perch. In winter, the lake is popular for ice fishing. Opposite the campground turnoff, the Magpie Creek Road leads to a back route (trail #248) that connects with the Hanging Valley National Recreation Trail, which climbs and then drops through a narrow rocky chasm to an overlook above Trout Creek Canyon.

The campground sits on an open grassy slope speckled with a few cottonwoods and junipers and flanked with large trees and willows along the lakeshore. The gravel campground loop connects the grassy, sloped, uneven parking pads. Most of the campsites are sunny and open with no privacy; the four campsites on the shore gain partial afternoon shade from the trees. The shoreline camps are muddy and overused; one even floods in high water. The remainder of the campground doesn't see much use, so you can feel like you have the place to yourself. At nighttime, the campground and bay quiet.

Campsites, facilities: The campground has 28 RV or tent campsites that can accommodate smaller RVs. Facilities include picnic tables, fire rings with grills, vault toilets, drinking water, garbage service, a boat ramp, boat dock, and campground hosts. Leashed pets are permitted. A wheelchair-accessible toilet is available.

Reservations, fees: No reservations are accepted. Campsites cost $8. Cash or check. Open year-round; however, services are available only May–September.

Directions: From I-15 in Helena, take Exit 193 to the east side of the freeway and go north on Washington Street for 0.8 mile. Turn east onto Canyon Ferry Road for 14.3 miles to the Canyon Ferry Dam. Cross the dam, driving another 3.7 miles around the head of the lake. At milepost 12.7, where you'll see the campground sign, turn right for 0.1 mile. The campground entrance sits at the junction between East Shore Drive and East Shore Drive N.

GPS Coordinates: N 46° 39.074' W 111° 42.484'

Contact: Bureau of Reclamation, Montana Area Office, Canyon Ferry Field Office, 7661 Canyon Ferry Rd., Helena, MT 59602, 406/475-3921, www.usbr.gov/gp/mtao/canyonferry/.

43 HELLGATE

Scenic rating: 6

on the east shore of Canyon Ferry Reservoir

Hellgate sits on along the south shore of a long, narrow bay at 3,800 feet on the east side of Canyon Ferry Reservoir, known for its fishing. While the bay is somewhat protected, this section of the lake is known for wind, and the nearly treeless peninsula housing the campground offers little protection from breezes. The bay lacks summers homes, making it a much more wild location than some of the campgrounds farther north.

The 1.2-mile-long campground offers a variety of terrain for camping. The first section flanks a creek with large cottonwoods and lush grass. Even though the sites here are south-facing, they are separated from each other by lush undergrowth (you can still see the campground road, though). On the bay, three loops with back-in gravel parking pads have waterfront sites. These vary between partial shade with willows and cottonwoods along the shore where you can beach a boat to full sun with overlooks of the water. Some have a little privacy, but you can see your neighboring campers from most of them. A last loop curves around the barren bluff at the end of the peninsula. The sites here garner grand views of the lake but are very windy and have zero privacy.

Campsites, facilities: The campground has 96 RV or tent campsites that can accommodate large RVs. Facilities include picnic

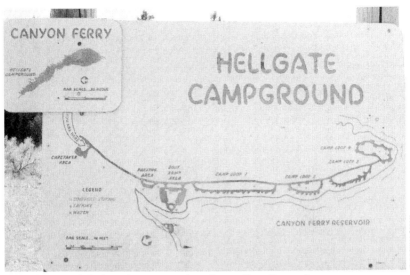

Hellgate is one of the largest campgrounds on Canyon Ferry Reservoir.

tables, fire rings with grills, vault toilets, one flush toilet, drinking water, garbage service, boat ramps, boat docks, a life jacket loan station, and campground hosts. Leashed pets are permitted. Wheelchair-accessible toilets are available.

Reservations, fees: No reservations are accepted. Campsites cost $8. Cash or check. Open year-round; however, services are available only May–September.

Directions: From I-15 in Helena, take Exit 193 to the east side of the freeway and go north on Washington Street for 0.8 mile. Turn east onto Canyon Ferry Road for 14.3 miles to the Canyon Ferry Dam. Continue driving for eight miles. At the campground sign at milepost 17.1, turn west onto the gravel road for 0.7 mile. The gravel soon gives way to rutted dirt with potholes and bumpy washboards as it descends to the campground.

GPS Coordinates: N 46° 39.079' W 111° 42.476'

Contact: Bureau of Reclamation, Montana Area Office, Canyon Ferry Field Office, 7661 Canyon Ferry Rd., Helena, MT 59602, 406/475-3921, www.usbr.gov/gp/mtao/canyonferry/.

44 GOOSE BAY MARINA

Scenic rating: 6

on the east shore of Canyon Ferry Reservoir

At 3,800 feet in elevation on the east shore of Canyon Ferry Reservoir, Goose Bay sits midway downlake in a remote area without crowds on the water for fishing, waterskiing, or boating. Contrary to the lake's rugged and semiforested north end, this section of the reservoir is surrounded by low, arid sagebrush, sparse grassland, and ranches. Trees are a rarity. The marina sits in a finger inlet protected from lake winds. The concessionaire's contract for this marina and RV campground runs out in 2010; call first to inquire on the campground's status and possible changes to its services.

The RV campground sits behind the store and adjacent to the marina; sites are stacked side by side in parking lot fashion with no privacy and no lake views. With no trees for shade, the campground is hot, but it's marginally protected by trailer homes, a few cottonwood trees, and the store if winds come from the west. The marina area also has 31 year-round trailer homes.

Campsites, facilities: The marina campground has 68 RV sites that can accommodate large RVs and 20 tent sites. Facilities include flush toilets, showers, hookups for water and electricity up to 50 amps, drinking water, garbage service, a disposal station, a boat ramp, a gas station, a convenience store, propane for sale, and a coin-operated launderette. The marina has 88 boat slips. Leashed pets are permitted.

Reservations, fees: Reservations are accepted. Campsites with hookups cost $17.50–19.50. Tent sites cost $12. Montana bed tax of 7 percent is added on. Cash, check, or credit card. Open April–early November.

Directions: From I-15 in Helena, take Exit 193 to the east side of the freeway and go north on Washington Street for 0.8 mile. Turn east onto Canyon Ferry Road for 26.5 miles, circling around the north end of the lake and down the east side to the Goose Bay sign. Turn right onto the rough gravel road and drive 2.8 miles. The road tours around one bay before reaching Goose Bay Marina. From Townsend at the lake's south end, drive east on Highway 12 for 3.3 miles and then north on Highway 284 for 20.3 miles to the Goose Bay turnoff.

GPS Coordinates: N 46° 32.513' W 111° 34.269'

Contact: Goose Bay Marina, 300 Goose Bay Ln., Townsend, MT 59644, 406/266-3645.

45 GOOSE BAY PRIMITIVE

Scenic rating: 6

on the east shore of Canyon Ferry Reservoir

At 3,800 feet on Canyon Ferry Reservoir's east shore, Goose Bay sits midway in a remote area less crowded than the north end. Goose Bay houses a marina, RV campground, a coin-operated launderette, and a store with gas, fishing tackle, propane, and minor groceries. Primitive undesignated campsites are scattered from the dirt-ramp boat launch west of the marina around the two peninsulas and two small bays to the north. The lake attracts anglers for its game fish and winter ice fishing. Five undesignated beaches surround the peninsulas, offering places to swim, water-ski, and beach boats overnight.

Primitive campsites flank the lake, offering solitude, privacy, quiet, and views. However, the undesignated area around the boat launch gets crowded with RVs. Away from the boat launch, sites tuck into the rare cottonwoods for wind and shade protection; others sit open on the barren bluffs above the lake, catching the brunt of winds and heat. Follow Leave No Trace principles in choosing an undesignated campsite, using only pre-existing fire rings. Scout the rough roads first for possible mudholes and large ruts as well as turnaround spots before driving in blind. Dirt roads circle both peninsulas, with campsites along the perimeters and plenty of flat space for tents.

Campsites, facilities: Goose Bay has 43 RV and tent campsites that can accommodate large RVs. Facilities include the occasional rock fire ring and two wheelchair-accessible vault toilets—one on each peninsula. Nine sites have picnic tables. Leashed pets are permitted.

Reservations, fees: No reservations are accepted. Camping is free. Open year-round.

Directions: From I-15 in Helena, take Exit 193 to the east side of the freeway and go north on Washington Street for 0.8 mile. Turn east onto Canyon Ferry Road for 26.5 miles, circling the lake's north end and dropping down the east side to the Goose Bay sign. Turn right onto the gravel road and drive 2.8 miles. The road tours around one bay before reaching Goose Bay. From

Townsend at the lake's south end, drive east on Highway 12 for 3.3 miles and then north on Highway 284 for 20.3 miles to the Goose Bay turnoff.

GPS Coordinates: N 46° 32.420' W 111° 33.663'

Contact: Bureau of Reclamation, Montana Area Office, Canyon Ferry Field Office, 7661 Canyon Ferry Rd., Helena, MT 59602, 406/475-3921, www.usbr.gov/gp/mtao/canyonferry/.

46 WHITE EARTH

Scenic rating: 6

on the west shore of Canyon Ferry Reservoir

At an elevation of 3,800 feet on the west shore of Canyon Ferry Reservoir, White Earth is named for its white sand and pebble beaches, although the sand is more like silty clay. As the reservoir level drops during the summer, the beaches get bigger. Call the Canyon Ferry Field Office for current water levels. The cement boat ramp, dock, and trailer parking aid those launching boats onto the lake for waterskiing, sightseeing, and fishing. In winter, anglers turn to ice fishing. The 29-mile-long lake is a trout fishery and also has ling, walleye, and perch.

The campground is open, treeless, windy, hot, and sunny. Many of the campsites line up along the north shore of a bay while others flank the main lakeshore. A few also rim a small lagoon. With no shrubs and trees, the grassy campground offers no privacy, protection from the afternoon winds, or shade. The campground does, however, gain good views of the sunrise over the Big Belt Mountains on the east side of the lake.

Campsites, facilities: The campground has 38 RV or tent campsites that can accommodate larger RVs. Facilities include picnic tables, fire rings with grills, vault toilets, drinking water, garbage service, a boat ramp, boat dock, and campground hosts. Leashed pets are permitted. Wheelchair-accessible toilets are available.

Reservations, fees: No reservations are accepted. Campsites cost $8. Cash or check. Open year-round; however, services are available only May–September.

Directions: From Winston on Highway 12/287 between Townsend and Helena, drive 5.3 miles northeast on dirt Beaver Creek Road, turning right at 2.3 miles to reach the campground.

GPS Coordinates: N 46° 31.292' W 111° 35.253'

Contact: Bureau of Reclamation, Montana Area Office, Canyon Ferry Field Office, 7661 Canyon Ferry Rd., Helena, MT 59602, 406/475-3921, www.usbr.gov/gp/mtao/canyonferry/.

47 CANYON FERRY LAKE KOA

Scenic rating: 6

on the west shore of Canyon Ferry Reservoir

At 3,850 feet on the west slopes of Canyon Ferry Reservoir, the KOA provides access to the lake even though it doesn't have waterfront. A Bureau of Reclamation boat ramp sits 0.2 mile to the east, and slip rental is available at The Silos Marina on Broadwater Bay. Designated swimming areas are also available near the marina. The campground is about five miles north of the 5,000-acre Canyon Ferry Wildlife Management Area, where birders and wildlife watchers can access trails to wildlife-viewing spots.

The KOA sits on an arid hillside above Canyon Ferry Lake, with views across to the Big Belt Mountains. Small pines and firs lend partial shade and windbreaks, but overall the site is very sunny and hot in midsummer. The campground road is gravel, along with the parking pads, which are stacked close together with no privacy in KOA fashion. The upper part of the campground is more open, drier, and dustier than the lower portion, which is built around patches of lawn. The KOA also runs the on-site Flamingo Grill, which is open for breakfast, lunch, and dinner.

Campsites, facilities: The campground has 47 RV campsites with a maximum pull-through length of 75 feet and 12 tent campsites. Facilities include picnic tables, fire rings, flush toilets, showers, drinking water, garbage service, a disposal station, coin-operated launderette, wireless Internet, a convenience store, a café, a playground, a dog walk, propane, a recreation room with TV, and horseshoe pits. Hookups include sewer, water, and electricity for up to 50 amps. Leashed pets are permitted. Wheelchair-accessible toilets are available.

Reservations, fees: Reservations are accepted. Hookups cost $25–43. Tent campsites cost $15–20 for one tent and $10 for a second tent. Tipis cost $45. Kamper Kabins cost $55–60. Rates are for two adults and two children under 16 years old. A 7 percent Montana bed tax will be added on. Use of the disposal station costs $4. Cash, check, or credit card. Open year-round.

Directions: From Townsend, drive Highway 12/287 north for 7.5 miles to milepost 70. Turn east onto Silos Road. (You'll see the two big, red brick silos.) Drive 0.8 mile east to the campground entrance on the left.
GPS Coordinates: N 46° 24.852' W 111° 34.839'

Contact: Townsend-Canyon Ferry Lake KOA, 81 Silos Rd., Townsend, MT 59644, 406/266-3100, www.canyonferrylakekoa.com.

48 SILOS

Scenic rating: 6

on the west shore of Canyon Ferry Reservoir

At 3,800 feet on the west shore of Canyon Ferry Reservoir, Silos is popular for its ease of access

off the highway. You only have to drive one mile of the dusty washboard, gravel road. Despite its popularity, this end of the lake is less congested than the more popular north end. The lake attracts boaters, water-skiers, windsurfers, anglers, Jet Skiers, and, in winter, ice anglers. The campground inlets contain beaches that grow larger throughout the summer as the reservoir levels drop. These work for swimming and beaching boats for the night. The boat launch includes cement ramps and docks. In the evening, the post-boating crowd heads to the Silos Bar and Restaurant, located at the highway turnoff to the campground. The campground is about five miles north of the Canyon Ferry Wildlife Management Area, which has trails for accessing wildlife-viewing spots to see waterfowl, songbirds, raptors, moose, and deer.

Located on large, flat, treeless, grassy plateaus, the campground comprises four main loops, each divided by a small, narrow inlet. Two additional small loops on the southern peninsulas contain undesignated campsites. The dirt loops kick up dust. The campsites offer a semblance of privacy because they are spread out, but since there is no vegetation taller than grass, you will still see neighboring campers. Some small willows flank a few of the more popular campsites along the inlets. Even from a mile away, you can hear some of the faint trucking noise at night along the highway.

Campsites, facilities: The campground has 63 RV or tent campsites that can fit larger RVs. Facilities include picnic tables, fire rings with grills, vault toilets, drinking water, garbage service, a boat ramp, and campground hosts. Leashed pets are permitted. Wheelchair-accessible toilets are available.

Reservations, fees: No reservations are accepted. Campsites cost $10. Cash or check. Open year-round.

Directions: From Townsend, drive Highway 12/287 north for 7.5 miles to milepost 70. Turn east onto Silos Road. (You'll see the two big, red brick silos.) Drive one mile east to the boat launch area. Turn right to access the campground loops.

GPS Coordinates: N 46° 24.687' W 111° 34.574'

Contact: Bureau of Reclamation, Montana Area Office, Canyon Ferry Field Office, 7661 Canyon Ferry Rd., Helena, MT 59602, 406/475-3921, www.usbr.gov/gp/mtao/canyonferry/.

49 CONFEDERATE

Scenic rating: 6

on the east shore of Canyon Ferry Reservoir

Located at 3,800 feet on the east shore of Canyon Ferry Reservoir, the campground flanks the north and south sand and pebble beaches of Confederate Bay. This remote area draws only a few people due to the rough condition of the access road, which waffles between ruts, washboards, jarring cattle grates, large potholes, and rocky sections. The road narrows to one lane and can be a mudhole when wet. Even though the campground doesn't have a boat ramp, you can launch from your campsite any hand-carried watercraft for fishing, sightseeing, or wind-surfing. In winter, the bay draws ice anglers. The beaches grow larger as the lake level drops throughout the summer.

The primitive campsites string along two sandy beaches. The south beach offers more trees and willows for a bit of shade and wind protection, but the north beach has only one cottonwood tree. While you won't have privacy from neighboring campers, the campground as a whole offers solitude, quiet, and privacy from the hubbub at the north end of the lake. Both beaches are sunny, hot in midsummer, and windy, but you can have your tent door a few feet from the water.

Campsites, facilities: The campground has 16 undesignated RV or tent campsites that can accommodate midsized RVs. Facilities include rock fire rings at some sites and two wheelchair-accessible vault toilets, one at each beach. Leashed pets are permitted.

Reservations, fees: No reservations are accepted. Camping is free. Open year-round.

Directions: From Townsend on Highway 12/287, drive east on Highway 12 for 3.3 miles and then north on Highway 284 for 16.8 miles to the Confederate turnoff. At milepost 25, turn west onto the gravel Lower Confederate Lane and drive 4.2 miles. Turn right to reach the north beach or continue 0.5 mile around the bay to reach the south beach. From I-15 in Helena, take Exit 193 to the east side of the freeway and go north on Washington Street for 0.8 mile. Turn east onto Canyon Ferry Road for 30 miles, circling around the lake's north end and down the east side to the Confederate sign.

GPS Coordinates: N 46° 29.324' W 111° 31.516'

Contact: Bureau of Reclamation, Montana Area Office, Canyon Ferry Field Office, 7661 Canyon Ferry Rd., Helena, MT 59602, 406/475-3921, www.usbr.gov/gp/mtao/canyonferry/.

50 INDIAN ROAD

Scenic rating: 6

on the Missouri River south of Canyon Ferry Reservoir

At 3,850 feet, Indian Road Campground, as its name implies, sits on an ancient Native American route that the Lewis and Clark expedition also followed. The campground, with its interpretive displays, is on the Missouri River just before it enters Canyon Ferry Reservoir. A lush oasis amid the arid surrounding hills, the park includes a children's fishing pond, which is ringed by a gravel walking trail and crossed by a bridge. Swimming is not permitted in the pond. Several breaks through the willows afford access to the Missouri River for fishing and wading. A paved bicycling and walking path parallels the highway into Townsend. North of the Missouri River, the

Canyon Ferry Wildlife Management Area also offers short trails to wildlife-viewing spots. It's an excellent place for bird-watching and good moose habitat.

A gravel campground road circles the park, with a few pull-through gravel parking pads. The remainder of the parking pads are short back-ins. A few cottonwood trees and shorter willows provide some shade, but the mowed-lawn campground affords no privacy between the close sites. You can, however, have views of the surrounding mountains. At night, the trucks on the highway are loud.

Campsites, facilities: The campground has 32 RV or tent campsites that can accommodate midsized RVs. Facilities include picnic tables, fire rings with grills, pedestal grills, vault toilets, drinking water, and garbage service. Leashed pets are permitted. A wheelchair-accessible toilet, paved walkway, and fishing platform are available.

Reservations, fees: No reservations are accepted. Camping is free. Open year-round.

Directions: From the north end of Townsend, drive Highway 12/287 north for 0.5 mile. (Turn off before the bridge over the Missouri River.) Turn east onto Centerville Road and drive 0.1 mile. Turn north into the campground.

GPS Coordinates: N 46° 20.065' W 111° 31.763'

Contact: Bureau of Reclamation, Montana Area Office, Canyon Ferry Field Office, 7661 Canyon Ferry Rd., Helena, MT 59602, 406/475-3921, www.usbr.gov/gp/mtao/canyonferry/.

51 YORK'S ISLANDS

Scenic rating: 6

south of Townsend on the Missouri River

Compared to the surrounding arid countryside, York's Islands is a lush oasis along the Missouri River, at 3,838 feet in elevation.

The area is named for York, Captain William Clark's servant, who accompanied him on the Corps of Discovery expedition, and is a place where the Missouri River fragments into different channels around eight islands due to beaver dams shifting the water flows. The campground is primitive, part of the fishing access site run by the state. Rafters, kayakers, anglers, and river floaters can launch eight river miles upstream at Tosten and float back to camp. A downstream float leads to Townsend and farther into the Canyon Ferry Wildlife Management Area, but no watercraft are permitted March–August to protect nesting waterfowl.

The grassy sites, which are crammed together and small, are partially shaded under tall cottonwoods. Junipers, willows, and lots of brush provide some privacy between sites, especially those ringing the outside of the loop. You can hear the railroad and the highway at night as the river here is slow-moving and quiet. You can find flat spaces on the grass for pitching tents.

Campsites, facilities: The campground has 10 RV or tent campsites that can accommodate trailers up to 30 feet. Facilities include picnic tables, fire rings with grills, vault toilets, and a concrete boat ramp. Pack out your trash. Leashed pets are permitted. A wheelchair-accessible toilet is available.

Reservations, fees: Reservations are not accepted. Campsites cost $7 with a Montana fishing license and $12 without a Montana fishing license. Cash or check. Open year-round.

Directions: From Townsend, drive south on Highway 287 for four miles to milepost 81.5. Turn west and cross the railroad tracks, driving one mile on the potholed gravel road. (Watch for cows on the road.) The road dead-ends at the campground.

GPS Coordinates: N 46° 15.995' W 111° 29.529'

Contact: Montana Fish, Wildlife, and Parks, Region 3, 1400 S. 19th Ave., Bozeman, MT 59718, 406/994-4042, http://fwp.mt.gov.

52 LOWER TOSTEN DAM RECREATION AREA

Scenic rating: 6

south of Townsend on the Missouri River

Lower Tosten Dam Recreation Area sits at 4,000 feet in a small canyon cut through dramatic sedimentary layers of orange and white stone amid surrounding sagebrush and juniper hillsides. Below the dam, the Missouri River rolls at a slow pace. Rafters, kayakers, and anglers launch boats from here to float down to Tosten fishing access site or farther to York's Islands. Above the dam, a small reservoir affords fishing, swimming, and boating. You can motor around a broad oxbow and islands in the river. Both sides of the dam are good for watching American pelicans.

The recreation area is divided into two campgrounds—one below the dam and one above. The lower area has two grassy, unshaded campsites adjacent to the cement boat ramp and squeezed between the road and the river. Large willow brush blocks the view of the river. The upper area has three grassy campsites on the shore of the lake formed by the dam. The picnic tables are covered, and small trees lend minimal shade. A cement boat ramp and dock are available. All five campsites are small, close together, and open, and you can hear humming from the dam in both areas. The road to access the dam is rough dirt with potholes, but the campground roads are gravel.

Campsites, facilities: The campground has five RV or tent campsites that can accommodate midsized RVs. Facilities include picnic tables, fire rings with grills, vault toilets, a boat dock, and boat ramps. Leashed pets are permitted. A wheelchair-accessible toilet is available.

Reservations, fees: No reservations are accepted. Camping is free. Open May–October.

Directions: From Townsend, drive Highway 287 south for 12.6 miles, passing Tosten and crossing the Missouri River. Turn east at the BLM sign onto Tosten Dam Road and drive 4.3 miles to the lower campground or 5.2 miles to the upper campground. The rough dirt road has a one-lane bridge. Watch for cattle on the road.

GPS Coordinates: N 46° 20.065' W 111° 31.763'

Contact: Bureau of Land Management, 106 N. Parkmont, P.O. Box 3388, Butte, MT 59702, 406/533-7600, www.blm.gov/mt/st/en.html.

53 WHITEHOUSE

Scenic rating: 7

in the Boulder Mountains in Beaverhead-Deerlodge National Forest

At 6,000 feet, Whitehouse sits along the Boulder River in the Boulder Mountains, a mecca for ATV riders. The river houses mountain whitefish along with brook, brown, and rainbow trout, although the stream shores are quite willowy. The 2.5-mile Cottonwood Lake Trailhead (#65) sits about three miles from the campground. From the lake, trails also climb farther to Thunderbolt Mountain and Electric Peak. Call the Forest Service on the status of this campground, as it may close temporarily for diseased tree removal. Be prepared for a rough, potholed, rutted road into the campground.

Of the three campgrounds on the Boulder River, Whitehouse is the most popular. The campground, which sits on the Boulder River, surrounds large meadows with a perimeter of aspens and a few lodgepole pines that are dying due to beetle attacks. The sites are spread out for privacy, but with the open, sunny meadow, you'll have views of neighboring campers. Some sites also command views of forested slopes as well as views of a few power lines. The meadows bloom in midsummer with harebells, yarrow, and purple asters. You'll find plenty of large, flat tent spaces here. Should the campground be full, you can find an additional five dispersed primitive campsites, also on the Boulder River, 0.5 mile east just opposite the junction the Red Rock Road. Other than the ATV noise, the campground is quiet.

Campsites, facilities: The campground has 10 RV or tent campsites. The Forest Service recommends a maximum trailer length of 22 feet. Facilities include picnic tables, rock fire rings or fire rings with grills, drinking water, and a vault toilet. Pack out your trash. Leashed pets are permitted. A wheelchair-accessible toilet is available.

Reservations, fees: No reservations are accepted. Camping is free. Open late June–November.

Directions: From I-15 between Helena and Butte, take Exit 151 (4.6 miles south of Basin). Cross to the west side onto Boulder River Road (Forest Road 82). Drive 3.25 miles, turning right at the fork and crossing the Boulder River. Continue for 3.9 miles. Turn left at the signed entrance to the campground. GPS Coordinates: N 46° 15.480' W 112° 28.755'

Contact: Beaverhead-Deerlodge National Forest, Jefferson Ranger District, 3 Whitetail Rd., Whitehall, MT 59759 406/287-3223, http://fs.usda.gov.

54 LADYSMITH

Scenic rating: 4

in the Boulder Mountains in Beaverhead-Deerlodge National Forest

Ladysmith, at 5,800 feet, is a small, little-used forest campground. The Boulder River near the campground is on private land, so you must drive three or so miles to public land, where you can fish for trout. As in much of the national forest here, the lodgepole pines are dying due to attacking beetles. Entire slopes of rust-colored trees in the area attest to the pervasiveness of the attack. This campground is scheduled for logging to remove the diseased

trees; call the ranger station to check on its status before visiting.

A rough-paved, potholed narrow road loops through the campground, which sits on a meadow and open forest slope. Buffalo berries, sticky pink geraniums, and yellow cinquefoil dot the slope. The dirt back-in parking pads are small, bumpy, and sloped. Much of the lodgepole forest is dead and marked for removal, which will convert the currently partial-shade campground to a sunny site. The upper campsites have views of meadows. While the access road has some noise during the day from forest travelers and ATVs, the night brings quiet.

Campsites, facilities: The campground has six RV or tent campsites that can accommodate only small RVs. Facilities include picnic tables, fire rings with grills, a large group fire ring with three benches, and pit toilets. Pack out your trash. Leashed pets are permitted.

Reservations, fees: No reservations are accepted. Camping is free. Open late June–September.

Directions: From I-15 between Helena and Butte, take Exit 151 (4.6 miles south of Basin). Cross to the west side onto the Boulder River Road (Forest Road 82). Drive 3.2 miles, turning left at the signed entrance to the campground. Drive over the cattle grate. GPS Coordinates: N 46° 15.127' W 112° 24.261'

Contact: Beaverhead-Deerlodge National Forest, Jefferson Ranger District, 3 Whitetail Rd., Whitehall, MT 59759 406/287-3223, http://fs.usda.gov.

55 MORMON CREEK

Scenic rating: 4

in the Boulder Mountains in Beaverhead-Deerlodge National Forest

Mormon Creek—also called Mormon Gulch—is a small, little-used forest campground at an elevation of 5,800 feet with a tiny creek trickling through the campground. The Boulder River near the campground is on private land, so you must drive four or so miles to public land, where you can fish for trout. As in much of the national forest here, the lodgepole pines are dying due to attacking beetles. Entire slopes of rust-colored trees in the area attest to the pervasiveness of the attack. This campground is scheduled for logging to remove the diseased trees; call the ranger station to check on its status before visiting.

Campsites are set close together in a grassy area blooming with wild roses, penstemon, cow parsnip, and bedstraw. The tree canopy, which provides filtered shade, is dead. Once this is removed, the campground will turn into an open meadow with a young crop of aspens growing into the shade trees. Some of the sites are overgrown and show little use. The flat spaces available in some sites will fit only smaller tents. The two sites at the top of the loop see the most use because of the partial privacy they afford.

Campsites, facilities: The campground has nine RV or tent campsites that can hold trailers up to 16 feet. Facilities include picnic tables, fire rings with grills, and pit toilets. Pack out your trash. Leashed pets are permitted.

Reservations, fees: No reservations are accepted. Camping is free. Open late June–September.

Directions: From I-15 between Helena and Butte, take Exit 151 (4.6 miles south of Basin). Cross to the west side onto Boulder River Road (Forest Road 82). Drive one mile and turn left at the campground sign. Climb on the single-lane, rough pavement over the cattle grate and dodge chuckholes 0.1 mile to the campground.

GPS Coordinates: N 46° 15.440' W 112° 21.735'

Contact: Beaverhead-Deerlodge National Forest, Jefferson Ranger District, 3 Whitetail Rd., Whitehall, MT 59759 406/287-3223, http://fs.usda.gov.

Index

www.moon.com

MOON.COM is ready to help plan your next trip! Filled with fresh trip ideas and strategies, author interviews, informative travel blogs, a detailed map library, and descriptions of all the Moon guidebooks, Moon.com is all you need to get out and explore the world—or even places in your own backyard. While at Moon.com, sign up for our monthly e-newsletter for updates on new releases, travel tips, and expert advice from our on-the-go Moon authors. As always, when you travel with Moon, expect an experience that is uncommon and truly unique.

MOON IS ON FACEBOOK—BECOME A FAN!
JOIN THE MOON PHOTO GROUP ON FLICKR

MOON OUTDOORS

"Well written, thoroughly researched, and packed full of useful information and advice. These guides really do get you into the outdoors."

—GORP.COM

MOON GLACIER NATIONAL PARK CAMPING

Avalon Travel
a member of the Perseus Books Group
1700 Fourth Street
Berkeley, CA 94710, USA
www.moon.com

Editor: Tiffany Watson
Series Manager: Sabrina Young
Copy Editor: Deana Shields
Production and Graphics Coordinator:
    Tabitha Lahr
Cover Designer: Kathryn Osgood
Interior Designer: Darren Alessi
Map Editor: Brice Ticen
Cartographer: Kat Bennett
Illustrations: Bob Race

ISBN-13: 978-1-59880-578-9

Front cover photo: Glacier National Park © Val Bakhtin/Dreamstime.com
Title page photo © Becky Lomax

Printed in the United States of America

ABOUT THE AUTHOR

Becky Lomax

Becky Lomax grew up camping. She cherishes fond memories of family camping trips in a yellow station wagon packed door-to-door with five raucous kids and their gear. Piled on air mattresses or cots in a canvas tent, she and her siblings would wake each morning to their mom doling canned grapefruit and mandarin oranges into plastic camping bowls while their dad pumped the green two-burner Coleman stove so he could cook pancakes.

Like any camping family, they had their share of rain, mosquitoes, vehicle breakdowns, and siblings who strip-mined the chocolate from the gorp bag. Her brothers still swear they didn't put that frog in her sleeping bag – but she's not convinced.

Today, Becky's favorite kind of travel still involves backpacking and camping. After ten years as a hiking and backpacking guide in Glacier National Park, she now travels the Northern Rockies as a professional outdoors writer and photographer. She uses her full-time writing career as an excuse to camp, hike, mountain bike, kayak, and ski, but her favorite research involves wildlife: She has followed biologists into the field to band raptors and radio-collar bighorn sheep and grizzly bears.

Becky is also the author of *Moon Glacier National Park*, and her work has been published in various magazines, including *Smithsonian*, *Backpacker*, *National Wildlife*, *Cross Country Skier*, *Montana Magazine*, *Montana Outdoors*, and *Northwest Travel*.